VENICE'S INTIMATE EMPIRE

VENICE'S INTIMATE EMPIRE

FAMILY LIFE AND SCHOLARSHIP IN THE RENAISSANCE MEDITERRANEAN

Erin Maglaque

CORNELL UNIVERSITY PRESS

Ithaca and London

First published 2018 by Cornell University Press
Printed in the United States of America

Library of Congress Cataloging-in-Publication Data

Names: Maglaque, Erin, 1987– author.
Title: Venice's intimate empire : family life and scholarship in the Renaissance Mediterranean / Erin Maglaque.
Description: Ithaca : Cornell University Press, 2018. | Includes bibliographical references and index.
Identifiers: LCCN 2017045852 (print) | LCCN 2017046527 (ebook) | ISBN 9781501721663 (pdf) | ISBN 9781501721670 (epub/mobi) | ISBN 9781501721656 (cloth : alk. paper)
Subjects: LCSH: Venice (Italy)—History—1508–1797. | Venice (Italy)—Intellectual life—16th century. | Venice (Italy)—Colonies—Administration. | Family life—Italy—Venice—History—16th century. | Humanism—Italy—Venice—History—16th century. | Bembo, Giovanni, 1473–1545. | Bembo, Giovanni, 1473–1545—Family. | Coppo, Pietro, 1469 or ? 1470–1555 or 1556. | Coppo, Pietro, 1469 or 1470–1555 or 1556—Family.
Classification: LCC DG678.235 (ebook) | LCC DG678.235 .M34 2018 (print) | DDC 945/.3070922—dc23
LC record available at https://lccn.loc.gov/2017045852

To my grandparents

CONTENTS

Illustrations

ACKNOWLEDGMENTS

It is a pleasure to thank the many friends, colleagues, and institutions that made this book possible to write. The initial phase of this project was made possible by the generous funding of the Clarendon Fund. I have since enjoyed three wonderful years as a junior research fellow at Oriel College writing the book. Thank you to Moira Wallace and John Elliott for making that possible, and for welcoming me so warmly to Oriel. I spent a semester at Harvard in 2015, which proved critical for further researching and revising the book manuscript. I owe a great deal to Jim Hankins for his support, and to the Lauro de Bosis Committee for making this possible.

My research in Italy was generously supported by ERASMUS, the Oxford History Faculty, the Fondazione Giorgio Cini, the Bibliographical Society, the Old Members' Trust of University College, and the John Fell Fund. At the Cini, many thanks to Massimo Busetto and Lucia Sardo for making my stays on the island so enjoyable and productive. I am also grateful to the archivists and librarians at the Archivio di Stato in Venice, Bayerische Staatsbibliothek, Biblioteca dell'Archiginnasio, Biblioteca Estense, Biblioteca Marciana, Biblioteca Trivulziana, Houghton Library, and Smith College for their assistance. I am particularly grateful to the archivists at the Archivio di Stato in Trieste, who patiently helped me make sense of crucial documents on microfilm.

Several colleagues read chapters of this book at various stages. I am indebted to Chris Carlsmith, John Elliott, Catherine Holmes, Oren Margolis, Sarah Ross, and Chris Wickham for their comments and advice. Hannah Murphy read, discussed, and cheered me on through multiple revisions of the manuscript—thank you, Hannah! I am especially grateful to Lyndal Roper and the members of the Early Modern Workshop for helping me test new ideas and for reading an early, crucial draft of the introduction to the book. I am also very grateful to John-Paul Ghobrial and Stephen Milner for their continuing support.

I benefited enormously from the supervision of Nicholas Davidson and Catherine Holmes. Nick has been a wonderfully supportive guide to Renaissance Venice. I am so grateful for his encouragement and expertise as I learned to navigate Venetian history and its archives. Catherine has been a wonderful mentor and teacher since I first arrived in Oxford as a master's student. I am more indebted to her intellectual generosity and patient guidance than I could ever possibly express here.

Karl Appuhn, Alex Bamji, Karen-edis Barzman, Tony Campbell, Georg Christ, Maya Corry, Lia Costiner, Cristina Dondi, Piero Falchetta, Patricia Fortini Brown, Tom Harper, Jim Harris, Holly Hurlburt, Claire Judde de Larivière, Mary Laven, Noel Malcolm, Nick Millea, Monique O'Connell, Sandra Toffolo, and Bronwen Wilson offered their advice and support at various stages of this project. Richard Scholar and Ita Mac Carthy are the best research (and spritz!) companions, from San Giorgio to Oxford. Many thanks also to Rachel Gibson, Natalie Lussey, and Renard Gluzman for their friendship and support, in and out of the archives. I have presented aspects of this project to seminar audiences in Oxford, London, Cambridge, and Norwich, and in conference panels at Renaissance Society of America meetings in San Diego, New York, Berlin, and Chicago. I am grateful to those audiences for their questions and critiques, which proved crucial for shaping the book.

Three anonymous readers closely read, critiqued, and made important, incisive suggestions for improving the book manuscript at two critical stages. I am enormously grateful to them for their time and careful consideration of this manuscript. It is a pleasure to thank Reader 1, in particular, who consulted this manuscript twice—it is immeasurably better for her or his interventions and suggestions. Emily Andrew has been a wonderfully supportive editor and has made it all seem easy. Of course, all errors remain my own.

Chapter 5 is a substantially revised version of my article "Humanism and Colonial Governance in the Venetian Aegean: The Case of Giovanni Bembo," published in the *Journal of Early Modern History* 19, no. 1 (2015). I gratefully acknowledge Koninklijke Brill NV for granting permission to reproduce this work. The publication of this book has been made possible by a grant from the Scouloudi Foundation in association with the Institute of Historical Research.

My family have sustained and encouraged me in countless ways, and in recent years have done so across an ocean. I owe them deeper thanks than it is possible to convey in print. My dad, stepmom, and brother have been a constant source of support. My mom even read the entire book—I am grateful to her for that, and for so much more. My sister has been my wonderful best friend and adventurous travel companion for almost three decades.

I finished this book manuscript a week before I got married to Tom. He has lived alongside this project since its very beginning and has been its most ardent cheerleader and most incisive critic. It simply would not have been possible—or nearly as fun—without him. Here's to many more books together, and long walks discussing them.

This book is dedicated to my grandmother, for teaching me the importance of a well-constructed outline; and to my grandfather, who encouraged me to keep asking questions.

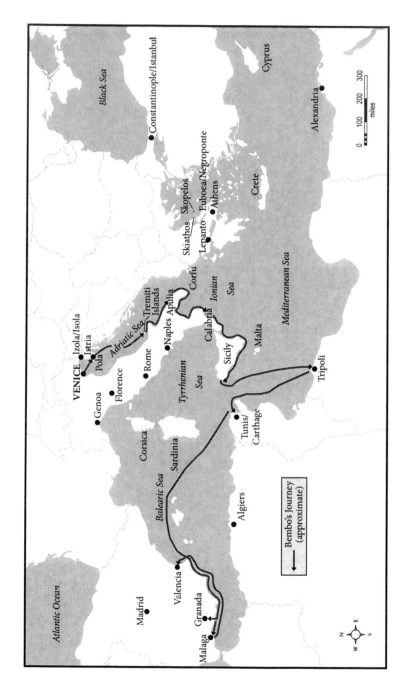

Figure 1. Map of Bembo and Coppo's Mediterranean world.
Cartography by Michael Bechthold.

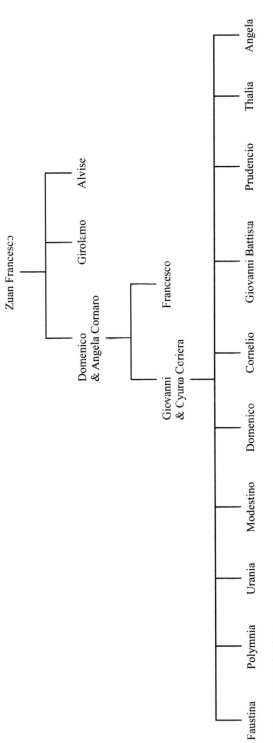

FIGURE 2. Bembo family tree.

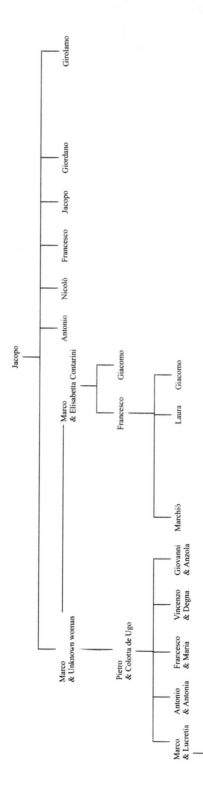

FIGURE 3. Coppo family tree.

VENICE'S INTIMATE EMPIRE

Introduction

Two Families

In Venice in 1536, Giovanni Bembo's world was turned upside down: because of "cruel fate and disordered nature," his dearest wife, Cyurω, and sweetest fifteen-year-old daughter, Angela, were dead within the space of a month. Bembo poured his grief onto the page in a long and complex Latin letter (figure 4).[1] Part self-consolation, part autobiography, the letter opens with a desperate cry: "Oh, what sorrow! My Cyurω died on the thirtieth of October in the tenth hour of the night. She was seventeen and I was twenty-four when we were united on Corfu."[2] The Venetian Bembo had spent time on the island of Corfu as a young man, and Cyurω, a Greek-speaking, Greek Orthodox Corfiote woman, had been his domestic servant. Evidently, for Bembo, there was no autobiographical time before Cyurω. He begins the letter with her death, before vaulting backward in time to the moment they met on the island. Bembo then narrates chronologically the events of his own life, from his adventures with Cyurω in the Mediterranean as a young man, to his studies of inscriptions and ruins in Spain and North Africa, to the highlight of his career as governor of two islands in the Aegean. The mood of the letter turns darker as he recounts the frustration of political offices in Venice, his political downfall on Skiathos in 1526, the deaths of his wife and daughter, and finally his deep mourning. Cyurω's death is the beginning and the end of Bembo's

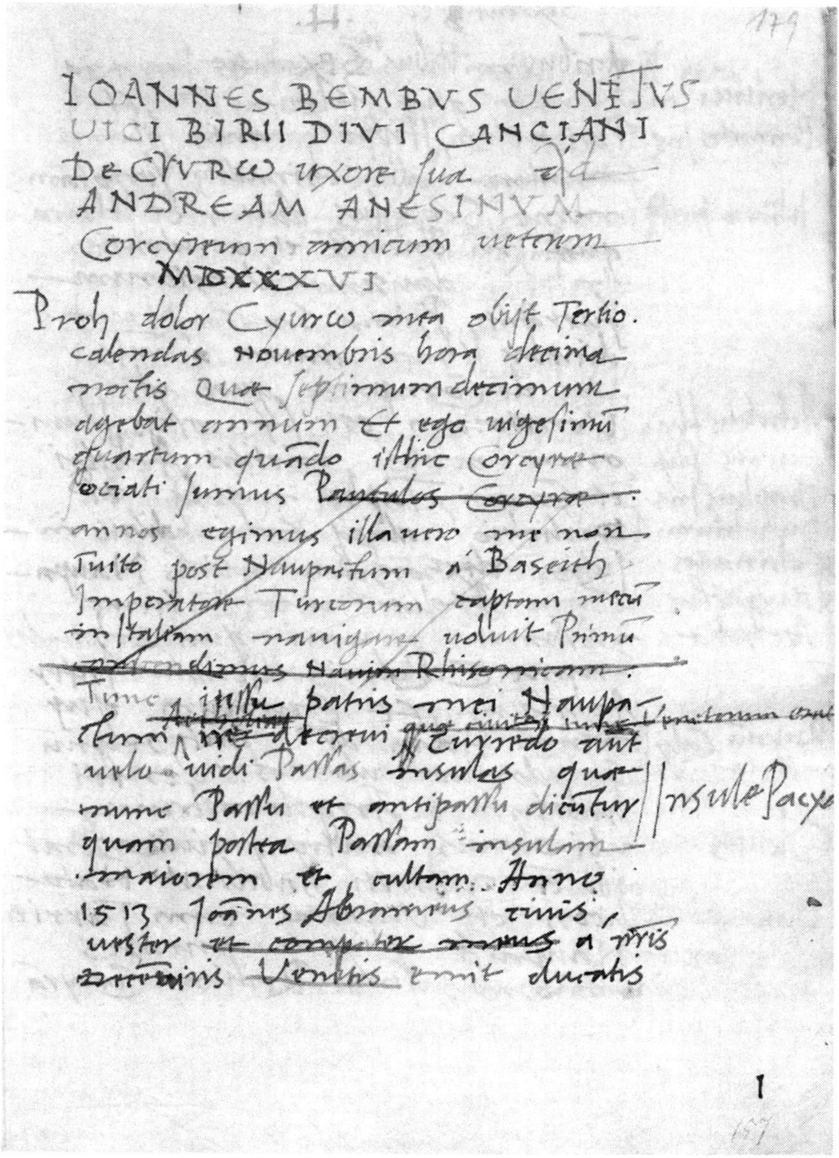
IOANNES BEMBVS UENETVS
UICI BIRII DIVI CANCIANI
ANDREAM ANESINVM
MDXXXVI

Figure 4. The opening page of Giovanni Bembo's Latin letter. Bayerische Staatsbibliothek München, Clm 10801, fol. 101r.

complicated letter, with memories of their life together punctuating its narrative.

In his letter, Bembo writes reflexively on the problem of transformation: what had he been, what had he become, who would he now be without Cyurω? His friendships with his patrician peers, now crumbled as his career lay in tatters; his family, now fractured, as he lay the blame for Cyurω's death at the feet of everyone surrounding him. Cyurω's death was caused by an accumulation of anxieties, Bembo wrote: their daughters wanted to marry, but Bembo and Cyurω could not afford the dowries set by Venetian law; to compound matters, those youthful suitors were useless, lazy, entitled, and inarticulate. Their son, Modestino, who was once so promising a scholar, "now hates books so much that he seems to be afraid to open them, nor does he study any other virtuous things."[3] These anxieties about her children's futures burdened Cyurω. Bembo used the evocative "macerabat" (wore down) to describe how these anxieties ate away at her, to describe her mind wasting away from distress. Importantly, this reflexive writing was inextricable from his wife's own transformation: from a domestic servant to the wife of a patrician governor, from a lively companion on his Mediterranean journeys to a woman deeply anxious, even ill, from her concerns about her own children. In this autobiographical moment, the troubling trajectories of his intimate relationships and his political career were laid bare.

Several years later, in 1550, the Venetian Pietro Coppo sat with his notary in his study in the seaside town of Isola. He was eighty years old and had determined that while still of sound mind and body, he should make his final testament.[4] On the Istrian peninsula, jutting out into the Adriatic Sea, Isola did not seem far from Venice, and yet Coppo had not lived in his native city for more than five decades. He had come to Isola all those years before as a notary himself, sent to help with the everyday administrative duties of running the colonial town. Coppo was born the illegitimate son of a Venetian patrician, and his career spoke to the opportunities offered to young men within the vast bureaucracy of the Venetian empire. But with his marriage to a local Isolan noblewoman, Colotta, Coppo had transformed from a youthful Venetian scribe of empire to an adviser, town planner, and council member greatly respected by the local Isolan nobility. The last time he visited his birthplace of Venice, where his natal family still lived, was to petition the doge for more flexible rights on behalf of the Isolans themselves. Looking back over the decades, Coppo had much to be proud of in the town of Isola: the beautiful new church he helped build, and a new quay and port, too; many years of service on the municipal council; and five sons who were already participating in the town's political life. By the time he came to write his testament, Coppo had given his sons substantial and promising properties, houses, vineyards, and gardens for their own marriages to Isolan women.[5] Coppo had transformed from a socially and politically precarious outsider to a powerful municipal figure; and Colotta had been central in this transformation, her own secure social status a foundation for his transformation.

Even as Coppo seemed to shake off his Venetian imperial identity for a new and more lucrative one as Colotta's husband and local Isolan dignitary, he seemed in his final testament to feel more keenly his emotional ties to Venice. He had been educated as an adolescent in Venice by Marcantonio Sabellico, a dynamic humanist teacher and great intellectual personality in late Quattrocento Venice. For Coppo, his days spent in Sabellico's humanist *gymnasium* were still a brilliant memory. He stipulated in his will that his finest manuscript, a luxury copy of an atlas he had authored and illustrated with woodcut maps, should be sent to the monastery of Santa Maria delle Grazie, between Poveglia and Malamocco on the Lido in the Venetian lagoon.[6] That monastery contained a library that held volumes of Sabellico's books, and Coppo wrote that he wanted his own precious book to sit on the shelves next to those of his Venetian teacher. Coppo's memories of Venice clearly had not faded over the many decades he spent in Istria. Just as Bembo reflected autobiographically on his own transformations, so did Coppo in his final testament.

Through their humanist writing and scholarship, their private writing in letters, miscellanies, and marginalia, and the documentary traces in the Venetian State Archives and the Isolan municipal archives, *Venice's Intimate Empire* constructs the parallel histories of these two families. Born only about three years apart in Venice, Bembo and Coppo were educated in the same humanist school in the city, journeyed into the Mediterranean, met and married colonial women, and formed families with them. And yet their origins were importantly different. Bembo was born to a marginal branch of a large patrician family; Coppo was the illegitimate son of a patrician father. On the boundaries of nobility, political power, and wealth, both men were particularly susceptible to the slippery opportunities and dangers of social mobility. Bembo, with his Corfiote, Greek Orthodox wife, would move between Venice and the Mediterranean empire as he took up the post of colonial governor of Skiathos in the Aegean. Coppo would become a local Isolan council member and an important figure in Isolan municipal politics and society. Tracing Bembo and Coppo from Venice to the Mediterranean, from adolescence in the humanist schoolrooms of Venice to their intellectual maturity, from natal families to their mixed conjugal ones, *Venice's Intimate Empire* addresses the multiple transformations these two men and their families underwent. These two family histories offer an unusual intimate insight into the history of the Venetian empire during the Renaissance.

In doing so, the book examines three primary themes: humanism, empire, and family. Bembo and Coppo were both humanists.[7] They were educated by well-known Venetian intellectual figures in the last decades of the Quattrocento, and went on to form scholarly friendships—and enmities—with the writers, editors, printers, and translators who made up the lively intellectual society of Venice in the last years of the century. In the Mediterranean, they encountered the physical remains of antiquity and carefully documented it in epigraphical albums and homemade woodcut maps, and in the margins of their books.[8] They produced their own scholarship: from traditional philological volumes to more innovative forms, as Coppo borrowed contemporary Roman methods for documenting antiquity and translated them for the Istrian-built environment.[9] They viewed the Mediterranean world—the setting for their political lives and imperial careers—through the eyes of highly trained scholars, and this had important implications for how they perceived their roles as governors. Bembo wrote about his own career in the Mediterranean in the epic language of the *Aeneid*, and recorded information about Skiathos that he found in Ptolemy and Livy in his geographical encyclopedia.[10] Humanism was the cultural framework through which they documented the empire and their own lives within it; it was the social foundation for some of their most personally important relationships, with teachers, fellow students, and friends. Bembo and Coppo drew deeply on their own scholarship to imagine, map, and, indeed in some instances, frame their political decision making. Thus, humanism forms a central theme of analysis throughout the book.

The second theme is that of empire. The Venetian Mediterranean empire, or the *stato da mar*, forms an important setting for Bembo's and Coppo's stories.[11] Both men met their wives there. Bembo met Cyurω on Corfu, a Venetian island, in 1497. Coppo married Colotta in Isola, part of the Venetian territory of Istria, in 1499. Both men also governed there—Bembo on Skiathos, and Coppo in Istria. They wrote texts describing the empire's geography and history, and put their education in Latin literature to use in crafting their own maps and texts to describe their places in the empire. Their children—Bembo and Cyurω had ten, and Coppo and Colotta had five boys—sometimes struggled to find their own place between the society of the Venetian metropole and that of its maritime state. The empire was a part of Bembo's and Coppo's everyday lives, as they created mixed families, studied its geography, and governed in its territories.

The final theme, and the most important throughout the book, is that of family. Bembo and Coppo moved from their natal families in Venice to the scholarly families of teachers, students, printers, and intellectuals that formed such an important component of Venetian patrician society. They formed their own families in the maritime state: Bembo moved his family back and forth between Venice and the Mediterranean, while Coppo and Colotta settled in Istria, becoming wealthy landowners there. Throughout, it was Bembo's and Coppo's concerns about their family life—particularly about marriage and reproduction—that drove their political decision making and even their scholarship. Marriage contracts, worries about dowries, sexuality, and childbearing were abiding anxieties for Bembo and Cyurω, Coppo and Colotta. These concerns about family shaped their experience of the empire and the possibilities they discovered in their humanist writing and mapping. By tracing Bembo and Coppo from their natal families in Venice to their conjugal families in the Mediterranean and finally to their plans and aspirations for their children, the book reflects these men and women's consuming deliberations and concerns for family life.

Historiographical literatures exist for each of these themes. But *Venice's Intimate Empire* is the first to analyze how humanism, empire, and family life were intimately related for the men and women who crisscrossed the early modern Venetian Mediterranean. In studying Bembo's self-consolatory letter written upon Cyurω's death, or in Coppo's final testament, we can see how humanist writing and scholarly friendships, the setting of empire, and the concerns of family life were inextricable. They wrote about the empire and their families in the Latin language of humanism, and the friendships formed in their Venetian schoolrooms shaped their affective sense of identity and geography for the rest of their lives. Their identities as governors in the Mediterranean world—one as a representative of Venice, another as an Isolan municipal figure—had important implications for their family life. Bembo's career would be in shreds after a family scandal on Skiathos. The futures of Coppo's sons in Istria would be secured with his landowning wealth and political capital. They perceived their empire through the literary and historical lens of humanism; they made political decisions based on their concerns for their families' futures. *Venice's Intimate Empire* puts forward a new picture of the relationship between humanism, empire, and family, as these were the perceptive lens, physical setting, and driving motivation for these men across their lifetimes.

Both Venetian humanism and colonialism have been limited by their boundaries as historical subfields. The social history of Venetian humanism, in particular, has not been subject to critical attention since the analyses of class-bounded uses of classical knowledge in governance described by Margaret

King in the late 1980s—an assessment she recently revisited, but the conclusions of which she did not substantially revise.[12] Venetian colonial historiography has proliferated because of recent interest in cross-cultural identities and experiences of empire, for which the archival records of the early modern *stato da mar* provide a rich record.[13] But just as the patricians who governed Venice did not govern only by principles of their humanist education but also from their experience as colonists and merchants, the histories of the early modern Adriatic and Aegean are not reducible to ethnic and religious exchanges and must account for local intellectual cultures. Margaret King's conclusions, which have shaped the historiography of Venetian humanism, along with the close focus of colonial historians on imperial identities, have created sometimes inward-looking subfields within Venetian historiography. It is my intention here to bring a history of Venetian intellectual culture into conversation with a history of Venetian colonial culture, with implications for our assumptions about each.

This book argues that we can see how humanism, empire, and family life were related only by studying how these individuals perceived them. Humanism was a deeply personal enterprise for Bembo and Coppo, as they used Latin literature to reflexively write and map their own lives and experiences in the Mediterranean empire. For these men, the empire itself was not only the collective enterprise elaborated and legitimated in Venetian humanist writing, but a physical setting for the personal triumphs and tragedies of their imperial careers and families.[14] As we shall see throughout the book, by understanding Venice and its empire through the eyes of Bembo, Coppo, Cyurω, and Colotta, much of what we think we know about humanism and early modern imperial life becomes far less certain. We will consider the empire from their perspectives, as they crossed the sea, mapped the empire in the margins of their books, carved woodcut maps, arranged dowries for their daughters, and allotted colonial property to their sons. *Venice's Intimate Empire* argues that when we see the Venetian maritime state, humanism, and imperial families from this intimate perspective, our understandings of each of these must alter and become more capacious.

An Intimate Approach

How did these families perceive their own empire, and their identities within it? How did their intimate relationships shape their perceptions and experiences of empire? These questions are at the heart of the book. And indeed, Bembo and Coppo, and Cyurω and Colotta offer us an unusual level of insight into their perceptions of their empire and their families. The combination of their social status, level of education, and the fortunate survival of a great variety and depth of sources related to their lives means that these families offer us an unusual opportunity to see the Venetian empire from the inside: from the imaginations and charged emotional experiences of the men and women who lived and governed in it. As we will see, this shift in perspective to the interiority of these subjects will have important historiographical implications for the study of early modern empire and humanism. But this emphasis on interiority also provides a fresh methodology for studying early modern empire, one that puts its subjects' emotional responses and reflexive writing about the self at the forefront of its analysis.

Bembo's and Coppo's social conditions are important determining factors in allowing us to write their intimate histories. Bembo was a patrician, but born on the outer circles of patrician political society. Coppo was the illegitimate son of a patrician father, a boy who witnessed his half brothers—born legitimately—gain all of the social and political benefits of noble status. Both men were at the slippery boundaries of social hierarchy.[15] Bembo was precariously balanced on the outer boundaries of patrician life and faced the possibility of swift upward or downward social mobility based on his political career. His catastrophic tenure on Skiathos, as well as his toxic combination of resentment toward his own class and a clear ambition for their patronage, meant that he would eventually become even more alienated from the inner circles of political and social power. Coppo, though excluded from the significant privileges of patrician class belonging, proved himself to be an impressive student and took advantage of all the opportunities of his humanist scholarly networks. The vast bureaucracy of the Venetian empire meant that a well-educated, if socially insecure, young man such as Coppo found a career as an imperial notary, and he transformed that career into a much more ambitious Isolan one with his marriage to Colotta.

Cyurω was also socially mobile, though for her the stakes were much higher. A Corfiote servant, she became the wife of a Venetian patrician and, after much strife, the mother to a patrician son, effectively flouting all the rules of patrician membership. Of all the figures in this book, Cyurω experienced the greatest highs and lows of social mobility. As we will see in chapter 3, this oscillation of social status was tightly related to her spatial mobility, as she moved from her native Corfu to Venice as the wife of a patrician, back to the empire as a governor's wife, and finally, in social disgrace, back to the metropole. As we have seen, Bembo ascribed her illness to the great anxieties these concerns about mobility caused her, as she worried about her eldest son's humanist education, her daughters' dowries, and her youngest son's patrician status. Conversely, Colotta was perhaps the most stable throughout her life. Born into the noble Ugo family in Isola, she further cemented her status in the town with her marriage to a Venetian almost-patrician. But Colotta's stability was the springboard for Coppo's mobility, as his marriage to her proved the foundation for his later political success and wealth. These families were particularly vulnerable to social mobility, and thus become valuable subjects for an analysis of the personal dimensions of encounters with social structures of empire across their lifetimes.

The historiography on the social conditions of the patriciate, therefore, is central to much of the research undertaken here. Monique O'Connell's social history of the *rettori*, or colonial governors, is foundational in this regard, as she elaborates the responsibilities, patterns of office holding, and legislative processes that supported and controlled the patrician colonial administrators.[16] Many studies on the social history of the patriciate have been published in the past thirty years, including Donald Queller's analysis of the ideologies and office holding of the patriciate, Dennis Romano's history of the social networks of patricians within Venice and the *terraferma*, and important articles by Stanley Chojnacki, as well as Alexander Cowan's work on patrician marriage.[17] Bridging Monique O'Connell's work on the *rettori* and earlier social histories of the patriciate in a methodological sense is Yuen-Gen Liang's *Family and Empire*.[18] Concerned with a very different imperial history of late medieval and early modern Spain, although taking the Mediterranean as its setting, Liang demonstrates the central position of the history of the family to a social and administrative history of empire. While O'Connell's book and earlier studies of the Venetian patriciate are essential for the research that follows here, I am also interested in incorporating Liang's approach to studying the multiterritoriality of empire through tracing the history of individuals in the colonial Mediterranean, and what these intimate histories can reveal about their negotiations of the different social, administrative, and cultural worlds in which they took part.

This sense of precarious social mobility also characterized Bembo's and Coppo's status as humanists. On the fringes of Venetian intellectual life, they produced unusual scholarship from their Mediterranean vantage points. Bembo is now known primarily for producing a fairly unexciting volume of philological scholarship and for being a friend-of-a-patron of Aldus Manutius.[19] Coppo is known for having produced the first regional geographic and historical description of Istria, which became an important text for historians such as Pietro Kandler, who documented Istrian history during the political upheavals in the region throughout the nineteenth century.[20] And yet, as we will see, both Bembo and Coppo had considerably more complex relationships to

Venetian humanism than these historiographical legacies imply. They were on the fringes of Venetian intellectual circles, like many of their peers. They were educated in the humanist schools of Venice but were not exceptionally talented intellectuals. Like many of their school friends, they journeyed into the Mediterranean in their early twenties and discovered a new way of engaging with antiquity. Within the setting of their scholarship, they were deeply engaged in the particularly Mediterranean dimensions of Venetian humanism. But once they took up posts in the empire, their scholarship turned inward: to describe their own experiences of empire, as part of its ranks of officeholders, as husbands to colonial women, as travelers through its space, and, in Coppo's case, as a settler in colonial territory. By studying their evolving scholarship across their lives, we gain an unusual insight into the ways in which humanism provided a language and literature for their lifetimes, and how Latinity could be molded and shaped according to individual circumstances and needs.

Precisely because they lived on the boundaries of social and intellectual circles in Venice and its empire, we have an unusual number and diversity of sources charting their social, intellectual, and political development. For Bembo, the primary source used throughout the book is his autograph composite manuscript.[21] Containing a collection of copied inscriptions from around the Mediterranean, as well as Greek schoolroom exercises, lists, and fragments of letters, the manuscript contains most importantly his lengthy autobiographical letter. This letter is a source for Bembo's reckoning of not only his own life but also that of his family and particularly of his wife, as the letter was written as a consolation following her death. Like many humanist scholars of his time, Bembo was also a book collector and active reader. I have traced four printed books that he owned and annotated, and one manuscript. We have a good sense of the rest of his library from studying his annotations to these printed books: he certainly owned many more than have survived today. The surviving annotated books include a printed copy of all of Petrarch's Latin works; a copy of Lucretius's *De rerum natura*; a Greek textbook, printed by Aldus Manutius; and a heavily annotated *Isolario*, or geographical encyclopedia of Mediterranean islands. His manuscript, which he gave to a close school friend, contains copies of texts by Cicero.[22] Finally, Bembo also published his own work of philological scholarship in Venice in 1502, drawing on the scholarly work of Venetian friends, classmates, and teachers.[23] With the annotations Bembo made to his miscellany manuscript, his scholarship across several genres, and of course his long autobiographical letter, Bembo's world of scholarship, family, and governance comes alive across the mass of his writing and reading.

Pietro Coppo, unlike Bembo, did not leave behind personal autobiographical writing. But he was a prolific scholar, particularly fascinated by geographical study of the Mediterranean. He wrote a substantial geographical encyclopedia, *De toto orbe*, which survives in two manuscript copies. He also wrote a summary of this text, the *De summa totius orbius*, in both Latin and Italian. This exists in three further manuscript copies. Several of these geographical manuscripts are illustrated with woodcut maps that Coppo cut and printed himself, providing an unusual insight into the ways in which Coppo reconciled his study of Ptolemaic geography with the Mediterranean world he witnessed, particularly the Istrian peninsula. Coppo also wrote and cut maps for a printed *Portolano*, or list-format sailing directions. Finally, Coppo wrote the first regional geography, or chorography, of the Istrian peninsula: *Del Sito de Listria*, written in the 1520s but printed in Venice in 1540. This is his most remarkable work, a close study of the history, mythology, topography, and built environment of his adopted homeland.[24]

Finally, this book also draws extensively on documentary sources. Bembo was a patrician and an officeholder in the empire, and so we can trace him through the social institutions that regulated his political participation and family choices. Coppo was not a patrician, so he is missing from the extensive Venetian documentation of patrician families, as we will explore in depth in chapter 1. But he was at the center of the municipal politics of Isola, in Istria, which, like many eastern Adriatic towns, kept extensive records of its proceedings. It is possible, then, to compare Coppo's administrative life with his scholarly one, to attempt to untangle how his geographical writing and mapping were linked to his new life in Isola. If Coppo did not write self-reflexively, the complex administrative world of Cinquecento Istria—on the one hand, deeply locally rooted, and on the other, connected in multiple ways to the empire and to Venice itself—provides a set of sources that can tell us a great deal about one man's relationship to the broader structures of empire. Very few early modern people were tracked by as comprehensive a state bureaucracy as that of Venice, educated to the high degree required to produce Latin scholarship, and in a social and cultural position to write about their own intimate lives. But this unusual set of circumstances provides us with a lens through which we can study the intimate experiences of early modern empire.

Across the range and variety of sources deployed here, it is Bembo's and Coppo's private writing that remains at the heart of the book's approach to intimate experience. Within Venetian historiography, the book's reliance on Bembo's and Coppo's private writing engages with James Grubb's question: Why did Venetians not write family *ricordanze* like their Florentine counterparts?[25] Where Grubb suggests that Venetian patricians memorialized their families in the documentary sources of Venetian central government, this book finds that Venetians did write privately about their families alongside those public family memorials such as the *Libro d'Oro*. It simply looks for this private writing in different places: not in *ricordanze* or in *libri di famiglia* but in the considerably less generically defined writings of marginalia, miscellanies, and private letters between scholars. While the book focuses on these two families, one implication of the research here is that to study Venetian private writing, we must not look for *ricordanze* or only in public records but rather look in the margins of printed books, in the flyleaves of miscellanies, and in the hundreds of letters that flew between Venetian elites. This is particularly true for men such as Coppo, who is missing from the records of the *Libro d'Oro* and other patrician record-keeping repositories due to his illegitimacy. By focusing on these public repositories, we may miss the men who wrote about their lives from more unstable social conditions. Seeking private writing in the margins of early modern sources, we are able to see Venice and its empire from the intimate perspectives of the men traversing them.

As Adam Smyth has written, reading early modern forms of life writing means attending closely to both its diversity of forms and the intertextual, mediated nature of these kinds of sources—from commonplace books and miscellanies to marginalia and even maps.[26] In Bembo's case, we can examine not only his autobiographical letter but the miscellaneous, composite manuscript in which it is contained, and compare these with the annotations in his printed books, which often overlap. As Smyth has found, the relationship between early modern forms of life writing and subjectivity is one of affiliation, of retrospectively identifying with narratives, texts, and figures of one's own life and of one's rich literary landscape through a process of associative connections and comparisons.[27] Through classical references in marginalia, overlapping annotations and prose, and comparing archival documentation with Bembo's and Coppo's own writings and maps, we can begin to piece together their interior experiences of their empire.

Bembo's, Coppo's, Cyurw's, and Colotta's experiences of empire were shaped by bonds of affection and friendship, by sometimes irreconcilable desires and needs, by fantasy and self-regard. By using archival documentation alongside scholarship and private writing, and especially by attending to questions of intertextuality and associative writing, we are able to see "inward as well as outward, to focus on the constitutive elements of human subjectivity as well as its determinants."[28] In doing so, the book builds on feminist historical scholarship that has emphasized that early modern selfhood was not entirely the product of discursive self-fashioning, a cultural artifact structured and determined by "identity regimes."[29] Instead, we see throughout how the desires and fears of these four men and women were often irreconcilable with the social and political institutions of their imperial metropole, how their senses of belonging and of selfhood were pieced together through lifelong processes of "identifications and separations."[30] In a discussion of fantasy in the conclusion to the book, I consider the wider implications of this intimate, subjective approach for the main political narrative that has structured Venetian historiography: the myth of Venice.

Humanism, Empire, and the Family

Venice's Intimate Empire offers a view of the Venetian empire from the eyes of its governors and, in the case of Cyurω and Colotta, from that of its subjects. In doing so, it unsettles some of our fundamental assumptions about Renaissance humanism, the Venetian empire, and early modern imperial families. In arguing for the interrelationship between family, humanism, and empire, the book contributes in several ways to ongoing historiographical debates about each. First, the study of humanism put forward here argues that we must see humanist intellectual development over trajectories of both time and space. Bembo's and Coppo's scholarship—though begun in the cookie-cutter mold of adolescent Latin education—developed in unexpected ways later in their lifetimes. They offer salutary lessons about the difficulty of categorizing the typicality of humanist practice, and its relationship to wider social structures and institutions. Linked to this, the book suggests (particularly in chapters 1 and 2) that affective relationships, broadly conceived, must be considered as one of the most important social structures in which humanism as an intellectual practice happened. We know a great deal about the institution of the Venetian Scuole and the printing houses that were indeed crucial for the development of Venetian humanism and for shaping its unique character.[31] But we know much less about how the social and emotional life of these institutions shaped the kind of scholarly work produced within them.[32] Humanist schoolrooms were important settings for lifelong affective relationships between students and teachers, and created bonds that held strong across the space of the empire. Educational life took place first within the natal family household, then within the close emotional bonds of the Scuola, and finally in the tightly knit communities of humanist publishing, where friendships and enmities had important scholarly implications. We cannot separate the emotional lives of humanists from their social institutions; the first two chapters set out what this kind of integrated cultural and social analysis might look like.

Second, as we track their experiences from the schoolroom of the metropole to the islands of the Mediterranean, the importance of place in Venetian humanism becomes especially clear. We learn a great deal about the Mediterranean dimensions of Venetian humanism, as we examine how Bembo's and Coppo's scholarship evolved from its Venetian origins in the lecture hall of San Marco to documenting the antiquities of the Mediterranean world. Margaret King has considered the role of the Venetian expansion into the *terraferma* in the development of humanism in the metropole.[33] Patricia Fortini Brown demonstrated that the classical inscriptions, ruins, and Greek culture of the Aegean world—often encountered during mercantile activity in the islands—made a deep impression on artistic and literary production in Venice during the Renaissance, an argument I build on in chapter 2.[34] Similarly, Deno Geanakoplos explored the hellenistic dimensions of the Venetian Renaissance, writing about the patricians who pursued the study of Greek to serve the interests of the state, as well as researching the role of dispersed Greek intellectuals (especially those from Crete) throughout the Mediterranean world.[35] Two collections of essays look at the role of Renaissance culture on Crete and Cyprus, respectively, the largest and most economically important of the Venetian island colonies.[36] In a 1985 volume edited by Vittore Branca and Sante Graciotti, contributors were particularly interested in the ways in which a Venetian colonial presence in Istria and Dalmatia was formed, or responded to, indigenous intellectual movements.[37] Finally, and within the recent turn in Venetian scholarship toward questions of identity, several studies have looked at the ways in which writing and illustrating volumes about "others"—and particularly Ottoman Turks—provided "a crucial moment of cultural self-definition," a way for humanists and artists to "craft a compelling notion of Western society."[38] Nancy Bisaha, Kate Fleet, and Margaret Meserve have written about humanistic and textual representations of Ottoman "others," while Bronwen Wilson has turned to Venetian print culture, including maps and costume books, to discover the ways in which Venetian metropolitan identities were formed in response to images of the city and its other.[39]

Scholarship on the identities, negotiations, coexistence, and representations of and between the many ethnic groups sharing the space of the early modern Mediterranean has informed my research, as it has opened up the field of Venetian colonial history to perspectives beyond that of the city of Venice itself and emphasized the processual and dynamic nature of coexistence. However, rather than a history of early modern Mediterranean identities, I hope to contribute here to a history of Mediterranean culture, and specifically to a history of the colonial intellectual culture of the Venetian polity.[40] Although cultural histories like those of Bronwen Wilson and Nancy Bisaha are important for understanding the perspectives of Venetians living in the metropole, the history of Venetian intellectual culture as it was produced, transmitted, and reshaped outside Venice is one that has yet to be written. This emphasizes how important the Mediterranean was to the particularity of Venetian humanism, and that Venetian humanist practices changed and evolved when confronted with the scholars of the Mediterranean colonies, the Mediterranean landscape, and especially its antique material culture. Moreover, it emphasizes that the stage of Mediterranean antiquity became especially important as a setting for imperial office holding. The literature of humanism met with the physical evidence of antiquity in the Mediterranean, and this provided a history and set of images for the humanistically educated officeholders who governed there. This book aims to elaborate an intellectual history of the Venetian empire by examining how humanism related to the task of governing in the eyes of the men who filled the empire's imperial offices.[41] It puts forward a history of the integration between humanism and the practical, subjective politics of empire as it was perceived by Venetian humanist governors.

Finally, as discussed briefly in the above consideration of social status and sources, *Venice's Intimate Empire* is interested in what might be called "secondary" humanism: in the scholars and texts that have not typically been studied within the intellectual history of humanist practice.[42] These texts are humanistic documents in the sense that Paul Oskar Kristeller outlined in his well-known definition of humanism as a mode of literary criticism focused on the rhetorical imitation of particular modes and styles of composition.[43] Although Kristeller's definition is usually taken to refer to the polished Latin texts of influential scholars and teachers, Kristeller's own *Iter Italicum* reveals the huge range of commonplace books, encyclopedic texts, miscellanies, poetry, and historical writing that were important features of the rhetorical, imitative literary criticism and composition that was Renaissance humanism.[44] Equally important to consider are the imitative traditions outside of those modeled on Cicero and Livy: those humanists who modeled their composition after their contemporaries, after minor classical writers, and especially after humanist literature that emerged from non-Italian centers, such as Dalmatia or Crete.[45] Finally, Thomas Dandelet has drawn attention to the enormous political importance of a strain of imperial humanism—as distinct from the republican civic humanism usually associated with Florence and Venice—in early modern empire building from Spain to Britain.[46] Recent studies of the civic humanism of the Renaissance Italian republics have called into doubt its coherence and significance as a movement within Renaissance political thought.[47] *Venice's*

Intimate Empire builds on this interest in expanding the kinds of political configurations with which Renaissance humanism has typically been affiliated.

In its focus on men on the fringes of Venetian intellectual life, and on their letters, marginalia, and even vernacular texts, the book puts forward a picture of Venetian humanism at a social and intellectual level different from that articulated in Margaret King's *Venetian Humanism in an Age of Patrician Dominance*. King's selection criteria included "activity," "significance," "residence," and "generation." Of these, "significance" is perhaps the most opaque: King writes that she includes humanists who wrote "substantial" works as well as those who wrote "minor" works but who were engaged in intellectual correspondence and conversation with others, or who were renowned as teachers and scholars. The parameters of a particular work's significance, however, are not elaborated.[48] I expand the parameters employed by King, including sources that were not necessarily "substantial" and men whose intellectual activity in the *stato da mar* was as significant for Venetian metropolitan intellectual and political culture as that of the men who were lifelong residents of the city. Coppo, after all, was not a patrician, even as he was a devoted student of one of the most famous Venetian humanists of the day, Marcantonio Sabellico; and Bembo, who was a patrician, was hardly dominant in either intellectual or social life, instead eventually alienating himself from his humanist-patrician peers. For those studying Renaissance humanism more broadly, then, this book offers lessons in studying the movement "from the margins": on the margins of social class, of the page itself, and from the Mediterranean margins of empire. In doing so, it provides the first major reassessment of Venetian humanism in thirty years.

Bembo and Coppo did not use humanist practices and antiquarian scholarship to justify Venetian rule in the Mediterranean, or indeed to elaborate sophisticated, conceptually unified theories or histories of their empire. Humanism was first and foremost a set of linguistic tools, literary images and figures, fragmentary historical narratives, and methods of recording the physical evidence of antiquity: intertextual and overlapping modes of documentation cobbled together in composite form. Humanism offered a subjective, highly personal mode of engaging with the textual and material evidence of antiquity, and this went hand in hand with the sociality of the humanist circles in which Bembo and Coppo participated. As we will see, Bembo's and Coppo's friendships with their teachers, fellow students, and intellectual peers were deeply and personally important to them and, indeed, structured their experiences and ways of writing about their imperial careers. Viewed from the margins, this book puts forward a more expansive vision of humanist practice in Venice than previous scholarship, which has emphasized a relatively rigid, formal relationship between patrician society and its political uses of humanism as an ideology and mode for state-oriented political thought.[49] Humanism was rather improvisational and informal, a scholarly framework for integrating a variety of both textual and material evidence, modes of authority, and documentary practices in order to imagine, map, and interrogate the space and history of the empire as Bembo and Coppo subjectively experienced it.

The book also offers a new picture of how we might study early modern empire and the history of families within it. Throughout, we see how the problems of family life—of marriage, reproduction, childhood, and adolescence— were central to the Bembo and Coppo families' experiences of empire. Bembo's marriage to Cyurω had serious implications for his own social status within the empire. Cyurω's experience of being an imperial subject underwent a series of sometimes painful transformations as she moved from Corfu to Venice and back to the Mediterranean, and as she took on the responsibilities of Venetian patrician motherhood. As we will see, Bembo and Cyurω's children, especially their teenage daughter Urania, encountered serious problems on the fringes of the empire in the northern Aegean. In this graphic episode of sexual scandal and violence, we will see how sexuality, the body, and the visceral physicality of reproduction defined the Bembo family's experience as governing representatives of Venice in the Aegean.[50] In the case of Coppo, reproduction had a much more positive set of consequences: from their five sons and their marriages to Istrian women, Coppo and Colotta cemented their position as a mixed family in the colonial territory of Istria. The book argues that these problems of family life, the sometimes messy, sometimes violent problems of sexuality and reproduction, were actually central to the way that empire worked in the early modern period. Questions of family life, and related concerns about the body and sexuality, structured these men and women's experiences of empire. They made decisions not based on an abstract imperial ideal, or indeed even necessarily based on an individual sense of social, political, or intellectual ambition, but rather based on family matters: How would they raise dowries? Who would be the most appropriate spouses for their sons and daughters, and how could they prevent the wrong kind of sexual relationships from unfolding? How could they accumulate, and then parcel out, land and other resources to the next generation? These questions drove their actions, and so must also be understood as a central subject of analysis for historians interested in the ways in which the Venetian empire worked in the early modern period.

In arguing for the central role of the family throughout, this book builds on an extensive Italian and Anglophone literature on family life during the Italian Renaissance. It has long been understood that the family, or more broadly the clan, was a fundamental building block of Italian Renaissance society. Indeed, some of the most influential studies of Italian Renaissance history have focused on the social history of the family, as in Christiane Klapisch-Zuber's work.[51] Within Venetian historiography, this literature is based on the intensive study of marriage contracts, dowry arrangements, and especially women's wills, and was aimed at illustrating a bird's-eye view of the choices that women faced as they moved from their natal household to a conjugal household and sometimes back again. This literature is particularly noteworthy for its nuanced portrait of gender relations in early modern Venice.[52]

From its origins in social history, the study of the Italian Renaissance family moved toward more culturally inflected studies of the family. For Renaissance Venice, Patricia Fortini Brown's study of the domestic environments and material culture of Venetian families is particularly important.[53] More recent work has aimed to historicize childhood, the body, and gender as they were experienced within Italian families and religious institutions.[54] Providing a foundation for these social and cultural studies, the historiography of the Italian Renaissance family has also long concerned itself with economic relationships to uncover the strategies patrician families used to consolidate power, and sought to understand the patriciate class as an economic and social institution in its own right.[55] In Venice, economic historians of the family have focused on the uniquely Venetian institution of the *fraterna*, under which a father's patrimony was shared equally and jointly by his sons; brothers also often lived together in the family *casa di statio* and often undertook domestic and business transactions within a fraternal partnership.[56]

This book builds on this increasingly diverse historiography and particularly extends the implications of Italian Renaissance family history into the realm of the Venetian empire. There is an emerging literature in early modern history on the importance of family in imperial structures. But this has largely been confined to the ways in which families monopolized certain imperial offices or created particular economic links with the colonial territory under their governorship.[57] *Venice's Intimate Empire* borrows more from the modern imperial historiography that emphasizes the importance of the cultural features of family life—particularly sexuality and the body—within imperial history.[58] This book builds on this emerging literature by analyzing the family through the subjective lens of personal experience and private writing.

It is able to do so largely because of the distinctiveness of Venetian intellectual culture itself. The patrician men who were educated as humanists read the canonical literature of Latin and, to some extent, Greek antiquity; this literature was entirely set on the same landscapes and coastlines that made up the Venetian empire itself. As we will see, Bembo and Coppo were especially interested in mapping the coordinates of their own imperial and intellectual careers against the ancient topography, figures, and historical narratives that they read about in classical histories and geographies. The personal, subjective writings and maps that they produced not only are evidence of a scholarly encounter with antiquity but chart their families' experiences across that same landscape. Early modern historians, particularly of the Atlantic world, have emphasized the importance of family and intimate approaches in studying empire.[59] However, the distinctiveness of Venetian humanism—its Mediterranean geography and its possibilities as a mode of life writing—means that we are allowed to see with an unusual depth and clarity the ways in which family matters, from reproduction and childbearing to marriage and death, structured men and women's experiences of early modern empire.

Transformation and Agency

The book began with an emphasis on the transformations undergone by our subjects. As Bembo reflected on his life, he interrogated his own social and political identities as he simultaneously mourned his wife's illness, which he ascribed to the anxieties caused by her own vast transformations. In Coppo's testament, we saw how his transformation into a local Isolan dignitary, husband to an Isolan noblewoman, was ambivalent in his own mind. He still mourned his close friendship with his teacher Sabellico, his affective thread to Venetian society, and memorialized it at the end of his life. Humanism, empire, and the importance of family are the three themes that emerge from these end-of-life private writings. These are the themes that make up the primary analytical focus of this book, alongside an attentiveness to the medium of private writing itself. But the processes of personal transformations—and the opportunities and exclusions that transformation incurred—are at the core of Bembo and Cyurω's, and Coppo and Colotta's stories.

To understand these transformations, we need a lens that can reveal early modern lives across both time and space. *Venice's Intimate Empire* is composed of these personal histories, which track their subjects' lives across multiple transformational trajectories: transitions from adolescence to adulthood; of social mobility; of intersections of gender, ethnic, and class identities; of evolving emotional histories, political subjectivities, and methods of private writing. Here, these parallel histories can perhaps be compared to the methods of long-exposure photography. In a long-exposure photograph, the camera's shutter speed is delayed in order to capture the passage of time. The path of moving objects becomes sharply visible. This book captures the transformations wrought and experienced by its moving objects, across the passage of their lifetimes.

Across the course of a long lifetime, our subjects may be typical at some points and unique at others. One was born into unusual circumstances and through education and political office achieved a prototypical career. Another began with an education and social condition similar to many others of his class, and veered from his path with a disastrous marriage and one catastrophic decision as governor. A snapshot from any particular moment in these individuals' lives, therefore, may or may not be representative of wider cultural trends. For example, the traditional humanist philological volume that Bembo edited in his early thirties looks like a perfectly representative source from this period of Venetian humanism, and indeed it has been used to exemplify contemporary trends in intellectual history.[60] But a glimpse of his later annotations to his geographical encyclopedia, which he used as a repository for classical information about the islands he was sent to govern, represents an entirely unique, subjective use of humanism for his personal imaginative ends.[61]

By studying these men and women as if through a long-exposure photograph, *Venice's Intimate Empire* shows that historical people can be both perfectly ordinary and perfectly extraordinary across the scope of single life. Their lives were made of both remarkable and completely unremarkable events and transactions. We can begin to see that the remarkable or unusual, understood through a lifelong analysis, indeed makes no sense without the context and contrast of the usual. Bembo and Cyurω, and Coppo and Colotta are both representative of wider cultural trends and phenomena, and entirely extraordinary, at different moments in their personal histories. As modern imperial historians have found, this intimate, long-exposure approach reminds us that "imperial processes, discourses and trajectories were ones that were lived, resisted and confounded by people . . . who lived out familial and individual lives in all of their complexities."[62]

One of the most intriguing implications of this approach is that it problematizes the analytical concept of agency in studying these individuals' lives. By taking the long-exposure approach to our two families, studying the lives of men and women across the decades and physical space, we can see more clearly the moments at which they were unable to shape their circumstances. Despite his political and social capital as a member of the vast Bembo clan, Bembo simply could not reintegrate into patrician political society after his catastrophic tenure on Skiathos. Though Coppo eventually achieved political success and wealth, the stage for his success was Isola, not Venice—was this a lasting legacy of his illegitimate birth? While Domenico, the youngest of

Bembo and Cyurω's sons, gained entrance to the patriciate despite his non-Venetian, low-born mother, their eldest son, Modestino, did not, and their daughters' social fortunes were imperiled by their lack of dowries. When could these men and women exercise change, and when did they fail? What circumstances conditioned these possibilities?

Throughout the book, we will see that it was the hierarchy of belonging and identity that most profoundly shaped these families' experiences. In Cyurω's story told in chapter 3, the intersection of gender and ethnicity had particularly powerful effects on her ability to shape her own social fortunes in Venetian society. In Bembo's words, she was—despite her defense of her husband, her anxieties for her children—still "a Greek woman, and the Greeks are not much loved."[63] That patchwork of gendered and ethnic identity proved unshakable. Gender and citizenship had particularly important effects for Coppo, too, although being a Venetian "man of empire" resulted in a considerably more positive outcome for him. As we will see in chapter 4, Coppo was able to leverage his Venetian identity, which was problematic at home, into social and political success in Isola. In the way that these families broke particular social molds and expectations, they reveal a great deal about how individuals encountered the larger social structures of their empire. Agency failed or succeeded at points across lifetimes, at intersections of class, gender, religious belief, ethnic belonging, and political cultures. Rather than ascribing our men and women a uniformly optimistic degree of agency, we can see how their experiences of agency rested on their highly mutable experiences of identity.[64] These questions of transformation, agency, identity, and belonging are threads running throughout the book, and to which we will return in its conclusion.

Chapter 1

Venetian Families

From the Household to the Scuola

Introduction

This chapter has two central aims. The first is to explore what it meant to be born on the boundaries of the Venetian patriciate. Around 2,600 patrician men were living in Venice toward the end of the fifteenth century.[1] Pietro Coppo and Giovanni Bembo were born on the slippery boundaries of this tightly defined aristocratic class: Coppo, born illegitimately toward the end of 1469 or in early 1470, and Bembo, born to patrician parents on the fringes of noble society just a few years later in 1473. The first section of this chapter describes Bembo's and Coppo's relationships within their families: to their mothers, fathers, grandfathers, and uncles. Their marginal status brought uncertainties and ambiguities to their sense of kinship, shaping their sense of personhood and subjectivity through contested family relationships. This part of the chapter explores the consequences of illegitimacy and marginality for Coppo and Bembo, respectively. It is particularly important to understand the fine gradations and tensions in social status for both of these young men within their natal families, as these subtle distinctions would condition their trajectories of social mobility for the rest of their lives.

Both boys were educated as humanists, first in their family homes, and then in the Venetian Scuola di San Marco. Bembo's and Coppo's transformations into adults provide an unusual insight into what was the experience of many humanistically educated adolescents in Renaissance Venice. Existing on the margins of Venetian intellectual society, they give us an unusual window into the secondary humanist culture of Renaissance Venice. Following the transformations of Bembo and Coppo from boyhood to adolescence to adulthood, we are able to give not only a specificity and richness to the data amassed by social historians but also a level of descriptive detail usually available only for the most unusual individuals.[2]

The Scuola provided a new scholarly family for these young men, particularly in the intensely affective relationship between student and teacher. Both Bembo and Coppo were taught by renowned personalities in Venetian intellectual society in the last decade of the Quattrocento. Both formed important relationships with these men, founded on both intellectual endeavor and more emotional bonds. Tracking Bembo and Coppo from their natal families to their scholarly ones, the second aim of this chapter is to discover the ways in which these affective intellectual relationships shaped Bembo and Coppo from a very early age. The chapter traces the effects of these relationships from their scholarly careers to their political ones, and even to their conjugal families in the Mediterranean. At the heart of this chapter is a consideration of the bonds of family: the families these men were born into, and the families they made for themselves among their classmates and teachers.

The emotional landscape of the schoolroom has not always been well understood by historians of the Italian Renaissance. This chapter takes us through Venetian Renaissance schoolrooms through the eyes of Coppo and Bembo, allowing us to perceive its formative emotional significance to young Venetian men. In doing so, the chapter navigates between several fields of research: the social history of humanism, the social history of Venetian families, and the history of education. Our understanding of the social histories of humanism has recently become much more nuanced. Brian Maxson's study of the social history of Florentine humanism has made our picture of who participated in that city's intellectual culture far more capacious. Sarah Ross's study of the upwardly mobile, aspirational middling classes of Venice— of the physicians and apothecaries who owned Latin texts, gave their children classicizing names, and wrote profusely of their intellectual life in their testaments—has given us a far more textured social history of humanism in sixteenth-century Venice.[3] As Ross has found, humanism was not simply a dry, dusty intellectual endeavor undertaken in ascetic solitude, but one marked by individual and family aspirations, a way to consolidate close emotional ties, and undertaken with a keen sense of the social value of a classical education.

In putting an examination of Bembo's and Coppo's social conditions along-side a study of the affective power of their education, this chapter aims to unfurl the complex relationship between social status, education, and interior life.

On the Boundaries of the Patriciate

Both Bembo and Coppo were born on the boundaries of the Venetian patrici-ate: one benefiting from all the privileges of membership but without the il-lustrious family history and wealth required to join the inner circle of patrician society; the other born illegitimately but able to potentially gain a foothold in political society through family connections and education. Though Giovanni Bembo and Pietro Coppo were born with family names that indicated mem-bership in the Venetian patriciate, their social statuses were in fact much more complicated than their names might first suggest. The Bembo clan sprawled throughout the city, with members in the most esteemed posts of government and moving in the most elite intellectual circles; but Bembo's own immediate family was far less fortunate. Bembo was born a patrician and participated in all the rituals that demarcated a young patrician man's social and political ma-turity. But there was an elite within the patrician elite in Venice, and neither Bembo nor any male member of his natal family could claim membership to that inner circle.[4] Pietro Coppo was born the illegitimate son of Marco Coppo, who, along with his father and his brothers, had held some of the more impor-tant posts of the Venetian imperial bureaucracy. But we know nothing of Coppo's mother, only that she was likely not patrician and that Coppo was born out of wedlock. With patrician births closely scrutinized, Coppo was both socially effaced and politically disenfranchised, his name missing from Coppo family genealogical chronicles as well as the central repositories of patrician social life in Venice.

Commemorating Giovanni Bembo's branch of the family was (and is) the Ca' Bembo in the Campiello Santa Maria Nova, just down the street from the parish church of San Cancian, a palazzo that belonged to Gian Matteo Bembo (1490–1570). Gian Matteo memorialized his brilliant career in Zara, Cattaro, Famagusta, Candia, and the *terraferma* with sculptures and inscriptions installed in the facade of his palazzo.[5] Giovanni Bembo did not grow up in what would be Gian Matteo's palazzo, though, but rather in a similar *casa di statio*, or a family palazzo divided into apartments for its members, also near San Can-cian, perhaps even in the same *campiello* as Ca' Bembo.[6] Unlike Gian Matteo, he would not have much to commemorate in plaques or inscriptions. The house had belonged to his grandfather, Zuan Francesco (born in 1426), and then to his father, Domenico (born in 1459). It contained a garden as well as an apothecary shop.[7]

Giovanni was born in 1473, three years after his father had married Angela Cornaro. Bembo did not write much about his father in his lengthy autobiographical letter. Neither his grandfather, Zuan Francesco, nor his father, Domenico, nor even Domenico's brothers, Girolamo and Alvise, had held any particularly important posts in the Venetian state. Bembo's only discussion of his father is Domenico's death: he was posted as *castellano* in Soncino in 1500, but he died that same year and was buried in the newly built church of Santa Maria delle Grazie there.[8] Giovanni's brother, Francesco, embarked on a more notable career than his father and grandfather: in 1494, he was appointed to a series of important posts at Modon, starting as *castellano* and eventually becoming *capitano* and *provveditore*.[9] But Francesco died of syphilis not long after.[10] If "the story of Venetian expansion is the story of men," none of Bembo's immediate male family members could claim much of a role in that imperial history.[11]

Much more important in Bembo's own accounting for his life was his mother, Angela Cornaro. Angela appears throughout Bembo's letter. She played an important role in urging Bembo to finally marry Cyurw and put an end to his shameful arrangement of cohabitation. Bembo was particularly proud of his connection to the Cornaro family, the wealthiest in Venice, through his mother. He repeatedly writes that Angela was related by blood to Caterina Cornaro, the then-deposed queen of Cyprus. This kinship loomed large in Bembo's imagination of his family history, even if there is no evidence of a direct family relationship between the queen and Angela Cornaro.[12] Bembo even named his third son Cornelio to commemorate this link between his own conjugal family and the famed Cornaro. As Holly Hurlburt has explored, the figure of Caterina Cornaro was important in Venetian culture as a cipher for thinking about the role of women in the Republic.[13] It was through Angela's (probably imagined) kinship to Caterina, rather than the more immediate history of his paternal family, the Bembo, that Giovanni Bembo crafted a sense of connection to the elite circles of patrician society.

Bembo followed the well-regulated trajectory from a prolonged patrician adolescence into political adulthood. His odyssey began at eighteen years old with an application to the *Balla d'Oro*, a lottery that allowed a lucky few to join the Great Council at age twenty instead of waiting until twenty-five, the usual age for inclusion. Enrollment in the *Balla d'Oro* became hugely popular among adolescent patricians at the end of the fifteenth century: the years 1471–90 saw a 185 percent increase in participation from the lotteries held in the first quarter of the century.[14] Bembo and his brother Francesco were entered into the *Balla* on 22 October 1501 by their parents Domenico Bembo and Angela Cornaro.[15] Their registration was witnessed by six patrician men who were likely friends and neighbors of the family; Benedetto Sanudo, for example, lived nearby in San Cancian.[16]

When patrician boys like Bembo, born legitimately of two patrician parents, turned eighteen, they would be registered in front of the State Attorneys, bringing along their fathers or male kin—perhaps even their male neighbors—to present evidence of their age. Finally, at twenty-five, they would earn their seat at the Great Council. Through their later twenties, these men would toil in minor, undesirable, and yet competitive positions in Venetian governance; in the 1490s, approximately 800 of the 2600 male patricians of the city held government posts.[17] These "political apprenticeships" served a number of purposes: they provided crucial training and education for young men, preparing them for greater political responsibility in more desirable posts; they provided them with a salary, even a form of social welfare for poor nobles; and they kept the young men out of trouble.[18]

Bembo had privileged access to all the markers of status that defined adolescence and young adulthood for patrician men. And yet his branch of his paternal family set him on the margins of patrician society. His grandfather, father, and uncles had not amounted to much. Even his brother, perhaps destined for a more brilliant career in the empire, had his life cut short by syphilis. It was to his mother, Angela, rather than to his father that Bembo looked for blood relation to the patrician elite, through her tenuous kinship to Caterina Cornaro. As we will see, Bembo's life was marked by a simmering resentment to his own class, even as he attempted again and again to gain the political offices that would allow him to make his way into the patrician elite. It is easy to imagine that the conditions for this tension between resentment and ambition were laid in Bembo's early years, positioned as he was at the margins of the patriciate, with only his mother's tenuous link to Caterina a possible instrument of social mobility.

Pietro Coppo was excluded from these rituals and privileges that defined patrician adolescent life. He was born illegitimately in two senses: his father was unmarried when Pietro was born, and Pietro's mother was almost certainly not a patrician woman. As Thomas Kuehn has elegantly written, illegitimate children in Renaissance Italy had "a personhood of uncertain dimensions," as their legal and social status in relation to their natal families was often ambiguous.[19] Coppo was raised in the family home, and so was part of the social relationships of his paternal family.[20] The Coppo family were never especially politically important in Venice, but they were one of the oldest patrician families in the city. Their family home was in the parish of San Paternian, just a few winding streets behind San Marco.[21]

Pietro's father was Marco Coppo, who was one of seven Coppo brothers and one of the most politically successful.[22] Marco (born 1443) had held several administrative positions in *terraferma* cities (Brescia and Verona), and was the *castellano* of Mocco (1471) and the *podestà* of Piran (1492) in Dalmatia. He was also *camerlengo*, or treasurer, on Crete (1484). Marco was married twice. He first wed the daughter of Nicolò Frizier in 1474.[23] The Frizier family were part of the *cittadino* class, a social group defined as "original citizens" of Venice and eligible to serve in valuable and sensitive roles in the state chancellery. As James Grubb has found, searching for a firm class or community identity for the *cittadino* is a difficult task, particularly as intermarriage was relatively common between patrician men and *cittadino* women—especially when a large dowry was at stake. Marco Coppo was part of the approximately 14 percent of male patricians to marry *cittadini* women across the Quattrocento and first half of the Cinquecento.[24]

Pietro was four or five years old when his father married his Frizier wife. We do not know the identity of Pietro's mother: was she the Frizier woman, whom Marco married several years after their son was born? Or was Coppo's mother a household servant, a common route of illegitimate relationships in fifteenth-century Venice? In Venice, patrician households commonly had several domestic servants. Venetian humanist writers as well as legislators were concerned with proper household rule and management, including the treatment of servants. Domestic service was a common occupation for lower-status women in the city; for them, it was usually a temporary occupation in preparation for marriage. Of course, the relationship between master and servant could be fraught with sexual tension. Dennis Romano has found that sexual relationships between patrician men and their servant women were looked at severely by the Great Council: men who had sex with a servant had to pay her entire salary and give her a dowry. In 1422, the Great Council legislated that any children who resulted from a sexual relationship between master and servant women were ineligible for council membership, and so effectively disbarred from the politically enfranchised patrician class itself, if not from the "cadet nobility" formed by what Grubb has called "noble commoners," still aristocratic but politically powerless.[25]

It is impossible to know Coppo's mother's identity, nor know with any certainty whether she was involved in his early childhood. Perhaps he acquired a stepmother with his father Marco's marriage to the Frizier woman in 1474. When she died several years later, Marco Coppo married again, this time to a patrician widow, Elisabetta Contarini, in 1483.[26] This marriage brought more children: twin boys, Francesco and Giacomo, were born two years later in 1485. Coppo was about fifteen years old when his twin half brothers were born. Coppo's early childhood was marked by two or perhaps three different mothers: his biological mother, whose identity and role in Coppo's life is impossible to know; the Frizier woman, Marco's first wife, who died during his adolescence; and finally Elisabetta, who introduced half siblings into the Coppo household.

Francesco and Giacomo were born into all the privilege of legitimate patrician status that Coppo had been denied. They were enrolled in the *Balla*, witnessed by a small group of patrician men: Giovanni Vincenzo Dandolo, Giorgio Loredan, and Pietro Friuli, who were likely friends or neighbors in San Paternian.[27] But perhaps nowhere is their legitimate status more clear than in Elisabetta's final testaments of 1540 and 1541. In this, Elisabetta bequeaths her entire inheritance to Francesco and to Francesco's two children, Marchiò and Laura. She even asks Laura to say mass for her soul in San Gregorio, because "it is not possible to ask anything else of my son Francesco."[28] It is possible that Giacomo predeceased his mother. But Pietro Coppo is not once mentioned in Elisabetta's testament. Did Marco provide separately for his illegitimate son upon his death? His testament does not survive, so we are left without clear answers. Even in households where illegitimate sons were raised alongside legitimate siblings, inheritance was often a highly contentious and ambiguous matter.[29]

If Coppo's link to family inheritance is murky, we can be much more certain about his place in family history and genealogy. In the seventeenth-century *Breve Trattato dell'Antichissima Famiglia Copa Nobile Veneta*, Pietro Coppo's name is meaningfully absent. Only Marco's two legitimate sons, Francesco and Giacomo, are recorded here. Francesco's three sons and Giacomo's two are recorded, while of course Pietro's descendants are entirely missing. Illegitimacy effectively scrubbed Pietro's existence from the family record.[30] We are largely left to imagine the emotional and psychological effects of this illegitimate status on Pietro, as well as those impressed by his three mothers and half siblings. But we have one possible insight into how Coppo conceived of his own family relationships, particularly to the men in his paternal family. Marco Coppo was, as we have seen, relatively politically successful in both the *terraferma* and maritime empires. But it was Pietro's uncle Nicolò (born 1465) who held the most impressive offices among the Coppo brothers, a career that culminated in his appointment to the very important office of *rettore* of Canea, on Crete, in 1501.[31] Pietro's grandfather, Iacopo Coppo, had held this post in 1450.[32] Another of Pietro's uncles, Girolamo Coppo, had been *camerlengo* on Crete in 1473.[33] Indeed, holding prestigious posts on Crete seemed to be something of a family tradition among the Coppo men, suggesting either that they acquitted themselves well enough to be repeatedly entrusted with these roles or that they developed relationships on the island that made them specialists in Cretan governance.[34] The other brothers—Antonio (born 1448), Iacopo, and Giordano—also held minor administrative posts, some in the *stato da mar*. Girolamo, before his prestigious appointment to Crete, had been the *rettore* of Aegina in 1462.[35] The posts on Crete, in particular, were glories for the Coppo family, who otherwise filled the routine administrative posts of the Venetian metropolitan government and that of its empire.[36]

One uncle, however, forms an exception to this otherwise honorable tradition of office holding in the maritime state. Antonio Coppo was the *rettore* of Lemnos in 1470, but while there committed an astonishing series of crimes on the island, terrorizing its inhabitants. These crimes included imprisoning a Greek nobleman in a well for forty days, strangling a Greek *protopapas* in a well, suspending a Candiote man by his hands over the well, cutting off the nose of another Greek subject "without any precedent or due process," torturing another subject by suspending him by the testicles, raping multiple women, accepting bribes to permit piracy, selling off the wheat and legumes of the island so that its inhabitants went hungry, and even permitting an illegal night wedding during which a Turkish raid captured three hundred islanders. In 1478, Antonio was banned for life from Venice, from the maritime state, and from Venetian ships, under threat of beheading.[37] This extraordinary series of crimes raises provocative questions about madness and justice in the maritime state. Closer to home in San Paternian, how did Antonio's criminal madness, exile, and reputation among the Venetian patriciate shape the ways in which he was remembered among his own family members?

Pietro Coppo would have spent his childhood in San Paternian hearing of his grandfather's, father's, and uncles' many exploits in the Mediterranean, from Candia, the crown jewel of the Venetian empire, to Antonio's scandalous exploits on Lemnos. His male family members' political careers seem to have made a deep impression on him. Once in Istria and starting a family of his own, he named four of his five sons after his grandfather, his father, and his uncles—including Antonio. Why would Coppo name his second son after his uncle, given Antonio's deeply scandalous reputation? He tied himself through his own male heirs to his paternal family line, an especially symbolic gesture given that Coppo himself held an ambiguous relationship to his evolving natal family. Coppo tied his new family to his old one in Venice, even as his own status within his natal family was unclear, and the reputation of one uncle intensely problematic. Coppo's emotional ties and family bonds, like those of many illegitimate children of Renaissance Venice, are perhaps difficult to perceive. His condition as a bastard was not straightforwardly exclusionary.[38] Raised in his father's household, exposed to the great deeds of his grandfather, father, and uncles, Coppo would carry a deep sense of his bonds with his paternal family out into the Mediterranean empire.

A Love of Learning: From the Household to the Scuola

Patrician sons, and occasionally daughters, received their earliest humanist education in the home. Like many other adolescents in Venice in the late fifteenth century, Bembo and Coppo began their Latin education within their natal families. Even though he was born illegitimately, Coppo was raised by a patrician father who may have himself benefited from a humanist education. Recent research has shown that these educational aspirations were held not only by patrician families but also by "middle class" parents in Venice, including physicians and apothecaries, during the sixteenth century. A humanist education was recognized as socially valuable not only for reifying one's patrician status but also for providing opportunities for social mobility.[39] If a humanist education could have been considered Bembo's birthright as a patrician son, it had potentially more value for Coppo, who could use his education to create social and political opportunities.

Both boys would have begun with learning Latin grammar and elementary Latin reading, before progressing to study rhetoric and composition. They would have begun at home, probably with a privately hired Latin tutor, and may have studied alongside their brothers or cousins.[40] There, Cicero would have held a special place in the life of any Italian Renaissance schoolboy. Bembo gave his school friend, the soon-to-be-famous humanist teacher Giovanni Battista Egnazio, a manuscript compilation of several of Cicero's texts, including his *Orationes, Quaestiones Tusculanae, De Oratore*, and *Topica*.[41] The result of this early education was that Bembo and Coppo had mastered Latin by the time they reached late adolescence. Though humanist education was rote, some historians of education have argued that it also provided a richer and more practical moral content.[42] Humanist teachers claimed that memorizing passages of Cicero's letters would equip students for civic life. Not only could Cicero's stylized and persuasive writing be mined for students' own compositions, but the ways in which Cicero described personal moral dilemmas—with his friends or with his political rivals—had real potential to be analyzed and then applied in students' own lives.[43] Anthony Grafton has written that students of humanism could find "practical lessons in the classics" that could not only be applied to real-life circumstances such as administration but also be used in public duties such as orations or letter writing.[44] Moral philosophy was not necessarily taught as a separate subject, but moral lessons and actions were analyzed and interpreted in every classical text, including poetic works like Virgil's.[45] In this view of humanist education, the aim of the *studia humanitatis* was not pedantically grammatical, but instead it equipped students with practical and applicable moral lessons for their own lives as governors, administrators, and diplomats.

But Bembo and Coppo not only learned a set of lessons, morals, or rules to apply to both written composition and real-life decision making. What emerges from studies of the Renaissance Latin classroom is a picture of total immersion in Latin through repetition, memorization, and extended analysis. From declining nouns and conjugating verbs out loud, to memorizing lengthy extracts from Cicero's letters and Virgil's poetry, to atomizing complex texts and reorganizing them in commonplace books, as Ann Blair has revealed, these students lived the Latin language, Latin literature, and ancient culture with a deep mental involvement in classical literature and history.[46] This total immersion in Latinity did not "produce a specified effect," to use the language of modern cognitive psychologists of reading: reading and memorizing a lot of Cicero did not necessarily or straightforwardly imprint Cicero's moral compass on the young reader, no matter what the humanist teacher may have intended.[47] Rather, these psychological studies of the effects of reading have found that literature produces changes on perception and personality in unpredictable and idiosyncratic ways.[48] The effect of Latin literature on Renaissance students, who lived alongside Cicero and Virgil over many years, was profound, long lasting, and unpredictable. As young men, Bembo and Coppo not only learned Cicero's framework of morality as it could be applied to everyday life. But, having spent their entire childhood and adolescence absorbed in learning Latin, they gained an imaginative relationship to Latin literature and antiquity that would color their lives far beyond the doors of the schoolroom.

This childhood Latin education in grammar and adolescent education in rhetoric were complemented, from the early fifteenth century, by the establishment of public schools that were funded by the Venetian state. The first public school was founded at Rialto in 1408, devoted specifically to the study of philosophy. Two further public schools were founded at San Marco in 1446 and 1460; the first was intended for those young men destined for careers in the Venetian chancellery, and the second was presided over by a *lector* who gave a daily lecture in poetry and one in rhetoric or history.[49] By the later fifteenth century, the Scuola di San Marco was a center for humanistic learning in Venice, commanded by high-profile "chairs" who gave crowded daily lectures under the Campanile; it was more of an intellectual club for young patricians than the chancellery school originally envisioned.[50] Both Bembo and Coppo attended the Scuola di San Marco: Bembo, under the lecturer Benedetto Brugnolo, and Coppo, under the lecturer Marcantonio Sabellico.

Both Bembo and Coppo likely began attending lectures in the last years of the 1480s or 1490, when they were in their late teens; Coppo wrote that he was taught by Sabellico for three years, perhaps until 1493, when he left for Rome and Naples. Although they heard lectures delivered by different teachers, it is tempting to imagine that their paths sometimes crossed among the bookish crowds gathering at San Marco. For both, it was at the Scuola that their intellectual transformations from schoolboys to scholars began to take place. At the Scuola, they formed close relationships with the fatherly Brugnolo and the captivating Sabellico. In a sense, they were intellectual apprentices, guided into the world of scholarship by these two distinctive personalities of Renaissance Venice.

This intellectual apprenticeship at the Scuola, undertaken during Bembo's and Coppo's late teens and early twenties, closely matched the earliest phase of the transition into political maturity that all patrician adolescents undertook. At the same time as they attended the Scuola, Bembo enrolled in the Balla d'Oro. Just as Stanley Chojnacki has suggested that young patrician theater and dining clubs like the Compagnie della Calza were forums in which men too young for government posts were initiated into patrician membership, so too should the Scuola be considered as an alternative community in which intellectual and political maturity progressed along parallel tracks.[51] Like the Compagnie, the Scuola was a place where young patricians could form friendships with their aristocratic peers; and these friendships would extend beyond the Scuola, binding them as a political class before their political enfranchisement.

Benedetto Brugnolo was a humanist teacher from Legnano who held the first chair established at San Marco from 1466 to his death in 1502.[52] Brugnolo's chair was the most prestigious in Venetian education at the time, a position that "from its inception [was] the most essential to the Venetian state as a training-ground for its civil functionaries and the future members of its governing councils, equipping its students with well-stocked minds and fluent pens and tongues."[53] He was indeed a renowned scholar in Venice and an experienced editor of classical texts, appointed by Bernardo Giustinian to edit his important history of Venice, and had already edited volumes of Cicero, as well as George of Trebizond's Rettorica in 1472.[54] His school at San Marco was the meeting place for many well-known humanists in Venice toward the end of the fifteenth century. One of these humanists was Giovanni Battista Egnazio, Bembo's friend who would have a prominent career in Venetian intellectual life, including a high-profile rivalry with Sabellico, the second chair at San Marco and Coppo's own beloved teacher.[55] As Bembo wrote in his auto-biographical letter, his other "condiscipulus" included the poet Domizio Palladio Sorano; Giovanni Quirini, who was the "regulus" of the island Astypalea (and who also funded the construction of Brugnolo's tomb in the Basilica dei Frari); the doctor and lawyer Bernardino Cabalino; the Cretan teacher of Greek Marcus Musurus; the secretary of the Council of Ten Giovanni Battista Adriano; and the poet and teacher Nicolaus Gambus.

Bembo valued his intellectual circle of Venetians, as well as Greek scholars, in Venice and the Aegean, and nowhere is this more evident than in his retelling of the births and baptisms of each of his ten children.[56] At his eldest daughter Faustina's baptism was the Venetian governor of Pesaro; at Polymnia's, Aldus Manutius (in Bembo's words, "literarum reparator et latinorum librorum propagator"),[57] the lecturer of Greek Scipio Crateromachus, and Hieronymus Amaserius of Forlì, a humanities teacher in one of the public chairs in Venice. Present for Urania's baptism was the mathematician Nano Germano. Modestino's godfathers were Bartolomeo Fin, a Venetian doctor and lawyer, and the Corfiote humanist and book collector Giovanni Abrame.[58] At the baptism of Bembo and Cyurω's second son, Domenico, were Matteo Fideli and Bernardino Cabalino, both doctors and lawyers who attended Brugnolo's school with Bembo. Cornelio, a son who died in infancy, was baptized by Bartolomeo Zamberto, "graecae latinaeque linguae bene erudito": Zamberto was the first to translate Euclid into Latin.[59] A third son, Prudentio, was baptized by Giovanni Baptisa Egnazio; also present were two Cretan scholars of Greek, Marcus Musurus and Arsenios Apostolis; the secretary to the Council of Ten Giovanni Battista Adriano; and the poet Nicolaus Gambus, all of whom studied with Bembo at Brugnolo's. This baptism was also attended by Raphael Regius, a public lecturer in Padua. Thalia's baptism was attended by a doctor and orator in Venice. Angela's baptism was attended by the poet Domenico Palladio Sorano, who was a classmate of Bembo's at Brugnolo's academy.[60] More than fifteen years after the birth of his youngest child, Bembo remembered and reconstructed in his autobiographical letter each of his children's baptisms according to the eminent humanists and Venetian aristocrats who were present, many of them classmates from Brugnolo's school at San Marco. The intervening years, and his careful elaboration of the social networks in which he used to take part, speak to the lifelong significance of these friendships and of the continuing importance of this masculine scholarly community.[61]

Coppo was also part of a network of Venetian humanist scholars, one that spanned the Adriatic world. This intellectual society, which included Istrian as well as Italian humanists, was—much like Bembo's—bound by personal friendships developed in school, as well as by textual exchange and imitation. From his experience in the Scuola di San Marco under Marcantonio Sabellico, Coppo was integrated into Sabellico's circle. Not only did Coppo imitate Sabellico in his writing, but the friendships that he made through Sabellico's school proved important throughout his life. We will explore these affective and literary relationships in greater depth in chapter 6. Indeed, Coppo traveled with Pomponio Leto, the famed Roman academician and Sabellico's own teacher, throughout Rome and Naples; and, as we have seen, he dedicated his chorography *Del sito de Listria* to Giuseppe Faustino, a classmate from the San Marco school.

Sabellico was one of the central figures of Venetian humanism of the late Quattrocento, as the owner of the first copyright for a printed work, a prolific writer who taught an entire generation of Venetian scholars and noblemen, a historian of Venice, and a polemical figure who took part in that famous scholarly feud with fellow Venetian teacher and Bembo's friend Giovanni Battista Egnazio.[62] Born in Vicovaro in Lazio around 1436, Sabellico was trained as a humanist in Rome under Gaspare Veronese, Porcellio, and Domizio Calderini and, most importantly, was a member of the scholarly circle the Accademia Romana, formed by Pomponio Leto. His first teaching post was in Udine in Friuli, a Venetian territory, in 1473.

Arriving in Venice in 1484, Sabellico quickly wrote and published three short works on the geography and administration of the city of Venice itself: *De Venetis magistratibus*, written in 1488–89; the topographical work *De Venetae urbis situ*, composed in 1490 and 1491; and finally, *De praetoris officio*, written in 1491–92. But perhaps his most popular work was *Rerum Venetarum ab urbe condita*, a thirty-three-volume history of Venice conceived in Livian periods and presented to the doge in 1487.[63] Sabellico was appointed to lecture at the Scuola di San Marco in 1485; after the previous holder of the second San Marco chair, Giorgio Valla, died in 1500, Sabellico replaced him. In this second chair, Sabellico emphasized the teaching of eloquence and gave lectures in poetry, rhetoric, and history. His "sensationalist reputation" ruffled feathers among his contemporaries, but he was clearly a compelling and memorable teacher.[64] With Sabellico, Valla, and Brugnolo at the helm of the Scuola, "the last fifteen years of the Quattrocento were something of a golden age for Venetian public education."[65] And, although Sabellico did not write as an official historiographer of the state—he was rather a state-employed teacher who happened to write history—the *Rerum Venetarum* and the series of three works on Venetian geography and governance reified his central place in the intellectual and political culture of the city.[66] Indeed, Sabellico's repeated use of imagery relating Venice as the new Rome, his populist, "eyewitness" literary style, and his huge range of correspondents in Venice and beyond meant that his mode of historical scholarship was particularly influential.[67]

There was perhaps no relationship more emotionally important to Bembo, Coppo, and their classmates than that which they fostered with their teachers. This is particularly evident in the consolatory literature penned by Brugnolo's students when their beloved teachers died—Brugnolo died in 1502, and Sabellico only a few years later in 1506. Indeed, Sabellico gave a funeral oration for Brugnolo, as the diarist Marino Sanudo recorded.[68] But it was the Venetian patrician Niccolò Quirini, Brugnolo's student and Bembo's friend and classmate, who most eloquently expressed his relationship to his teacher in his oration for Brugnolo. This relationship clearly exceeded the Scuola di San Marco, as Brugnolo did not just teach Quirini Latin: he "desired not only to teach his pupils erudition and learning: indeed truly he strove to deter them from vice, and to imbue them with good character."[69] This transcended the teaching of moral philosophy to take the form of a deep affective relationship that imprinted on his students' personalities. As Quirini wrote, Brugnolo "always taught his students with such kindness, it was as though he himself had fathered them."[70] The Scuola became a kind of alternate houschold for these young patrician men, who shaped their personalities and their most intimate relationships around the teaching of their lecturers in rhetoric, poetry, and history. It was a scholarly household that Bembo himself tried to re-create as a grammar teacher in Pesaro, where his wife Cyurω "loved [his students] as if they were her own sons."[71]

Coppo recalled this affective, almost paternal relationship with his own teacher when he recorded his final wish for his precious manuscript to be sent to Santa Maria delle Grazie: "[It is] in the library of the said monastery that the excellent M. Marcantonio Sabellico—author of the Venetian Histories, who has 200 ducats per annum as provision for a public lecturer in the study of humanities in Venice, of whom I was his dearest pupil for three years—left his works composed in his hand, and my work will remain in the said library near to his, for my remembrance."[72] When Coppo composed his will in 1550, he decided to leave his *opera*—a manuscript copy of his most ambitious work, a Latin geography titled *De toto orbe*—to the monastery of Santa Maria delle Grazie. Suppressed in 1810, the church and monastery were on a lagoon island of the same name, only a short distance beyond San Giorgio Maggiore, and were devoted to a miraculous image of the Virgin that had been brought to the island from Constantinople.[73] Coppo's precious *De toto orbe* sat on the monastic library shelves next to the manuscript works of his beloved teacher. These "libri ornati," mentioned in Sabellico's own will, were perhaps his *Rerum venetiarum ab urbe condita*.[74] Sabellico had also arranged to be buried in the monastic church and for a tomb tablet to be placed into the wall of the church, with the modest epitaph: "This small urn contains Coccio, the writer whom neither the events of history nor the whole of time could contain."[75] Sabellico probably composed the Latin epitaph himself, which was framed by the poet's laurels, the writer's quill, and a blank heraldic shield, an evocative symbol of Sabellico's (supposedly) lowly birth as the son of a blacksmith.[76] Here was a man who had made his career through scholarship, writing, and history: an evocative model for Coppo, his own origins effaced from the repositories of patrician membership and family history.

Sabellico chose the lagoon island of Santa Maria delle Grazie as his final resting place because of his particular devotion to the Virgin. But Coppo arranged to have his most treasured manuscript sent to its library simply because his teacher was present there, in both mind and body. These lines in Coppo's will suggest his continuing identification with the Venice of his youth and create a bond with Sabellico and with Sabellico's *gymnasium* at San Marco, where Coppo spent three happy years as Sabellico's "carissimo auditor" (most attentive pupil). Coppo had dedicated his most popular work, his chorography of Istria, to a schoolmate, Giuseppe Faustino: "our most youthful age was spent in the learned school of the most cultured Sabellico," as Coppo wrote loyally in the dedicatory preface to the book.[77] Sabellico's personality, teaching, scholarly publications, and the friends formed in his "litteratissimo conturbenio" (most learned academy) were threads woven through Coppo's work and life, knitting together his life on the Istrian peninsula with those three rosy years at the Scuola di San Marco. Those three years were deeply meaningful to Coppo, and he chose to commemorate them by linking his own scholarship to that of his beloved teacher. Coppo's dedicatory letter and will, his precious manuscript, the monastery shelves creaking under the weight of teacher's and student's Latin tomes, evoke an intellectual society and culture grounded in literary relationships that were freighted with emotional significance.[78]

Friendship and Enmity: Bembo's Scholarly Communities

Jacob Burckhardt wrote that the "decline" of humanism around the turn of the sixteenth century could be attributed to the young humanists who were "led to plunge into a life of excitement and vicissitude, in which exhausting studies, tutorships, secretaryships, professorships, offices in princely households, mortal enmities and perils, luxury and beggary, boundless admiration and boundless contempt followed confusedly one upon the other."[79] Burckhardt's colorful description of the enmities and competitiveness of humanist society during the later Renaissance captures some of the frictions among the teachers, students, printers, and editors of Venice at the time. These were the sinister, though no less affective, counterparts to the relationships between students, teachers, and classmates: bickering and infighting sustained by the printing presses, and that created divisive, exclusionary scholarly communities within communities.[80]

One of the best-known scholarly sparring matches of late Quattrocento Venice was that between Sabellico (Coppo's teacher) and Egnazio (Brugnolo's student and Bembo's schoolmate and friend). Bembo himself played a key role in this debate by editing and publishing the bitter scholarship that fanned the flames of their enmity. While we know very little of Coppo's early education in Venice, Bembo's role in this philological debate allows us to draw a case study of the ways in which affective scholarly relationships worked to shape both communities and intellectual debate in Renaissance Venice. These affective bonds were not only those between attentive students and beloved teachers but also those between fractious intellectual communities, divided by questions of scholarly interpretation and academic method, which were deeply important in crafting a sense of intellectual identity.

Bembo edited an untitled collection of works by contemporary humanists, printed by Jacopo Pencio da Lecco in Venice in 1502 and reissued by Giovanni Tacuini (the printer whose edition of *Vitruvius* Bembo admired) in Venice in 1508.[81] Bembo dedicated the book to Andrea Anesi, his friend on Corfu. The book is a compilation of commentaries and miscellanies, a collection of texts that drew a defining line between Sabellico's and Egnazio's scholarship as well as inaugurated a new method of approaching classical texts. The authors whose work Bembo collected in his edited printed volume, particularly Domizio Calderini and Angelo Poliziano, initiated and developed a method of selective collecting of commentaries on classical texts. This was a reform of the previous method of writing commentary, which explicated every single line, sometimes every word, of a classical text, recording disparate information about etymology, mythology, history, and geography, sometimes only loosely related to the passage at hand. Interestingly, perhaps the epitome of this copious commentary style was Niccolò Perotti's *Cornucopiae*, which Brugnolo himself edited in 1501. Even considering Bembo's real regard for his former teacher, his role as editor of this new commentary style can be seen as a generational intellectual transition, a break with his teacher's old ways.[82] This was one, definitive method by which even the most devoted students could create a sense of scholarly identity, indicating the individuality of their approach to classical texts.

In his edited volume, Bembo included texts that participated in this new method of commentary and were also closely connected to his own educational and social world in Venice. This included Giovanni Battista Egnazio's *Racemationes*, or "grape-gatherings," a metaphor that brings to mind the comparative literary scholarship of Poliziano and Calderini, also included in the volume. These "grape-gatherings" were commentaries on passages from Virgil's *Georgics*, on Pliny, on Ovid's *Metamorphoses*, and on other classical texts. But the *Racemationes* is also known for its bitter attacks on Sabellico's scholarship and for disparaging Sabellico's attempts to undermine Egnazio's reputation.[83] In his early twenties, Egnazio had opened a very popular humanist school, a decision that perhaps threatened Sabellico, the older and more established teacher.[84] To give readers the opportunity to judge for themselves, and perhaps to aggravate their troubled relationship for the sake of better book sales, Bembo also included Sabellico's *Annotationes* on passages from Pliny and Livy, the very text that Egnazio was attacking. But Bembo did not stop there. His publication also sharpened the enmity between Domizio Calderini and Poliziano. Using his new method in the *Miscellanea*, Poliziano dismantled Calderini's interpretations of the relationship between the Latin writer Propertius and the Greek Callimachus (as detailed by Grafton).[85] Bembo's edited volume did not simply represent a debut of the new historical philology being developed by these scholars at the turn of the century, but it intensified in print their bitter divisions, accusations, and enmities. By staking his own claim in these intellectual divisions, Bembo created a new scholarly identity for himself: he was innovating on his teacher's methods and drawing intellectual and affective links to the fashionable Egnazio.

The new historical philology that emerged in Venice during this period was closely linked to the lively intellectual scene of the Venetian printing houses. Benedetto Brugnolo was, for instance, renowned for his work as an editor and corrector working with the Venetian printers. Sabellico, too, largely owed his fame—and perhaps his reputation for superficiality—to the market for his works created by the printing press. Indeed, he commented on just that expanding market for Latin texts in his dialogue *De lingua latina reparatione*, written around 1490.[86] But perhaps no printing shop was busier or more spirited than that of Aldus Manutius, the famed humanist printer and publisher. Bembo drifted on the outer edges of the intellectual society drawn to Aldus's print shop, among the many correctors, editors, typesetters, investors, and others who swarmed his shop, sometimes making it impossible for him to work.

When Aldus first arrived in Venice in 1490, it was Bembo's friend Egnazio to whom he went for support and to find an opening in the intellectual society of Venice (and not to Sabellico, possibly another cause for their intense rivalry).[87] In his autobiographical letter, Bembo wrote that his friend Santo Barbarigo's father, Pierfrancesco, was a shareholder in Aldus's enterprise.[88]

Bembo and his family were also more intimately connected with Aldus. He attended the baptism of Bembo's daughter Polymnia—named for a Greek muse, a fact that Aldus certainly would have appreciated—after which the family dined at Aldus's house.[89] Polymnia was born in Venice in 1505 or 1506, perhaps just before Aldus married Maria Torresani and moved into her family's home in San Paternian. We have an account, if a satirical one, of what such a dinner party would have looked like in Aldus's family home in San Paternian. Erasmus stayed with Aldus in his home in these years, famously working shoulder to shoulder with Aldus night and day to bring out his *Adagia* from his press in 1508.[90] Erasmus liked to eat well. In a later dialogue, *The Ciceronian*, he mercilessly exaggerates the claims of the self-promoting workaholic humanists who proved their devotion to scholarship by eating only "ten very small raisins" and "three sugared coriander seeds" for their dinner.[91] Erasmus did not find Aldus's dinners satisfactory: in his *Colloquies*, he satirically reimagined Aldus's dinner table—under the tyrannical supervision of Andrea Torresani, Aldus's father-in-law—as a culinary desert of weak wine, rotten eggs, and stale bread mixed with potter's clay. The women ate the leftovers and the workers at the press ate the women's leftovers.[92] Aldus gave Erasmus permission to eat alone in his room.[93]

But if the food left something to be desired and Torresani was a boor, the intellectual company was brilliant and generous, as Erasmus himself acknowledged. In the *Adagia*, Erasmus wrote that "every one of the scholars" who clustered around Aldus "offered me, without being asked, copies of authors which had never been printed, and which they thought I might be able to use. Aldus himself kept nothing back amongst his treasures. It was the same with John Lascaris, Baptista Egnatius, Marcus Musurus, Frater Urbanus. I experienced the kindness of some whom I did not know either by sight or by name."[94] Aldus and his male family members, the motley intellectuals of Venice, and honored visitors from abroad all dined together under one crowded roof. Was Bembo one of those nameless friends, alongside Egnazio, offering scholarly kindness to Erasmus at Torresani's dinner table? Through his friendships with Egnazio and Barbarigo, Bembo could craft his own scholarly identity as one of the privileged and innovative intellectuals flocking around Aldus.

Just as the affectionate relationships between students and teachers came to shape the scholarly communities of Renaissance Venice, so too did their enmities. They provided a drama in which the young humanists of Venice participated eagerly: as when Egnazio came to reconcile melodramatically with Sabellico at the elder scholar's deathbed, and later even penned a funeral oration for Sabellico and published his unfinished work.[95] And, after the days of the schoolroom and the lecture hall had ended, new scholarly families formed. One of the most progressive was around Aldus and his print shop, but others formed among hellenistically inclined scholars, the new historical philology, those interested in Aristotelian thought, and other communities within communities dotted throughout the city. These groups provided the context for the culmination of the young patrician's transformation from student to scholar, as friendships and enmities allowed young scholars like Bembo to claim academic methods and interpretative positions. Bembo, in editing his own book, surrounding himself with scholars of Latin and Greek, and enmeshing his family life with Aldus's own, reached the beginning of intellectual adulthood. This was a period in which he became a scholar in his own right, producing scholarship that, while it drew on the social connections formed at Brugnolo's school, operated independently from his teacher, even representing a definitive break from his teacher's philological method. These affective bonds, whether of deep regard or of professional enmity, shaped Bembo's scholarship and intellectual identity.

Conclusion

At twenty-three and twenty-two years old, respectively, Coppo and Bembo left Venice. As we will explore in more depth in the next chapter, Coppo was bound for Naples, where he would study ancient ruins and epigraphy with the Roman teacher Pomponio Leto, Sabellico's own teacher, and so Coppo's intellectual "grandfather." During his travels, Coppo would also study in Crete, mobilizing his uncle's political career for his own scholarly gain. And, Coppo would be appointed to his first post in the Venetian empire in the late 1490s and marry in 1499, when he was twenty-nine. Coppo's first post was as an imperial notary, sent to Istria as a scribe working under one of the many governing officeholders of the Venetian imperial bureaucracy on the peninsula. This was not a highly paid or highly regarded post of governing, but it was an important one. That Coppo could achieve a post within the empire at all is a testament first to the career opportunities presented by the many offices of the empire. But it is also evidence of the socially transformative powers of his education. Originally founded to produce scribes for the Venetian chancellery from among the *cittadino* class, the Scuola of San Marco had a similar social effect for Coppo: transforming him from an illegitimately born son of a patrician to a scribe of empire.

Bembo departed for Corfu, where he would study Greek with Ioannis Moschi. He also met Greek scholars while in the Aegean: he was reunited with Apostolis on Skiathos and met during his travels the Greek artist Joannes Dominicus Methoneus, known now as Domenico delle Grèche, who had painted a topography of Greece as well as produced an illustrated version of Ptolemy's *Cosmographia*.[96] Both Bembo's and Coppo's continued education in the Mediterranean world would be shaped by the intellectual networks they had forged at home in Venice. Their families, the Scuola, and their scholarly communities in Venice formed important staging grounds for their later lives and provided friendships that would continue to shape their intellectual work.

These tracks of political and intellectual development and transformation mutually shaped the young lives of patrician adolescents. Their Latin education provided a language, imagery, historical sensibility, and geography that deeply shaped their perception of the Mediterranean empire and their role within it, as we will see in the next chapter. The friendships formed in the Scuola and in scholarly communities of Venice continued to anchor them to the intellectual society of the city while simultaneously expanding to accommodate new humanist friends and family members from across the Venetian Mediterranean. But most significantly, this early interrelationship between family life, learning, and social transformation meant that these spheres of activity and identity would be inextricable in later life. We will see throughout the rest of the book the ways in which this early relationship between social status, education, and interior life shaped Bembo's and Coppo's scholarship, conjugal families, and identities as governors and administrators of empire.

CHAPTER 2

Documenting the Mediterranean World

Introduction

Giovanni Bembo left Aldus's print shop for the Mediterranean, but he did not leave behind the material world of Venetian humanist scholarship. In February 1526, Bembo inscribed his printed copy of a Venetian edition of Lucretius's *De rerum natura*, writing that he had read it "with friends" while he was the colonial governor of Skiathos and Skopelos in the Aegean.[1] If there was indeed a small book club of readers of Epicurean philosophy on Skiathos in 1526, Bembo does not reveal their identities. Instead, his annotations to the book reveal a rather more pedantic reading. After a few pages of underlining words and copying them into the margins, he gave up on this exercise and switched to conscientiously correcting the Latin grammar of the text. His copy of Lucretius suggests an intellectual project deserted, here, for a more mechanical grammar exercise. Giovanni Bembo and his friends made a half-hearted attempt from the Aegean to engage with one of the most complex texts to have been rediscovered by Italian humanists.[2] Even so, humanist intellectual inquiry was the medium of connection between Italy and the Mediterranean world for these Venetian and Venetan scholars and governors who wrote and exchanged Latin books on a geographical axis that stretched from the gates of Milan to Skiathos.

On the one hand, then, the Mediterranean world shaped Venetian intellectual culture, which was not bound within the confines of the lagoon. This has been well understood and explored by historians of the art, architecture, and print culture of the city, if less explored by intellectual historians.[3] But this chapter investigates, conversely, how deeply Bembo and Coppo were tied into these humanist ways of understanding the Mediterranean classical past. The chapter tracks through their scholarship how they intellectually and even emotionally confronted the materiality of antiquity in the Mediterranean.[4] If Bembo could not quite make sense of Lucretius on Skiathos—and so resorted to the grammatical exercises he had learned in school in Venice—other aspects of his humanist intellectual practice became heightened and intensified. The very physicality of antiquity that Bembo and Coppo encountered in the Mediterranean, from the ruins on Crete to the Latin epigraphy scattered along the Spanish coast, changed the nature of humanist inquiry as they understood it. In the Mediterranean, their intellectual lives and pursuits were diversified, no longer confined to the philological squabbles of the city or to the networks of friends and scholars revolving around their teachers. When their deeply embedded knowledge of classical texts confronted the material remains of the classical world, the medium in which they worked changed dramatically. Bembo transformed a Venetian state-owned galley and its merchant trade route into the means for a tour of the ruins of the western Mediterranean, and—following the model of Cyriac of Ancona—wrote his own sylloge documenting the adventure. Coppo, relying on both his family connections and his scholarly ones, spent years in southern Italy and on Crete, eventually creating his own innovative woodcut maps out of their topography and ruins.

There were, of course, models for these kinds of multimedia approaches to the physical landscape of the Mediterranean, and these will be an important part of our story throughout this chapter. When these models were filtered through firsthand, personal encounters with the antique landscape of the Mediterranean, this led to these new modes of creative expression for Bembo and Coppo. Confronted with the materiality of antiquity, they brought their humanist education to bear on physical evidence, creating different modes of documenting and thinking about the classical world than those they had learned in Venice. Not only did the Mediterranean world captivate humanists in Venice and the Veneto, but Venetian humanists—once they set sail from Venice—were entranced by what they found there, and responded by creating new and eclectic ways of documenting the physical world.

Beyond simply demonstrating the importance of the Mediterranean world to Venetian humanism, then, this chapter investigates the materiality and the media of this encounter, arguing for the intensified creativity and eclecticism of the intellectual work that Bembo and Coppo pursued from Granada and Crete, Corfu and Istria. Perhaps this was especially true for Coppo, who

transformed his teacher and schoolmates' journalistic written style into vividly graphic form, producing both regional and Ptolemaic maps of the Mediterranean world and beyond. This chapter explores how, as young adults,
Bembo and Coppo were transformed by their encounters with both the local
scholars of the Mediterranean world and its material evidence. In their encounters with Greek teachers and local guides, and with the fragmented
physical remains of the classical past, their humanist practice underwent its
own transformation to become documentary, composite, and fragmented in
response.[5]

A Mediterranean Adventure

Bembo was part of a small community of scholars in Venice, particularly circling around Aldus, involved in Hellenistic scholarship. Of course, Aldus is
perhaps best known now for his visionary editing and printing of a number
of important classical Greek texts. But Bembo was also one of the relatively
small number of Venetian men at this date to learn ancient Greek formally,
and as his many friendships with Cretan scholars and Greek lecturers attest,
he seems to have considered Greek an important aspect of his scholarship.[6]
Bembo owned a Greek grammar, the *Institutiones Graecae grammatices*, brought
out by Aldus himself in 1497. But it seems that, at least during this initial foray
into learning Greek, Bembo did not progress very far: he annotated only the
first six folios, after which the pages are crisp, white, and seemingly unread—
even in the five centuries since.[7]

At twenty-two, Bembo left Venice for the first time, traveling to the island
of Corfu at the mouth of the Adriatic. He would meet Cyurω there two years
later, in 1497; and it seems that he spent those first two years on the island
immersed in the study of Greek, expanding beyond the little he learned from
Aldus's grammar book. His Greek teacher was Ioannis Moschi, known to us
through Bembo's own heading to his Greek exercises: "Scripsit Joannes Bembus Venetus Corcyra in ludo Joannes Moschi 1498 menses Augusti," underneath which Bembo practiced making Greek characters and then copied a
number of Greek texts, perhaps at the instruction of his teacher.[8] The ten
folios of Greek texts are themselves composite, made up of schoolroom exercises and copied practice texts from grammar books: Libanius's "Monody on
the Daphnean temple of Apollo," on the destruction of that temple by fire or
lightning; alchemical recipes for making different kinds of ink and glue, and
for the use of Monemvasian wine; a collection of short hortative orations ("On
the attraction to women," "Seek the truth, avoid lies," and so forth); and a copy

of one of Aesop's Fables, "The Hen and the Golden Eggs." On Corfu, Bembo's Greek learning extended beyond his meager annotations to his Aldine Greek grammar, to include creating a kind of schoolroom composite manuscript-within-a-manuscript that combined classical texts, recipes, and fables.[9] Perhaps learning Greek in the Greek-speaking Mediterranean took on a different set of meanings and allusions than it had in Aldus's Hellenic circles in Venice, moving from grammatical pedagogy to a more diverse, lively study of fables, recipes, and dramatic classical texts. That Bembo studied these texts on Corfu with a Greek teacher hints, too, at the Greek intellectual cultures of the islands and contributes toward a picture of their local methods of teaching.[10] Finally, Bembo undertook this more serious study of Greek in the same years as he met his future wife, Cyurω, on Corfu; as we will see, she wrote letters to Bembo and would educate their children. Cyurω's own literacy may have lent a more personal urgency to Bembo's newfound commitment to Greek learning.

After these years on Corfu, in the spring of 1505, Bembo banded together with a few friends to bid for a charter to operate one of the state-owned galleys of Venice. The *incanto di galere*, as this state-operated galley auction was known, was a quintessentially Venetian operation.[11] Once a year, at the Rialto, the mercantile galleys that were intended to sail set trading itineraries throughout the Mediterranean and beyond that would be auctioned off to noble bidders. These "great galleys," manned by up to 180 rowers, loaded down with tons of pepper, cinnamon, ginger, nutmeg, silk, or silver, sailed a number of well-established trading routes: to Flanders, to Alexandria, to Beirut, departing from Venice at a time appointed by the Senate, making only approved stops along the way, and staying at port for a length of time previously determined.[12] The galleys, setting off from Alexandria back to Venice groaning with the precious weight of pepper, silk, nutmeg, helmed by the virtuous patricians of the city, are a central element of the "myth of Venice." The *incanto* evokes several important elements of Venice's mythology: the foundations of the city's wealth on the exotic eastern shores of the Mediterranean, the savvy initiative of the joint partnership, the collective integrity of the patriciate. In Lane's work and in others', it was the *incanto di galere* that became a symbol for the capitalist ingenuity and collective mercantile spirit that made the city so unique.[13]

Bembo and his friends hardly lived up to that mythology. In his autobiographical letter, Bembo wrote that he was awarded the ship in partnership with Carlo Contarini, Battista Mauroceno, Giorgio Cornaro, and Giovanni Querini. Bembo had close links with these men: Mauroceno had stood witness to Bembo's age at his entry to the *Balla d'Oro*; Cornaro, the brother of the deposed queen of Cyprus Caterina Cornaro, was (obscurely) related to Bembo through his Cornaro mother, Angela; and Querini had been a schoolmate at Brugnolo's Scuola. As Bembo wrote, it was Querini who commissioned Brugnolo's tomb in the Frari. Bembo wrote that they traveled with another galley (state-owned mercantile galleys always sailed in convoy), the *Santa Maria*, whose *padrono* was Sebastiano Dolfin.[14] The route that Bembo goes on to describe matches that of the so-called Barbary route, which sailed down the Adriatic to Sicily and then Honaine (in Algeria), along the western coast of North Africa, along the coast of Spain, from Malaga and Valencia to the Balearic Islands, and then returning via Sicily to Venice.[15] And indeed, in the records of the *incanto di galere*, Giovanni di Domenico Bembo appears as one of the noble patrons of the 1505 state galley sailing the Barbary route.[16]

The journey was far from typical. The Barbary galleys usually left in the late spring, as did most of the mercantile and pilgrims' galleys, timed to coincide with the favorable weather and sailing conditions across the Mediterranean. This trip round Sicily, North Africa, and the Spanish coast typically took about six to seven months; but Bembo's galley did not reach safe port in Venice for nearly a year, returning eleven months after they departed.[17] Their journey was likely delayed for two reasons. First, Bembo and his friends used their time as merchant captains to view ancient ruins and transcribe inscriptions, taking long days in Syracuse, Carthage, and Sagunto to explore these ruined cities. Second, Bembo and his friends seem to have been kidnapped. In a short text copied into his autograph manuscript, dated 10 April 1506 and written "in carcere," Bembo began a letter: "Giovanni Bembo of Venice, of the Barbary cargo galley, to the Bishop of Kefalonia: On Tuesday I was captured . . . and led to a castle where I am now imprisoned," perhaps somewhere in the vicinity of Syracuse, on the coast of Sicily. He wrote that he was taken along with Pietro, the son of Battista Mauroceno ("a man of greatest authority"), and that—though he is "poor, and [I] have no investment in the galleys"—he darkly threatened that he had important and wealthy friends.[18]

Bembo and his partnership of patrician men did not embark on the Barbary route simply to trade precious North African metalwork in Spanish markets. Nowhere in Bembo's account of their travels, nor in his letter from prison, does he mention anything remotely associated with trade or the mercantile nature of the Barbary route. Instead, Bembo's account is littered with details about his family and friends, modern and ancient toponymy, descriptions of ruined sites, epigraphy, and references to Pliny and classical authors.[19] Bembo began the account by listing the friends with whom he auctioned the galley, taking care to note their more illustrious connections. Setting off down the coast of the Adriatic, Bembo wrote that they visited "the Diomedeas islands, now called Santa Maria de Tremiti," giving both the classical toponym (probably from Pliny) and their contemporary Italian name. Passing Apulia and Calabria, they then sailed to Sicily. Bembo was particularly fascinated by the geography and classical landscape of Sicily. He peppered his travel narrative with both natural and ruined points of interest: "Leucopetra, now Capo dell'Arme," a promontory of white rocks that featured in Pliny, Strabo, Ptolemy, Thucydides's history of Demosthenes, and Cicero;[20] an ancient temple ("The Temple of the Sun"), where "the sun, during the equinox, passes through two small and perfectly round windows";[21] and in "ancient Syracuse," a "great amphitheater."[22] They sailed through the Aeolian Islands and Vulcano Island, "where the sacred fire still burns, and always spits out smoke and ash."[23]

Leaving behind Sicily for Africa, Bembo had concerns that were both contemporary and scholarly: he wrote of the island of Djerba as "the shelter for pirates," before turning his attention to the aqueduct "forty *millia passuum* in length" (the Zaghouan Aqueduct to Carthage). Bembo then listed the Arabic names of the villages surrounding Carthage, all "planted with trees and gardens, which yield the best fruit—especially pomegranates."[24] Carthage was an area of particular interest for Bembo and his humanist friends, and so too was "Caesarea or Cyrta," which he identified as the birthplace of Augustine of Hippo.[25] The journey to Spain was also eventful: they saw "three great, monstrous fish, which the sailors called *cao de oio*." In Malaga, they saw two white camels; two panthers "chained with great stones around their necks"; and women "wearing short tunics, with bare arms."[26] They viewed the ruins of Sagunto, including the Temple of Diana and a "complete amphitheater, with its *scaenae*," and described its inscriptions.

Bembo recalled that Cyurω was pregnant when they set off, and so—sending Bembo off with admonishments to write often—she stayed behind in Venice. He interrupts his travel narrative to record that Cyurω had indeed "sent me many letters during this sea journey, in Sicily, Africa, and Spain." Her demand for information about Bembo's "health" made at the galley's departure from Venice was apparently repeated at intervals throughout Bembo's journey.[27] As we will explore in greater detail in the next chapter, Cyurω's literacy would become a source of family identity and even pride. Finally, Bembo wrote, after eleven months, the galley returned to Venice.

Their journey was ostensibly for mercantile purposes and on Venice's behalf, but it seems to have been rather appropriated by these young men for scholarly reasons. Bembo's consuming interests on the journey were the remains of antiquity he witnessed, the match between classical literature about Mediterranean geography and the coastlines and towns he saw himself, the social status of his Venetian friends, and his intimate relationship with Cyurω as it took epistolary form. Underneath this quintessential ritual of patrician partnership and commercial enterprise lay a reality of friendship, intimacy, and scholarship that was considerably messier and much less mythically ideal. Perhaps inspired by his Greek studies on Corfu and by his initial firsthand encounter with Mediterranean antiquity, Bembo and his friends' unconventional journey around Mediterranean shores suggests just how captivated these men were by the built environment of antiquity they found there. On this adventure around the western Mediterranean, Bembo began to thread together his contemporary experience of the Mediterranean landscape with its antique past.

Bembo's Epigraphical Album

Alongside his prose travel account within his autobiographical letter, Bembo's large collection of ancient inscriptions, titled "Inscriptiones antiquae ex variis locis sumptae" and included in his autograph manuscript, may be seen as a kind of parallel documentation of his journey.[28] Certainly Bembo recorded inscriptions from places he had been, both on his 1505–6 journey in the central and western Mediterranean, and from his later travels in the 1520s to the Aegean. Copied inscriptions from Syracuse, Malaga, Valencia, and Sagunto litter the sylloge, reflecting Bembo's travels there and his interest in their ruined landscapes (figure 5). And yet others—from Rimini, Mantua, and, most especially, the vast number of inscriptions and sketches from Rome—do not reflect Bembo's own eyewitness documentation of the antique ruins, but rather the popular circulation of epigraphical collections throughout Renaissance Italy at the time. Even his inscriptions from Skiathos and Skopelos, where he lived for two years, had already been documented by the famed Cyriac of Ancona. The inscriptions are not in the order of his travels; some are neatly copied, some hastily scribbled, and some interrupted with sketches of monuments, beginnings of letter drafts ("A la mia signora Isabela . . ." reads one), and even a sketch of his own dagger.[29] The sylloge is a complex collection, which suggests that Bembo's encounter with antiquity was composite: it was made in the complementary practices of eyewitness documentation of the physical world, copying of circulating epigraphical texts, and the miscellaneous compilation practices of humanist manuscripts.

There was good precedent for this jumbled compilation, probably most widely known from Cyriac of Ancona's heavily circulated *Commentaria*. Cyriac was perhaps the single most important figure who translated the physical world of Aegean antiquity into text and image during the Renaissance. He

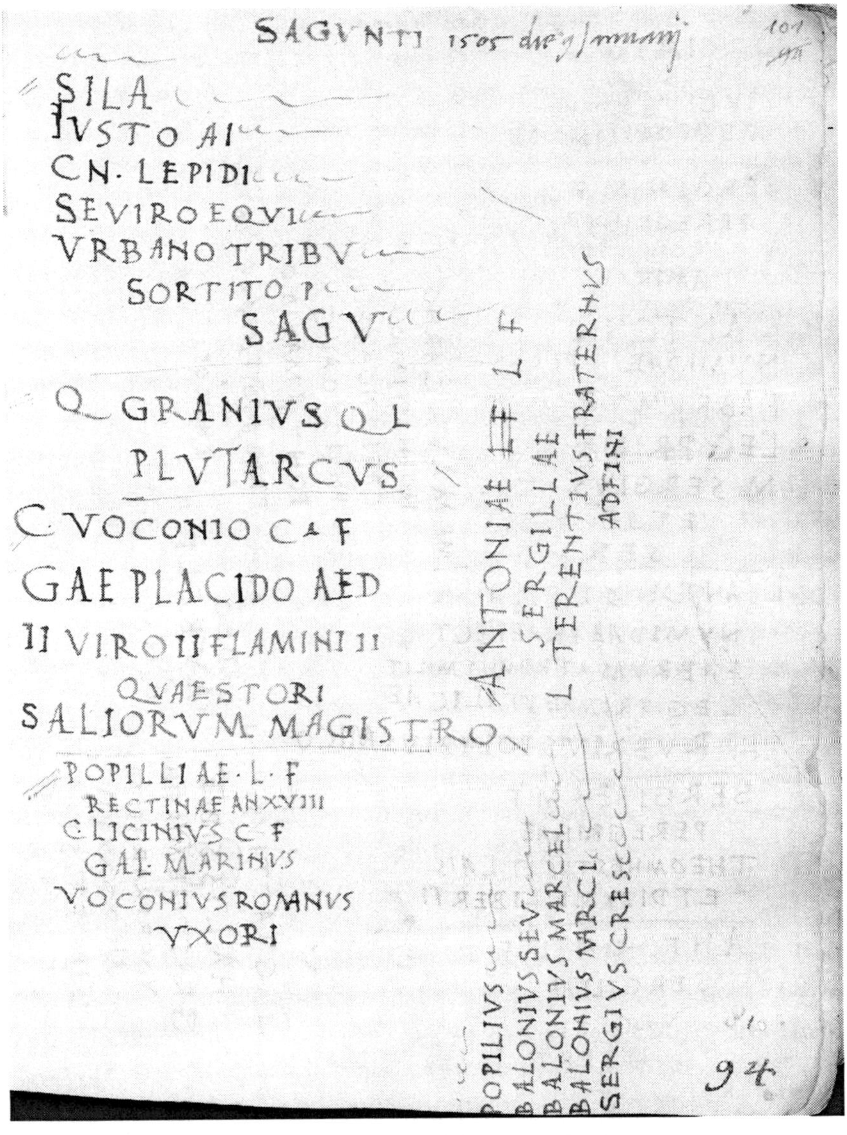

FIGURE 5. A page of Giovanni Bembo's sylloge. Bayerische Staatsbibliothek München, Clm 10801, fol. 179r.

By kind permission of the Bayerische Staatsbibliothek.

traveled extensively around the Mediterranean world collecting inscriptions, dealing in books and antiquities, and working as a diplomat and merchant, even staying at the Ottoman court of Mehmed II.[30] His extensive notes of Latin and Greek inscriptions, travel diaries, and geographical descriptions— probably at one point reaching six volumes, known as the *Commentaria*— were lost in the Sforza library fire at Pesaro in 1514.[31] Only one autograph excerpt from the *Commentaria* has survived, known as the Trotti manuscript, and it is from this excerpt that we can glean what the entire original *Commentaria* might have looked like.[32] However, Cyriac's miscellaneous collections of inscriptions, notes, and drawings were circulated widely throughout the Renaissance, and Cyriac himself made copies as gifts for important friends. Theodor Mommsen even speculated that it was not a library fire but the voraciousness of Renaissance collectors that was responsible for dispersing the original *Commentaria*.[33] These excerpts circulated all over the Mediterranean and Italian diplomatic and humanist world: from Genoese Chios, to Constantinople, to Venice and the Veneto. Like the Florentine geographer and humanist Cristoforo Buondelmonti, Cyriac was known in the humanist circle of Nicolò Niccoli: in a *Vita* written of Cyriac by his friend Francesco Scalamonti (produced at the insistence of the Venetian humanist Lauro Quirini on Crete), Scalamonti writes that Cyriac received a dignitary's tour of Niccoli's library and antique coin and sculpture collection.[34]

The editorial history of Cyriac's texts and the survival of only one excerpt from the *Commentaria* make the heterogeneous nature of his compilation of inscriptions, drawings, and prose difficult to perceive. Like Bembo, Cyriac did not copy inscriptions or write his travel accounts chronologically or according to his travel itineraries; and these already "out of order" accounts were then dispersed through various manuscript copies. E. W. Bodnar, who has published most of Cyriac's texts, has tried to "reconstruct" his journeys by editing Cyriac's letters and accounts into a chronological order—producing a coherent narrative, but not necessarily an accurate picture of Cyriac's *Commentaria* or of his approach to the material culture of the Mediterranean. Furthermore, several composite manuscripts preserve "Cyriacana": those collections of inscriptions, drawings, and miscellaneous texts (including the *Liber*) that were probably copied and circulated from Cyriac's own manuscript collections.[35] The popularity of "Cyriacana" collections, in which the *Liber* was copied together with Cyriac's letters, drawings, and geographical texts that Cyriac owned (including the fourth book of Poggio's *De Varietate Fortunae*, which reports Nicolò di Conti's Indian travel account, and Pomponius Mela's *Cosmographia*), indicates the diffusion of the Mediterranean encounter with antiquity through heterogeneous compilations of text, epigraph, and image.

Where Bembo's prose travel account provides classical information and descriptions of the ancient sites scattered around the western Mediterranean, his sylloge provides no historical context or interpretation of the inscriptions. The only context provided is the heading of the folio with the name of the city or location, "Roma" or "Pola," and even this is not done uniformly throughout the sylloge. This descriptive sparseness is a feature of Cyriac's *Commentaria*, too. Besides a brief line associating the inscription to a particular building, Cyriac simply copied the Latin and Greek inscriptions into his book, without parsing the inscription itself. There is often no relationship between the inscription or diagram and the main body of the narrative text, just as Bembo's prose account—embedded within his autobiographical letter—is contained in the same manuscript as his sylloge, and yet he does not make cross-references between them.

In the narrative text, Cyriac and Bembo describe their travels in detail: recording who they traveled with and what they did on each island or city, and relating myths and geographical descriptions. Their prose travel accounts are vividly drawn, filled with glimpses of the many local Greek subjects and intellectuals of the Mediterranean world who shaped both Cyriac's and Bembo's own intellectual endeavors. These meetings sometimes evoked an encounter not only between Italian humanist and local Greek epistemologies, but indeed between contemporary and ancient temporalities that stretch the imagination. Cyriac, for example, writes of stumbling across a dramatic waterfall on Crete, where local Greek priests tell him they have "sometimes seen Diana herself with her dazzling nymphs, their white robes cast aside, nude bathers submerged in the translucent waters."[36] On Chios, he relies on the local Greek islanders who have preserved the ancient names of ruins to discern their original context, name, and use in a pattern of research with striking parallels to textual philology, aided only by local actors.[37] Bembo studied under Moschi on Corfu, but his account is littered with proud references to other Greek scholars; later, on his return voyage to Venice from Skiathos, he spent time on Crete, where he met a number of learned Greek scholars, including Domenico delle Greche, "who painted the sites and places of Ptolemy's *Cosmographia*," as well as Giorgio Madiota, known for his great skill in Greek letters.[38] If the precise nature of Bembo's intellectual interactions with these men is left obscure, his evident pride in knowing them is scrawled across the pages of his manuscript. His conspicuous, repeated insistence of having experienced Greek scholarship not only at home in Venice but also from within the local intellectual societies of Crete and Corfu suggests that these relationships were intellectual achievements within the social world of Venetian humanism.

In the sylloge format, though, these encounters with the Mediterranean become material, documentary, and intensely fragmented. Cyriac, a more conscientious antiquarian than Bembo, copied in descriptive evidence of all of his encounters with the antique material culture of his travels: dimensions of Roman temples and their columns; lists of manuscript incipits from his book purchasing on Mt. Athos; bits of poems written in his honor; new inscriptions he devised by copying antique ones; and encomia that he penned to Paros, to Chios, and to the pagan gods of the sea, all inspired by the Siren (and in vernacular). Beyond copying material into the volumes, Cyriac also attached fragmentary manuscript leaves into his *Commentaria*, folios that contained excerpts from antique Greek letters.[39]

The composite nature of Cyriac's *Commentaria* and of Bembo's own sylloge, with their jumbled texts and images, was not conducive for extended narrative analysis of the fragments and inscriptions that these men recorded and copied. The heterogeneity of the *Commentaria* allowed a kind of documentation that was authoritative in its variety and extent, rather than in Cyriac's successfully parsing of Greek and Latin inscriptions for their meaning or historical import. This matrix of authority-through-variety also explains why Bembo did not distinguish, neither formally nor conceptually, between inscriptions he personally viewed and those he copied from other documentary sources. The fragmentary mode of compiling these documentations was considered by both Cyriac and Bembo to be the best way of textually approaching and recording the fragmentariness of antique material culture itself, as the composite book was the most accurate way of documenting the ruined, obscured, and scattered evidence of antiquity.

Bembo's sylloge documents the ways in which his mode of intellectual inquiry, and the media of his humanist practice, changed once he set sail to view the ancient sites of the central and western Mediterranean. Bembo had progressed through the ritualized stages of political, social, and intellectual development at home in Venice. Indeed, when he successfully bid on the Barbary galley in the 1505 *incanto*, he participated in one of the central civic rituals of adult male patrician society. The patrician men who won a ship (and its trading route) in the *incanto* at the Rialto would take payments from other merchants for cargo to be shipped. Because these great galleys were so expensive to build, maintain, and man, only the most expensive cargo—mostly spices and precious textiles and metals—would be transported. These nobles, banding together in "a joint venture," needed to be trustworthy and reliable. The head of the partnership, the *patrono*, had to be at least thirty years old, and needed to be able to provide security for the galley and for the full payment of its crew—no small feat, and yet another signal of a patrician male's incorporation into social (and economic) maturity.

In the Mediterranean, the friendships and social bonds of male adolescence continued to be important. Bembo proudly recalled Giovanni Quirini's devotion to their teacher Brugnolo, and he relied on the reputations of his wealthier friends when subject to capture and imprisonment. And yet the nature of his humanist inquiry changed, as this social world expanded to incorporate Greek local learning as well as alternative humanist methods of documentation. In Venice, the culmination of Bembo's maturity as a scholar was his editing of a compilation of philological texts, produced within the scholarly community revolving around the Aldine Press. This philological inquiry was translated to the physical world in the Mediterranean, as Bembo used the medium of the sylloge to document his encounter with antique material culture. In the sylloge, different claims to authenticity and a different kind of affinity to the ancient world drove his documentary practice. Like Cyriac's *Commentaria* decades before, the medium of composite documentation became central to understanding the physical environment. The fragmented evidence of Mediterranean antiquity, broken, incomplete, and scattered down the coasts of Africa and Spain, required also a kind of fragmentary documentation to truthfully record its ancientness.

These developments in Bembo's humanist practice demonstrate that space, as well as time, must be central to our understanding of Renaissance intellectual culture. If Bembo's intellectual maturity was placed alongside the social rituals of maturity and gradual political enfranchisement, the spatial axis of humanist practice—from Venice to the Mediterranean and back again—must also play a role in how we understand humanism to have changed and developed. In the Mediterranean, Bembo's deep intimacy with classical texts was confronted with classical materiality, and so the ways in which he engaged in humanist textual practice changed too, becoming documentary, heterogeneous, and fragmented. As we will see in chapter 5, this had consequences for the way in which Bembo perceived the world around him, and especially for how he perceived his own experiences within the empire, as both a governor and a husband.

"A diligent and thoughtful man" in Rome

"I have travelled through all of Italy and sailed all around the Mediterranean Sea," Coppo claimed in the preface to his magnum opus, the Ptolomaic geographical encyclopedia *De toto orbe*. Coppo wrote the text of his major work between 1518 and 1520, at a time when he had been permanently settled for several years in Istria, was married, and had five sons. But he had undertaken those journeys through Italy and the Mediterranean years before as a bachelor, who, like Bembo, had set off from Venice to study and observe the physical remains of antiquity. Coppo departed from Venice in the early 1490s with his Venetian patrician friend Pietro Trevisan. They were headed for the house and academy of Pomponio Leto (1428–98): Coppo's scholarly "grandfather," as it were, Marcantonio Sabellico's own Roman teacher. Coppo would learn from Leto, participate in the vibrant intellectual life staged in Leto's household academy, and travel with Leto and Trevisan through Naples. Like Bembo's extended network of school friends, the relationship Coppo formed with Sabellico in the Scuola di San Marco would prove to be crucial when he decided to continue his education in Naples and Rome.

Pomponio Leto's Accademia Romana was one of the most important communities of scholars—and collection of objects—in the development of Renaissance antiquarianism. Like Cyriac of Ancona, Leto provided a model of engagement with antique material culture that proved influential for generations of Renaissance scholars. The members of Leto's academy adopted ancient Roman names, recited classical poetry, and assembled a large and varied collection of antique inscriptions, mounted on the walls of Leto's house and displayed in his garden. The group was temporarily disbanded due to fears of heresy in 1468 after Leto was arrested in Venice (1466), but it was allowed to regroup in 1471 after the election of Pope Sixtus IV. Situated near the ruins of the baths of Constantine, Leto's house was the ideal setting to study inscriptions and stage the plays of Plautus and Terence.[40] It was the convergence point for scholars who wanted to live and breathe Roman antiquity, a scholarly household animated by a passion for *Romanità*. Although Leto did not publish prolifically, his historical work, *Romanae historiae compendium*, was his most successful publishing project.[41] The *Compendium* was published in Venice in 1499, a year after Leto's death in Rome. Leto sent the manuscript text to Sabellico in Venice, who corrected it and arranged for it to be published at Bernardino Veneto's Venetian press. Leto may have even arranged for Coppo to take the work to Sabellico: in one of Leto's letters, he writes of a certain "Pietro, a diligent and thoughtful man, who will take the *Compendium gestorum romanorum* back with him [to Venice] to show to you."[42] Coppo may very well have been Leto's "diligent and thoughtful" messenger, liaising between his beloved Sabellico and Sabellico's own highly regarded teacher. Sabellico would pen a glowing posthumous *Vita* of Leto printed alongside the *Compendium*.[43]

Coppo was deeply influenced by Leto's approaches to the material evidence of Roman antiquity; as we will see in chapter 6, he imported these methods to his adopted homeland of Istria. Though the *Compendium* was Leto's most successful published work, his antiquarianism and interest in Roman archaeological and epigraphical remains were influential primarily through the tours he gave to visiting scholars of Roman ruins, and through notes his students disseminated from his lectures on the same subject.[44] His *De antiquitatibus urbis Romae* was printed in Rome in 1510 and was the only instance in which his guided tour of Roman antiquities was made available to a wider audience. Comparing his visual impressions of Rome's buildings and monuments with his reading of Pliny and Cicero, Leto's itinerary of Roman ruins and topography was one of the most successful experimentations with writing an archaeological, regional history derived equally from experience and scholarship.[45] Leto wrote a brief physical description and history of single elements of the larger urban fabric—from the Arch of Constantine, through the Pantheon, to the Esquiline Hill—which he broke into roughly alphabetical headings. He then moved to categorize the city differently, by listing all of the elements present in a single neighborhood; for instance, all of the monuments, ruins, and geographical features surrounding the Porta Capena.[46] He included fourteen of these regional distinctions, before alternating to another mode of classification, by type of monument. Leto listed all of the bridges, *campi*, fora, basilica, baths, bodies of water, and roads that survived of the ancient city. There is very little descriptive language, and no narrative, in *De antiquitatibus*; the book rather reflects the kinds of taxonomies of information that Leto used to categorize and compare the classical remains of Rome, both as an observer of the city and as an antiquarian who collected fragments. This composite construction of the regional topography of the ancient city probably reflects that the text was written from Leto's experience giving tours of Rome to his students, as it attempts textually to map Leto's spatial encounter with discrete antique elements within a larger, complex urban built environment. It also likely reflects the intended audience for the text: humanist visitors to Rome who wanted a small and well-organized account of the names, places, and antiquity of the ruins they saw.

Was Coppo the beneficiary of one of Leto's famed tours around Rome, at some point before Leto's death in 1498, or in Naples, during their eighteen-month stay there between 1493 and 1495? Coppo never wrote reflexively about these early journeys, so it is difficult to know. But in his later geographical works, and particularly in his woodcut maps and chorography of Istria, it is plain that he was deeply influenced by Leto's passion for ancient Roman history and material culture. Coppo was undoubtedly also a reader of another highly influential writer about Roman antiquity, Biondo Flavio. Flavio wrote *Roma instaurata* (Rome, 1446), his attempt to reconstruct ancient Rome as co-existing with the contemporary city, by interpreting his eyewitness account of the ruined and even partially submerged monuments and buildings of the classical city. He wove together textual, archaeological, and epigraphical information about the ancient cityscape. Flavio dedicated the text to the pope Eugenius IV, writing that the pope's decision to preserve Rome's classical ruins had returned order and stability to the city: invoking the ability of the ruined city to intervene into contemporary political and social life.

In an attitude reminiscent of the ways in which Cyriac's antiquarianism was perceived by Scalamonti and other contemporaries, Flavio saw his own project as intrinsically more stable and more long-lasting than the built environment of the city, however Eugenius attempted to preserve it. He wrote that future readers will attest "whether the restoration wrought in marble, rick, cement, stone, and bronze, or the restoration in literature, will last better and longer."[47] Like Leto, Flavio understood his written project as one that could not decompose, in which the built archaeological and epigraphical remains of the city could be preserved indefinitely. Like Cyriac's composite manuscript documentation, Leto's and Flavio's printed reconstructions of Rome were composed of heterogeneous kinds of evidence (textual, archaeological, visual, and epigraphical) and compared against one another to determine—in what Leonard Barkan has called a "philological reconstruction"—the most historically accurate picture of the classical Roman cityscape.[48] As Roberto Weiss has written, the kind of philological scholarship practiced on manuscripts by humanists was, by the Quattrocento scholars interested in the physical remains of antiquity, able to be adapted to study the physical world.[49] Leto and Flavio were central figures in that enterprise for the Roman cityscape; and, as we shall see in chapter 6, their texts and methods of scholarship proved able to be adapted from the Roman context to the sites of Coppo's Istria.

Cretan Antiquities and Venetian Colonialism

Because none of Coppo's writings, notes, or books from his time in Rome or Naples survive, we must cast our eyes backward in time from Coppo's major works completed in the 1520s and 1530s in Istria to discover how these Roman approaches to ancient Roman remains may have shaped his writing and mapping. We may focus on one particular source that reveals the way in which Coppo melded his experience with Leto and Roman traditions of archaeological writing with his own experience in the Mediterranean: his maps of Crete.[50]

Coppo spent six years on Crete during this early period; although the precise dates are not clear, this was probably during the very first years of the sixteenth century. His paternal uncle Nicolò was posted to Candia (modern Heraklion) on Crete as *rettore* in 1501 and as *provveditore* in 1502; it was likely with these prestigious appointments that his nephew came along to Crete. Coppo married Colotta in Isola in 1499 and received his first municipal post there in 1505, so perhaps he traveled between Isola and Crete; in any case, he returned permanently to Isola by 1505. Coppo spent a great deal of time on Crete soon after his tours of antique Roman and Neapolitan remains with Leto, and his encounters with the *Romanità* of Leto's academy and Flavio's texts are plain in his documentation of the Cretan landscape.

The landscape and built environment of Crete offered up a rich body of material evidence of Greek and Roman antiquity for Coppo and other Venetian humanists. It was a dramatic and experimental setting for humanist inquiry, where the antiquarianism of the peninsula could be tested on the very stage of ancient myth and literature. Perhaps no other humanist offered as emotional a description of Cretan ruins as Cristoforo Buondelmonti. Born around 1380 in Florence to a cadet branch of a patrician Florentine family, Buondelmonti left Florence for the Aegean in his mid-twenties in order to learn Greek. There, he wrote a geographical and archaeological description of Crete dedicated to Nicolò Niccoli, the *Descriptio insulae Cretae*, which may have originally contained a map.[51] Five years later, in 1420, he produced his *Liber insularum archipelagi*, an encyclopedia of the Aegean Islands that matched a geographical description, some discussion of toponymy and classical history, and archaeological information with maps of each island; the *Liber* also contained a chapter on Crete.[52] The *Liber insularum* was enormously popular in the late Quattrocento and Cinquecento and is known in sixty-four manuscript copies—only thirteen fewer than Marco Polo's travel account.[53] The book was also popular among Venetian readers. The Latin text was translated in two copies into the Venetian vernacular in the late fifteenth century. Three Latin copies of the *Liber* can be attributed to specific Venetian owners. One copy now in Berlin was in the collection of Antonio Venier.[54] A volume of the *Liber* now in the Biblioteca Civica in Padua contains an inscription recording that Taddeo Quirini—brother of the more famous humanist Nicolò on Crete—gave the book to Jacopo Zeno, the Venetian patrician bishop of Padua (1418–81).[55] Finally, Francesco Barbaro (1390–1454), one of the most well known of the Venetian patrician humanists, owned a composite volume of geographical writing in which the *Liber* was included.[56]

Venetian readers may have been interested in Buondelmonti's writing about their own colonial possessions in the Mediterranean, and perhaps especially in his descriptions and mapping of Crete, one of the most important of the Venetian holdings in the maritime state. Buondelmonti wrote about Crete both in the *Descriptio* devoted solely to the island and in the *Liber*. In the *Descriptio*, he wrote particularly evocatively about the state of the antiquities on Crete: "Among [the columns] I found, near the huts of the peasants, sarcophagi made of a very white marble, where the pigs ate their grain. They tore all to pieces the magnificent sculptures which lay about. I have seen the busts of mutilated statues, in the midst of which, here and there, are marble monuments."[57] It is easy to imagine such descriptions tugging on the heartstrings of Venetian humanist patrician statesmen at home in Venice. And, while Buondelmonti "wept freely at seeing this ruined place,"[58] the Venetian colonizers of the island, by stark contrast, deserved praise. The Venetian patrician collector Nicolò Cornaro showed Buondelmonti his garden filled with antique sculpture where "he poses on a pedestal every statue that he discovers in the bushes and finds to his taste, and there are plenty of them . . . the ancestors of my host posed the busts of Marc Antony and Pompeius. There I saw pretty marbles brought from every kind of building."[59]

The accusations of neglect that Buondelmonti leveled at the peasant subjects on Crete were an inheritance of writing on Roman ruins. We might compare these to Petrarch's mournful description in his letter to Giovanni Colonna sometime after his visit to the city in 1337: "For today who are more ignorant about Roman affairs than Roman citizens? Sadly I do say that nowhere is Rome less known than in Rome."[60] It also emerged from a sense of Venetian political and cultural superiority as the local imperial power. Cyriac of Ancona's description of an archery competition on Crete in 1445 reinforces the sense that the Venetian imperial administration saw the island's antiquity, and the scholars who studied it, as useful to reinforce their authority. The Venetian governors of the islands organized the archery contest because "of the ancient worth of all the Cydonian and Cretan archers," publicly staged "under the gaze of the distinguished citizens and colonists."[61] The ancient ruins and myths of Crete were not simply scholarly fodder for visiting humanists, but part of the ways in which Venetian cultural authority was transformed into public spectacle for the "citizens and colonists" to witness.

Coppo's woodcut, hand-colored map of Crete in his *De toto orbe* is similarly a product of this provocative encounter between Venetian colonial governance and the physical stage of antique myth and history (figure 6). His map in his encyclopedia is littered with ancient toponymy and ruins. The fragmented pieces of dark stone scattered across a wide swath of central Crete represent its Greek and Roman period ruins. The Minoan Labyrinth and ruins of Knossos are depicted; so too are the ruins of "Cortina," or Gortyn, an archaeological

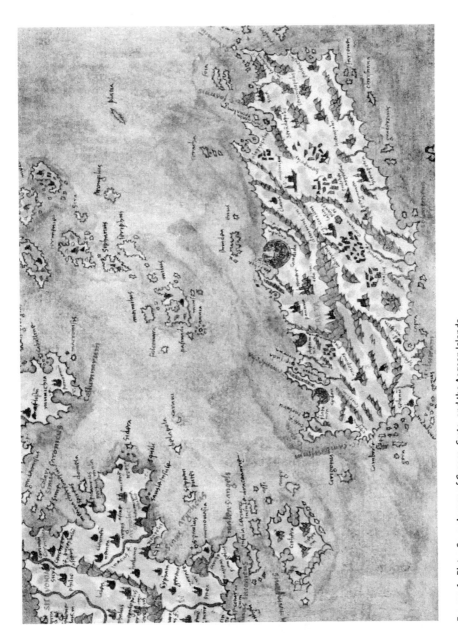

Figure 6. Pietro Coppo's map of Greece, Crete, and the Aegean Islands.
By kind permission of the Biblioteca dell'Archiginnasio, Bologna.

site that features ruins from the Minoan, Hellenistic, and Roman periods of the city. Coppo depicts Serandopolis, a city also discussed by Buondelmonti, as formerly inhabited by giants. He shows Pergamea, a city of classical literature, founded by Aeneas (in the wrong place: he was meant to found it in Italy). However, the map is not meant to show Crete as it stood in ancient times, indicated not only by the ruined state of the antique sites but by Coppo's depictions of the densely built modern cities of "Hierapetra" (now Ierapetra), "Candida" (Heraklion), and "Rhetimi" (Rethymno). These were strategically important cities for Venetians that they fortified with important harbors and governor's loggias.[62] Coppo's map of the island layers classical literature and myth, ancient physical remains, and modern Venetian cities. He must have witnessed firsthand the spaces of modern Venetian governance—walking the halls of his uncle Nicolò's loggia in Heraklion—as well as those of ancient ruins. His map integrated the ancient and modern physical landscapes of the island, even perhaps suggesting that these were mutually reinforcing.

In 1526, Coppo produced yet another woodcut and hand-colored map of Crete, this time for his *De summa totius orbius*, a summary of the larger *De toto orbe* encyclopedia.[63] Three manuscripts of the *Summa* exist, only one with maps. All of these are written in Coppo's own hand, suggesting that he was entirely responsible for their circulation.[64] While the *De toto orbe* included Crete within a small scale regional map of Greece and the Aegean, Coppo devoted an entire, and more detailed, chorographic map to the island in the *Summa*. Signed "P.C.F" ("Petrus Coppus fecit") and dated to 1526, the map is also titled "Lisola de Candia" and features a prominently printed description borrowed from Homer's *Illiad*: "In antiquity, the island of Crete had one hundred cities. The Greeks called it 'Centonipoli' and it was most fruitful."[65] Here, in finer detail, Coppo indicated the broken fragments of Knossos, of "Hierapolis," "Cortyna." In both the *De toto orbe* map and the 1526 *Summa* map, Coppo borrowed from a longer tradition of Italian mapping of the Aegean, from both Buondelmonti's *Liber* and perhaps the *Descriptio*, and likely also Bartolomeo dalli Sonetti's *Isolario*. A combination of Ptolomaic geography (in evidence especially in the regional European maps of the *Summa*, such as those of France and the Iberian peninsula), Latin and vernacular Italian geographies, and his own firsthand experience of the island, Coppo's maps of Crete are also uniquely his own. They are evidence of the six years he spent on the island, of his time there in the centers of Venetian governance (particularly in Heraklion, where his uncle was posted), and of his interest in its ruined antique landscape and ancient literary tradition.

Crete was an especially provocative site for Italian humanists, who melded their own antiquarian traditions with the physical remains dotting the landscape; and for Venetians, this scholarly project could take on political meaning as the stage for their own most distinctly imperial experiment in the Mediterranean state. For Coppo, his keen attentiveness to ancient ruins—an interest honed in Leto's house in Rome—was transported to the Mediterranean and combined with his everyday experience of Venetian governance there, as he lived with and witnessed firsthand his uncle's prestigious imperial career on the island. We know little of Coppo's humanist scholarship in Venice under Sabellico, before he left the city to travel through Italy and Crete. So it is difficult to know precisely how his intellectual trajectory developed over time and across space, as we can track Bembo's. However, Coppo's maps—in the *De toto orbe* and the *Summa*, and in his chorographic *Del Sito de Listria* as we shall see in chapter 6—are creative, even innovative productions. Of course, Ptolemaic geographies were popularly published, and so too were works like Buondelmonti's circulated widely in manuscript, but the hybridized combination of these traditions with Roman antiquarian sensitivity and eyewitness imperial experience was revelatory. Coppo's maps depict a layered world of classical geographies, ancient text and myth, antiquarian documentary practices, and modern imperial sensibilities, which is a faithful orientation to his own experience of the encounter between the ancient and modern worlds that took place on the stage of Venetian empire. Coppo was indeed a "diligent and thoughtful" cartographer of that experience.

Conclusion

In this chapter, we traced Bembo and his school friends as they toured the western Mediterranean by galley, and we saw how Coppo made the most of his close relationship with Sabellico, as he studied Roman ruins with Pomponio Leto and translated this study to the island-colony of Crete. Both of these young men and their friends seemed to desire a different kind of encounter with antiquity than the one they had learned in the Scuola di San Marco. In the Mediterranean, they found the physical stage of classical literature and myth: guided by Pliny, Ptolemy, and Strabo, these young men discovered the material remains of the antique world that they had lived and breathed through literature from their earliest childhood. They were guided through this encounter by the antiquarians who had carved a path of documenting these remains a generation before, through the wide dispersal of Cyriac's sylloge, the record of Pomponio Leto's tours, Flavio's textual excavations, and Buondelmonti's maps. Their texts and teaching were used by humanists like Bembo, Coppo, and their friends, who ventured out into the Mediterranean in their footsteps. These young Venetian men underwent their own intellectual transformations in the Mediterranean world, as they copied texts under the watchful eyes of local Greek scholars, or experimented with translating methods of documentation and scholarship between the textual and the material, Venice and the Greek islands, Rome and Crete. These texts were part of Bembo's and Coppo's intensely provocative encounters between humanist scholarship and the firsthand experience of the ruins of classical civilization, once they set out from Venice as young men.

What did they hope to find there? On the one hand, Bembo's and Coppo's journeys into the Mediterranean were the next stage in their social and intellectual development. As they partially let go of their intellectual communities in Venice, they maintained some friendships, which helped them navigate the new world of the Venetian Mediterranean. In encountering different kinds of evidence of the classical past, and local Mediterranean scholars, they formulated different kinds of documentary and scholarly practices. Bembo, like Cyriac, created a sylloge that provided an alternative documentation of his journey through the Mediterranean than his prose travel account embedded in his autobiographical letter. Coppo, following Leto's and Flavio's topographic interest in the ruins of Rome, turned to cartography to document the ruins of Crete. Perhaps Bembo's interest in philology, in atomizing and comparing elements of classical language, made the composite compiling of epigraphy a natural choice for documenting his journey. Sabellico's journalistic style of writing, which paid close attention to landscape and setting and often used tropes of the bird's-eye view to describe unfolding events, may have influenced Coppo's own choice to chorographically survey the ruined landscape of Crete. This is a possibility we will examine more closely in chapter 6. Though their documentary practices took different forms, forms potentially related to their own intellectual communities and teachers, both men found in the Mediterranean landscape and its people a new way of engaging with antiquity.

Of course, these new creative practices were at least in part due to the simple fact that all of the literature that these men had studied as children physically took place in the places they visited, and the traces left there were not only visible but referenced in classical authorities. Venice, as historians have noted, was conspicuously lacking in visible antique remains, especially for a city whose foundation myths often included the idea that Venice was the inheritor of, or even absorbed, the classical civilization of Rome (via Byzantium).[66] At one level, going into the Mediterranean to view the ancient sites discussed by Pliny and others was a necessity: Venice did not have the ancient physical landscape of Rome, or even of its subject *terraferma* cities, such as Padua (where Antenor's tomb was a venerated monument) or Verona.[67] But that the Mediterranean was also a Venetian imperial space gave these scholarly excursions a more complex political meaning. In some cases, as in the Venetian governors' archery contest on Crete, scholarship of the ancient world could be mobilized for political theater, much like the classicizing overtones of the Venetian governors' ritualized entrances to their subject cities upon their appointments.

But Bembo, Coppo, and their friends were not using their antiquarian scholarship to justify or glorify Venetian rule in a straightforward way, and they would not do so once they were themselves appointed to administrative positions within the *stato da mar*. Instead, the antique landscape of the Mediterranean colonies was incorporated into their scholarship, their imagination, and their perception of the empire, and they drew on this scholarship to understand how to govern. Maya Jasanoff has written incisively about how the collecting of antiquities can be used by historians as a way to understand the relationship between power and culture in colonial settings.[68] Much of our attention has been devoted to the public, ritual, and representative iterations of this: the spectacle of colonial rule, and its incorporation of Roman Imperial motifs, history, and antique-built environment.[69]

But with Bembo and Coppo, we will be able to perceive the ways in which humanism, and particularly antiquarian scholarship, was part of their subjective writing and experience of empire. The methods of scholarship that they developed during these years in the Mediterranean—methods of recording inscriptions and mapping ruins—would become important during their later political lives, as they described and mapped their own experiences as governors and husbands in the empire. The Greek, Istrian, and Dalmatian scholars they met during their travels around the sea were not only subjects but also scholarly collaborators, with their own perspectives and epistemologies related to the material evidence of the antique Mediterranean. The encounter with these local actors and with the material antiquity of the Mediterranean was as important for their understanding of governance as it was in their formation of families across the cultural and confessional boundaries of the Mediterranean colonies. It is to their wives and children and their Mediterranean experiences that we turn next.

CHAPTER 3

Gender and Identity between Venice and the Mediterranean

Introduction

In 1525, Giovanni Bembo set off from Venice to Skiathos, the island to which he had been appointed as colonial governor by the aristocratic Great Council of the lagoon city. He arrived on the island after a long sea journey with his family in tow: wife Cyurω and perhaps six of their children. The teenaged Urania and her siblings Faustina, Polymnia, Modestino, Domenico, and Angela (then only four years old) probably made their temporary family home on Skiathos, too. Bembo described their journey in a letter to his friend Andrea, written twelve years later. He described their travels from the towns of the Adriatic coast, to Crete and Negroponte, and finally to Skiathos. The family made a longer stop on the island of Crete, and Bembo described a remarkable exchange there: "Walking along through the city of Crete, my Cyurω heard passers-by and travellers saying: This is the wife and consort of the Rettore of the islands of Skiathos and Skopelos. They greeted her, saying, 'Hail to the Rettore's Wife!' [('Ipsam alii salutabant dicentes: "Χαίρε χυίρα ρετοῦρενα!')] You can imagine how glad and delighted my Cyurω was then, when she saw how the people, the sailors, the citizens, and the nobles were venerating her."[1]

As Bembo urged Andrea to picture the street scene, it is easy for us, too, to imagine a delighted Cyurω walking through the streets of the Cretan town, greeted in vernacular Greek by the people of the island, perhaps speaking to them in her native language. Cyurω had left her birthplace of Corfu twenty-five years before, and since then had been on long journeys around the Mediterranean, lived in the Bembo family home in Venice, given birth to ten children, and buried four who did not survive infancy. She faced pregnancy on galley ships; she oversaw her children's humanist education in the metropole; she fretted over dowries for her daughters. She had lived as Bembo's informal partner for nearly two decades before they married. She had fought for her son Domenico's inclusion into the nobility, despite her status as a low-born Greek foreigner. So as Cyurω was greeted in the vernacular Greek of the Mediterranean islands, in her native tongue as the proud wife of a member of the Venetian political elite, we can certainly understand her happiness and relief. She had returned to a place like home, but arrived there changed. As Bembo tells it, this moment on Crete was the joyful culmination of Cyurω's experiences as both Greek and Venetian: it was her triumphal reentrance to the Mediterranean empire.

But this street scene was only a fleeting moment in Cyurω's much longer life of travels and encounters. Her triumphal walk through the Cretan city came about through the happy but transitory intersection of her Venetian and Greek identities: the moment at which her native identity—what was once her colonial subjecthood—could, paradoxically, transform her into a member of the governing class. Cyurω was both colonial subject and an imperial woman; Corfiote, but the mother of Venetian aristocrats; Greek Orthodox, the daughter of a perhaps Muslim father; ambiguously servant and wife. In his autobiographical letter, Bembo even wrote her name in a mixture of Latin and Greek letters. If Cyurω's encounter on Crete was the happy intersection of these changing vectors of identity, she experienced many more encounters that were deeply troubled, moments in which her Greekness, her marriage, or her mixed-background children were sources of partial belongings and exclusions.

"Haec est uxor et marita Rectoris," Bembo wrote, reporting the Cretans' greetings and translating them into his more familiar humanist Latin. But what did it mean to become the wife and consort of a Venetian colonial governor when one had once been a colonial subject? What was gained, and what was given up? What kinds of exclusions were bargained for a new, if only partial, belonging? Cyurω's social and cultural identities and sources of belonging were constantly in flux, as she moved between Venice and the Mediterranean, encountered Venetian aristocrats and Greek scholars and subjects, was subject and ruler.[2] This chapter traces these transforming connections and ways of belonging through Cyurω's experiences and encounters, in Venice and in the Mediterranean world. Tracing these changing ways of belonging shows that categories of identity could be wafer-thin, permeating the boundaries between governor and governed, between wife and servant, between exalted mother of aristocratic children and scorned outsider who threatened the integrity of the nobility.

Cyurω's transformational experiences, and those of her children, suggest that the family must be a central element in our understanding of imperial society and political culture. Not only did Cyurω directly participate in the social dynamics of the empire, as we see so provocatively in her street encounter with the Cretans. But Cyurω's encounters with her children, her husband, native islanders, and the Venetian patriciate have left tracks that can tell us about the ways in which one woman negotiated, became enrolled in, and was sometimes excluded from the society and structures of the Venetian empire. A burgeoning field within imperial history has been the study of the colonial family and the domestic or intimate sphere, which has been convincingly shown to have been an important arena in which definitions and categories of identity—particularly concerning the intersections between race and gender—were renegotiated in colonial settings and at home in the metropole.[3] Like the women studied in these imperial histories, Cyurω transgressed, adopted, and negotiated categories of belonging that were central to the societies in which she lived, including political identities, ethnicity, religion, and class.

By tracking Cyurω's encounters and transformations, we can perceive the relationships between a woman, her family, and the social and political dynamics of a Renaissance Mediterranean empire. These relationships were characterized by hybridity and by spatiality. First, Cyurω spent her life crossing spatial, political, social, and religious borders: she appears to us as "an image of between-ness which does not construct a place or condition of its own other than the mobility, uncertainty, and multiplicity of the face of the constant border-crossing itself."[4] Crossing borders between Venice and the empire, Latin and Greek beliefs, Corfiote servant and Venetian wife, Cyurω spent her adult life neither entirely as a member of the colonizing or governing class nor entirely as a colonial subject. It is for this reason that she makes such an unusual and rich subject for a history of the early modern Mediterranean. Indeed, the ways in which Cyurω accommodated political, social, and religious senses of belonging as she moved through Venice and its empire give us a glimpse of the individualized lived experience of identity in the early modern world. It is this lived experience that can help us avoid the false historiographical dichotomy between, on the one hand, immutable (particularly religious) identity and, on the other, syncretic, shared spaces and practices that has characterized the history of the late medieval and early modern Mediterranean.[5]

But Cyurω's story also presents historical challenges, of which her complicated name is emblematic. "Cyurω" was the name given to her by her husband, Bembo, in the long letter he wrote to his friend Andrea upon her death. It is an odd name, neither Latin nor Greek. Perhaps, for Bembo, the mixed orthography captured her mixed identity as a Corfiote woman and subject, and as a Venetian wife and mother. Bembo's "Cyurω" was probably an adaptation of her Greek name "Κιούρω," a name that was common on fifteenth- and sixteenth-century Corfu. And finally, to the Venetian scribes and family historians who meticulously compiled information about Venetian patrician marriages and births, Cyurω/Κιούρω was fully Italianized. In the Venetian archival record, she became "Chiara." As she never wrote her own name, we can only trace her names and identities from the epistolary and archival sources created by her husband and by the institutions of the Venetian state.

The problem of Cyurω's name points to a wider problem in attempting to write her history, or in trying to write the history of any early modern woman whose life was shaped by a confrontation between the connectivity of the Mediterranean world and the structures of empire. The primary source from which we know about Cyurω is Bembo's letter, which begins with her death, before leaping backward in time to the moment at which he first met her, when she was seventeen and cohabiting with him on Corfu. Because the letter is one of consolation, addressed to a friend who had also known Cyurω as a teenaged girl on Corfu, Bembo spent much of the letter discussing Cyurω: what she did, what she said, and what she felt, from their first meeting until her death in 1536. The letter is indeed autobiographical, as the majority of the text relates Bembo's life, but his life was inextricably bound up with Cyurω's and their children's. Her death undoubtedly profoundly grieved and troubled him, even taking into account the hyperbole and literary conventions of Latin consolatory epistolary writing, and so she was the focus of the letter as he remembered her to Andrea. Bembo wrote particularly about her relationship with him, as wife, supporter, adviser. His letter is therefore not only an autobiography but also a biography of his wife.

At the heart of Cyurω's mixed identity, multiple names, and conflicts of belonging is the fact that she is knowable to us only through Bembo's letter. Bembo's way of writing her life—in a humanist consolatory Latin letter— was itself inextricable from the structures of knowledge and power that Cyurω encountered and often battled throughout her life. What we know of her life is accessible to us through a source that was itself constructed within humanist political culture. Bembo's remarkable biographical letter about his wife, in both its humanist form and its content, was itself a product of the social, cultural, and political structures of humanism and empire that Cyurω herself confronted.

Finally, Bembo's letter—though on one level, part of a well-established genre of Latin consolatory epistolary writing—does not present him or his authority as husband, father, or governor in a particularly favorable light. He relates a series of failures in his domestic life that spill over into his role as governor, most catastrophically surrounding his daughter Urania's affair with his scribe. His authority as father and governor, so intimately linked within Renaissance Venetian paradigms of masculinity, was seriously undermined in those domestic imperial failures, and yet he related them anyway to Andrea. He wrote so bluntly about his own failures as a Venetian patrician man that he seems to upend many of the central models of masculinity that Venetian society held dear; we will examine the implications of this in detail in chapter 5. The confessional nature of this letter, the very fact that Bembo wrote in such (sometimes excruciating) detail about his own mistakes and failures, suggests that his narrative concerning his wife is a perhaps unusually self-reflective accounting of their life together.

Κιούρω

Κιούρω, as her name was then, was born in 1480 on the island of Corfu. We do not know precisely where, although she probably lived in the city of Corfu by 1497, where Bembo remembers first meeting her. We do not know the name of Κιούρω's mother, but her father was Mustafa Coriera. Mustafa's name was entered into the documents of Venetian administration as a result of a powerful series of laws made by the Senate and Great Council throughout the fifteenth and sixteenth centuries that were intended to ensure the integrity of the patriciate by regulating patrician marriage and reproduction (we will turn to these in greater detail below). Increasingly, these regular evaluations by necessity also enrolled women into the regulatory documentary practices of the state. In the *Libro d'Oro*, a register kept by the State Attorneys to record noble births in Venice and instituted in 1506, under the entry for her son Domenico (born in 1517), Κιούρω's name is recorded as "Chiara Coriera."[6] A few years before she died, Girolamo Loredan, a Venetian patrician family historian, recorded in his genealogical chronicle that Giovanni Bembo had married the (nameless) daughter of Mustafa of Corfu, a woman who had been Bembo's household servant.[7]

When prompted, then, Cyurω must have given the Venetian State Attorneys the name "Mustafa Coriera da Corfu" for her father, a name that might have raised a few eyebrows among the gatekeepers of the city's aristocracy. Although it is impossible to be sure, Mustafa Coriera may have been a Muslim, perhaps from the Iberian peninsula. On Corfu from at least Κιούρω's birth in 1480, he was on the island for years before the waves of Jewish and Muslim migration across the Mediterranean, including to Corfu, caused by the Spanish expulsion of the Jews and then Muslims from the very end of the fifteenth century.[8] Indeed, there was no Muslim community in Corfu in the second half of the fifteenth century, at least so far as is recorded in the surviving notarial documents of the island's archive. Mustafa may have been a Spanish or Portuguese Muslim trader who settled in Corfu temporarily to do business, or perhaps even a Muslim slave, sold into service on Corfu.[9] Κιούρω's mother was probably a Greek woman from Corfu, as Κιούρω's own Corfiote Greek name and her Greek Orthodox religion suggest a Greek upbringing on the island.

In a view of the city of Corfu printed in 1486, we see Venetian galleys cut across the waves of the city's port, and sailors and merchants busy getting ready to unload the galley's cargo.[10] Figures on foot and on horseback gather at the entrance of the port to welcome the ships. Dominating the print is the towering Fortezza Vecchia, first a Byzantine fortification before being occupied and largely rebuilt by the Venetians. Amid the impressive fortifications and jutting cliff faces are houses densely packed and churches and monasteries nestled in shady groves. When the Milanese canon Pietro Casola visited Corfu in 1494 on the way to Jerusalem, when Κιούρω was fourteen years old, Casola observed that the people there were as densely settled. "There is a dense population of men and women . . . but for the most part they are of low class, although there are some of gentle birth."[11]

Κιούρω would have belonged among the women of "low class" whom Casola saw in the city. However, as Casola noted, Corfu did indeed have a local patriciate "of gentle birth." One lasting legacy of the Angevin rule of the island was that this Corfiote elite was divided into a Latin community and a Greek community, and it was the Latin Corfiote elite whose daughters could marry into the Venetian patriciate. Marriage to Corfiote Latin women could indeed be enormously beneficial for a Venetian patrician, as the local legal code of the island, the Assizes of Romania, allowed Corfiote women to inherit the family's property, and therefore pass the family's sometimes substantial landholdings to their husband's family.[12] Bembo could not have expected, however, to come into a Corfiote fiefdom when he married Κιούρω, who is recorded as having been his domestic servant.[13] But it is important to note these more subtle stratifications within the Corfiote community. Not only was Κιούρω not a landholding member of the Corfiote patriciate, but the only truly viable option for Venetian patricians was to marry women who belonged to one-half of that elite group. Both Κιούρω's Greekness and her low-born status were problematic in the eyes of the Venetian patriciate, as we shall see. Κιούρω spent her childhood among these competing religious and social identities, and experiencing the changing colonial landscape of the island.[14] Κιούρω's life after she met Bembo was marked by her awareness of social and cultural difference, and by her keen understanding of the reach of empire into her family life.

Cyurω

Bembo remembered having "been united" with Cyurω on Corfu when she was seventeen and he was twenty-four.[15] The Venetian *Cronaca matrimoni* records Cyurω as Bembo's "femena," or domestic servant.[16] This is likely simply a shorter version of the term "femena vil," most commonly used to refer to the slaves or "very low-ranking" women whom patrician men very occasionally married.[17] This term is not straightforward. Bembo and Cyurω did not marry until 1516, or almost twenty years and several children after they first met, so the identification of Cyurω as "sua femena" may reflect her status as Bembo's long-term informal partner, rather than her actual occupation or even servitude within his household. That she wrote Bembo multiple letters and, as we shall see, educated their daughters within the household raises questions about her status as a domestic servant. It is, of course, not impossible that they met when Cyurω came into domestic service in Bembo's household on Corfu. Whether Cyurω was Bembo's servant or whether this terminology was meant to evoke her objectionable status as Bembo's unmarried partner, that she was recorded as having been "sua femena" in the official records of the State Attorneys was problematic for the status of her family.

The first three years after Bembo and Cyurω were "united" were spent entirely outside Venice. Shortly after they met, Bembo's father, Domenico, sent him to Lepanto, probably for trade; there is no indication that Cyurω joined him there. He returned to Corfu but left again in 1499, this time with Cyurω, and after making several stops in the coastal towns of the Adriatic, came to settle in Pesaro on the Italian Adriatic. Here, Bembo joined Giovanni Sforza's mercenary army against Cesare Borgia and took up two municipal posts in the nearby small town of Candelara. After spending time studying theology at the monastery of St. Francis, Bembo was then dismissed from Sforza's army but given "a house with a garden" in Pesaro to start a school for children in the town.[18] Bembo wrote that, in this idyllic setting, Cyurω "loved [his students] as if they were her own sons." Even before Cyurω had children, her life with Bembo meant that her domestic life was melded with humanist scholarship, and that her identity as a mother was wrapped up in providing a humanist education. In 1500, however, their peaceful life as a scholarly family in Pesaro came to an abrupt end. Cesare Borgia, Pope Alexander VI's warmongering son, took the town; and Bembo's father, Domenico, died while at his post as castellan of Soncino in Cremona. Bembo's brother, Francesco, "rushed to Pesaro" to tell him that their father owed a fortune of fifteen hundred ducats to the Venetian State upon his death, and the State was threatening to take the family house, garden, and apothecary shop. Cyurω, in the same year, had her first child: a daughter named Faustina. With infant in tow, an army threatening the town, and the looming threat of great financial loss to the family, Bembo, Cyurω, and Francesco set off for Venice.[19]

Shortly after moving back to Venice with his family, Bembo was appointed to a minor administrative position on the Giustizia Nuova. In a matter of weeks, he resigned from the post in a fit of rage and disillusionment.[20] Cyurω rejoiced: "She wished passionately, hoped, and got the idea into her head that the Great Council would then appoint me to other honors and magistracies in your [Andrea's] city of Corfu: so that she might worship in her own country and be useful to her family and to her friends."[21] It seems that, at least in Bembo's recollection of three decades later, it was Cyurω's desire to return to Corfu that was most memorable of those years following their chaotic relocation to Venice. Particularly striking in Bembo's memories is that Cyurω wished to "worship in her own country," a phrase that raises questions about Cyurω's religious beliefs and practices in Venice and indeed on Corfu, and how this religious identity might have been perceived by Venetian society.

There was a large Greek community in Venice, particularly from the second half of the fifteenth century: between 1470 and 1540, approximately the years of Cyurω's lifetime, Greek immigration to the city doubled.[22] The Scuola di San Niccolo dei Greci, a confraternity established in 1498, was a crucial social institution for Greek men and women in Venice. And there seems to have been little pressure for Greek women to adopt Latin devotional practices, or even, as Ersie Burke has written, to learn Italian to speak to their husbands.[23] However, the members of the Scuola di San Niccolo and the Greek women studied by Burke were either non-patrician Greeks married to other Greeks or noble Greek women from important colonial or Byzantine patrician families whose marriages to Venetian men were potentially both financially and politically profitable. This picture of relatively easy coexistence between Greek women and Venetian men in the domestic setting, and between the Greek community as a whole and the urban society of Venice is predicated on these particular configurations of class identity.

As Sally McKee has found for Venetian Crete, even while religion was an important ethnic marker for Venetians, women's attachment to the Greek church was less important in terms of their social status than it was for men; and in general, there was no tidy hierarchy between the Latin population and the Greek population organized along lines of religious belonging.[24] Indeed, as McKee has shown, it was in the intersection of ethnic markers with class identity that the clearest expressions of ethnic differentiation can be found. Of course, it is impossible to say with any certainty exactly how Cyurω expressed her religious beliefs or the extent to which she participated in Greek religious life in Venice or on Corfu. But we might speculate that if Cyurω did indeed desire to return to Corfu to participate in Greek religious life there, it was perhaps because her status as Bembo's "femena" in the eyes of the Venetian patriciate effectively made her Greek ethnicity—and religious belonging—all the more problematic within her adopted city of Venice.

However, Cyurω evidently did recognize the potential of her new relationship with Bembo. As the mother of his child, she could return to Corfu with a newfound social status and financial power. Especially if Bembo was appointed to a colonial post on Corfu, she could wield this new social and political power to help her friends and family still living on the island. On the one hand, then, Cyurω may have missed her homeland after several years away from the island, and perhaps particularly after having become settled in the Bembo home in Venice. On the other, Cyurω seems to have glimpsed the possibilities that her new identity as a Venetian mother could afford her. She would return to Corfu as the consort of a Venetian governor, with all of the social and political benefits that went along with that position. Cyurω's unfulfilled apparent desire to return to Corfu captures the complex contradictions of her changing senses of belonging, and the new possibilities to which these transformations gave rise.

Becoming the consort of a Venetian humanist posed some serious challenges. As we saw in the previous chapter, in 1505, Bembo traveled with some of his patrician school friends across the central Mediterranean. It seems that Cyurω set off with them, but they did not make it far from Venice before she realized she was pregnant. "Then Cyurω was pregnant; she rejoiced on the trireme, called by the sailors 'the little ship.' The sea and the sad sight of the waves made my Cyurω terrified, and she dreaded the long and dangerous navigation circling Africa to the channel and the Columns of Hercules, and then the Spanish coast and the African one."[25] When they reached Pola, just across the northeastern Adriatic in Istria, Cyurω returned to Venice, "twice writing me letters admonishing me to write letters to her often."[26] Pregnant with their son Cornelio, Cyurω could not face the long sea journey. That she at first intended to go with Bembo and his friends, though, hints at her willingness—even desire—to adventure into the Mediterranean world, not only to return home to Corfu but to travel much further afield.

Pregnant and home in Venice, Cyurω anxiously posted letters across the sea, urging Bembo to write to her and relate his adventures in the Mediterranean. That Bembo records her letters to him suggests that Cyurω was indeed literate, but to what level? Intriguingly, Bembo uses the same Latin phrase—"dare literas"—to describe both his own letter writing and his wife's. Perhaps she was indeed as capable of writing letters as he was. As Bembo sailed throughout the western Mediterranean, Cyurω continued to send him letters asking for news of his health. Finally, as we will see in the next section, Bembo records that Cyurω taught their daughters their "letters." She was literate, then, and that Bembo praised her and encouraged her to teach the girls indicates that female literacy was perhaps valued within their family. Indeed, even the girls' names—Faustina, for a Roman empress, and Polymnia and Urania, for Greek muses—suggest that for both sexes, this was a scholarly household.[27]

Within a decade of first meeting Bembo on Corfu, Cyurω had been transformed from a Corfiote teenager and domestic servant to the mother of two half-Greek, half-Venetian daughters and the consort of a Venetian patrician. She had become "like a mother" to Bembo's schoolchildren in Pesaro, fled the town with her infant daughter, relocated to the Bembo family home, and begun a scholarly journey with Bembo into the Mediterranean. Throughout, she perhaps retained her Greek Orthodox beliefs, apparently a source of distress once she lived in Venice and found it difficult to practice her religion. Her new role as Venetian consort and mother brought with it new opportunities to help her family on Corfu and to travel across the Mediterranean; but neither of these could be fulfilled, as Bembo could not gain a post back on the island, and her pregnancy meant that it was impossible for her to face such a dangerous sea journey. During the first years with Bembo in Venice, Cyurω's Corfiote Greek subjecthood and identity as Κιούρω were transformed by partial connections and what may have been difficult separations.

A Mixed Family

In 1516, Cyurω and Bembo finally married. They had lived together for almost twenty years. Bembo's mother, Angela Cornaro, had urged Bembo fifteen years earlier to marry Cyurω, when they had first returned from Pesaro with baby Faustina in tow. After Faustina was born in 1500 or 1501, Cyurω had two more daughters, Urania and Polymnia, and finally, three sons in succession, Modestino, Domenico, and Cornelio.[28] She was probably pregnant again with Domenico when they finally married in 1517. Among the witnesses at their wedding was Giovanni Battista Egnazio, Bembo's close friend from his days in Brugnolo's lectures at the Scuola.[29] It seems that the births of their sons had finally prompted Bembo into action, as they were excluded from the patriciate.

But it was not until 1517, with the birth of Domenico, that Bembo and Cyurω argued passionately to have the baby enrolled in the *Libro d'Oro*, the "Golden Book" that recorded the birth of every patrician child. The *Libro d'Oro* had been relatively recently instituted in 1506, when the Council of Ten legislated that every noble male birth was to be registered by the State Attorneys. The book also had to include the birthplace and surname of the mother. Hence Cyurω's Corfiote identity and father's name were enrolled in Venetian state documentation.[30] This legislation was only one component of a complex patrician social world in which marriage was of the utmost importance. Francesco Barbaro, a Venetian patrician humanist, wrote *De re uxoria* ("The Wealth of Wives") in 1415 and it proved popular throughout the Renaissance.[31] The text speaks eloquently to the ways in which patrician men were educated to think about the relationship between marriage, reproduction, and their political lives. In the first section of the treatise, "On the Selection of a Wife," Barbaro wrote about nobility: "Let us esteem, therefore, the noble origin of both our parents, and communicate it to our children. While other things are uncertain, shifting, and transitory, this legacy of nobility is fixed with secure roots, can withstand any force, and will never be destroyed."[32] Even before the tightening of marriage legislation a few years later, Barbaro wrote anxiously about the power of a truly noble marriage amid the "uncertain" and "shifting" world around him. Barbaro, like the Council of Ten and the State Attorneys, felt that unquestionably fixing one's identity within a social class through noble marriage and reproduction was the most important way to retain a sense of permanence.

Permanence was important to Barbaro and to the Venetian patriciate because it would ensure the continuation of political stability in the city: "For [noble-born children] will realize that all eyes will be turned on them in expectation that they will in some way reiterate in their own lives the virtue they have inherited from their ancestors. So we may call those honorably born 'the walls of the city.'"[33] Noble marriage and reproduction were conceived as almost physical defenses against the "transitory" forces of historical change. And the mother was central in the reproduction of this permanence, because she was considered to transmit bodily her own noble qualities. Children from legitimate marriages between noble men and women were "more inclined to honor, are more responsibly reared, and ultimately make better citizens," while "those who were conceived in lust and outside of wedlock are for the most part violent and dishonest and inclined to all that is base."[34] This was not simply a matter of a mother's role in educating her child. Barbaro instructed even noblewomen to breast-feed their babies, as they could shape the mind, body, and emotional character of their children. For example, Barbaro wrote, "the hair of goats suckled on sheep's milk gradually becomes softer," while "the pelts of lambs who are suckled by goats are visibly coarsened."[35] A mother's nobility could physically transform her infant into a potentially virtuous citizen, a bastion of political stability who could defend the Republic from change.

To the Venetian State Attorneys, Cyurω could not have been a more unfit choice for a wife and mother. She was a colonial subject and not a Venetian citizen; she was not a member of the nobility—indeed, she had (at least for administrative purposes) been a domestic servant; and her first four children had been born out of wedlock. And yet Bembo wrote about her as the perfect *materfamilias*, mixing Venetian patrician expectations with classical mythology to describe her actions as wife and mother. He was nevertheless movingly aware of patrician perceptions of her. "My Cyurω took care that [our] daughters learn letters and the Palladian arts, to sew, weave, and spin silk; and she always practiced with them all of the domestic things that a good *materfamilias* would do. But she was a Greek woman, and the Greeks are not much loved."[36] Despite Cyurω's education of her daughters, which fulfilled perfectly the expectations of Venetian patrician mothers, Bembo understood that she would never be fully accepted into his class. She taught her daughters to read, and the image of this Greek-speaking woman educating her daughters— themselves named after the Greek muses of Sacred Song and Astronomy— calls to mind an idealized scholarly household, in which ancient and vernacular Greek, ancient myth and contemporary paradigms of motherhood, happily and easily coexisted. It is only in Bembo's brief final sentence that we gain a glimpse of the much more difficult reality that this scholarly family faced in patrician Venice.

With the birth of Domenico, though, Cyurω had produced a legitimate son as Bembo's wife. But the State Attorneys still "objected to the mother's *genus*," as Bembo writes, a difficult word to precisely translate but probably intended to capture all of these objectionable facets of Cyurω's identity, including her Corfiote origin, Greek religion, and previously servile status.[37] Against the background of the preoccupation of the patriciate with noble marriage as a social and political institution, it is easy to imagine its reluctance to allow Cyurω and her son into its ranks. Bembo finally convinced the State Attorneys by bringing his "patrons" in front of them, including Giovanni Battista Adriano, the secretary of the Council of Ten, and Battista Mauroceno, who was then a member of the Council. With this support representative of the legislative body that had created the *Libro d'Oro* in the first place, the scribe of the State Attorneys entered Domenico's name into the book.[38] Against the law and the expectations of the patrician class, Bembo and Cyurω's infant son—born neither Venetian nor Greek, neither noble nor servile—was given the kind of fixed identity that Barbaro so exalted in his *De re uxoria*. Domenico had become an official member of the patriciate, and so a member of the governing class.

Domenico was the only one of Bembo's children to become eligible for membership on the Great Council. In later Venetian patrician genealogies of the family, Domenico is in fact the only child included: he later married three times, to a Barbaro woman in 1543 (two years before his father's death), to a Malipiero woman in 1561, and finally to a Foscarini in 1567, with whom he had a son, Giovanni, named for his grandfather.[39] Domenico married Venetian noblewomen from prominent families and named his unimpeachably noble son for his father. Domenico's story is perhaps evidence, then, of the power of patrician legitimacy in Venice, and of the kinds of social mobility that could be achieved.

Bembo and Cyurω's hard-won fight with the State Attorneys for Domenico's enrollment in the *Libro d'Oro* had been an unqualified success, as Domenico solidified his status among the Venetian patriciate through a series of noble marriages. But what of Bembo and Cyurω's other children? Beyond our productively more complicated view of patrician membership described in the social histories of Chojnacki, Grubb, and others, even within a single family, multiple kinds of social and political membership and enfranchisements could coexist. And indeed, what of Cyurω's own experiences of pregnancy and raising her children? Ten pregnancies over the course of two decades, from the age of twenty to forty-one, was a physical trial in itself, even outside of the immense social pressure from Bembo's aristocratic peers who deemed her an unacceptable mother for noble children. This was compounded by the deaths in infancy of four children sequentially. Her experiences during these years of bearing and burying her children is all but opaque to us in Bembo's letter.

An Imperial Family

In 1525, Bembo was appointed to a post as governor of Skiathos and Skopelos, islands in the northern Aegean. This was a triumph for the family: it was the most important position of Bembo's career, and one that would take him and his family back to the Mediterranean empire. When Cyurω heard that Bembo had been appointed to Skiathos, it may not have been the possibility of practicing her religion or of seeing her family that came to mind, but rather the salary that Bembo could earn as a colonial governor. Bembo recalled in his letter that upon hearing of his appointment, "My Cyurω hoped, from the profit of Skiathos, that she could provide the dowries for [our] daughters, who are now three in number: Polymnia, Urania, and Angela."[40] Cyurω's daughters, their fortunes and futures in Venice, may have been foremost in her mind. Alongside increasingly stringent marriage legislation in Venice, patrician dowry requirements had been rising "relentlessly" since the fourteenth century.[41] Patrician families—wealthier ones than Bembo's—had difficulty keeping up.[42] What Bembo records as Cyurω's immediate thought—that her husband's salary could provide a much-needed source of income to supplement her three daughters' dowries—might hint how she, even as an outsider, engaged in the same kinds of negotiations and strategic planning as Venetian patrician women. If not a Venetian patrician woman herself, she perhaps thought and acted like one, at least when it came to provisioning for her daughters' future inclusion into the patriciate.

Bembo and Cyurω's journey to Skiathos took them to the coastal towns of the Adriatic and to Crete. We have seen Cyurω's triumphal entrance to Crete, as she walked the streets of the city, greeted in vernacular Greek by Cretan "people, sailors, citizens, and nobles."[43] The family then sailed on to Skiathos, where they were to make their home for the next two years, the usual length of the governor's appointment to the maritime state. It was a deeply traumatic time for the family, and it is Cyurω's experience and her daughter Urania's, rather than Bembo's governance and decision making, that is the focus here. Urania was Bembo and Cyurω's third daughter, one for whom Cyurω was so keen to build a dowry. She was born around 1510, although we do not know the precise date; she was a teenager in 1525–1526, perhaps sixteen or seventeen years old. On Skiathos, Urania began an affair with her father's scribe. Bembo described the following events: "My scribe had an illicit affair with my daughter Urania, and twice made her pregnant. Through his skills, the scribe made her abort the first born, by means of soaking the tar of mallow root. And again, the scribe tried so that the girl would abort the second infant, but she did not want to, because the first time, the girl was in grave danger as she delivered the aborted infant. I declare, in the middle of the city, crowded with my people, I ordered that the scribe's testicles be removed by the executioner, lest he might commit infanticide again."[44]

While we will turn to Bembo's reasoning in chapter 5, we might consider here Urania's experience and her mother's response. Although historians often consider abortion to have been secretly procured between women, Urania's male partner conspired with her to create an herbal abortifacient. Who was Bembo's scribe? In general, it seems that Venetian scribes were posted to the chancery offices of the empire. This was, of course, Coppo's first role in Istria. Monique O'Connell gives an example of the castellan of Coron, who worked with a Venetian scribe during his tenure in the mid-fifteenth century.[45]

Certainly it would seem that major governing posts, such as those on Crete or in Modon and Coron, would warrant Venetian scribes to assist with the complicated tasks of administering those important centers. As we will see in the next chapter, the vast imperial bureaucracy in place on Istria was also supported by Venetian scribes, such as Pietro Coppo, who often were *cittadini*. But on Skiathos, a minor post of the empire, one that did not even warrant a castellan, did Bembo have a Venetian scribe? Or was the scribe potentially Greek, one of Bembo's many scholarly, highly literate Greek contacts in the Mediterranean world? It is impossible to know. But it is also difficult to ignore the specularity of Urania's forbidden relationship with her father's scribe, and Bembo's own illicit relationship with Cyurω.

Somehow, despite the riskiness of the abortion and her "grave danger," Urania managed to keep her first terminated pregnancy a secret, at least from her father. Pregnancy out of wedlock, especially with a non-noble and potentially Greek scribe, was socially catastrophic for Urania. As we know, her mother hoped that she would make a noble marriage in Venice, and was indeed planning for her dowry. For the scribe, helping Urania get rid of the evidence of the affair was probably the best of several unfortunate options. If their relationship was known publicly, he would face either marrying Urania or having to pay her dowry.[46] If, on the other hand, he could keep the relationship secret by getting rid of any evidence, he could go unpunished. For Urania, a young woman in a tiny island community and the daughter of the only Venetian administrator on the island, the social stigma she would have faced in raising a child out of wedlock was grim indeed.[47]

It seems that it was only the potentially life-threatening physical danger of the second abortion that induced her to speak out. Urania may also have been anxious about the repercussions of aborting her pregnancy. Across early modern Europe, infanticide—which included both aborting a pregnancy and killing the infant soon after birth—was universally extremely harshly punished.[48] Perhaps her father feared the repercussions of Urania's complicity in the first aborted pregnancy, and so chose the course of justice that would protect his family. This was not a case of abortion or infanticide like those more commonly studied in Venice and the Veneto: cases reported to the authorities by watchful neighbors who heard abandoned infants' cries from sewers, or who became suspicious of the woman next door who disappeared to the countryside to give birth in secret.[49] Urania's abortion and second pregnancy were discovered within her family; although her father's choice to punish the scribe publicly, in the central square on Skiathos, may have been catastrophic. As we will see in chapter 5, the *fama*, or rumor, of Urania's scandalous affair and her father's equally scandalous response spread throughout the maritime state and to the ruling class in Venice itself. It was on this far-flung island of the Venetian empire that intimate relationships, including sex and reproduction, became a touchstone of imperial governance.

The traumatic events on Skiathos in 1525–26 were deeply disappointing for Cyurω. As the governor's wife, she had journeyed to Skiathos perhaps feeling proud and hopeful that this post would mean a secure future for her three daughters in brilliant marriages to young patrician men. Returning to Venice after her family's catastrophic time in the Aegean was a very different journey from the one taken to Skiathos only a few years before. Everyone in Venice seemed to know of her family's disgrace. Her husband was the subject of fierce gossip, mocked viciously by his patrician peers. Cyurω may have faced down this social catastrophe. "My Cyurω understood and felt that they held me in contempt as a shameless and ruined man, and her heart was crucified with great sadness: she consoled me, that I might maintain my legacy from poverty and I might survive; and she proclaimed publicly against those magistrates and honorable men."[50]

As Bembo tells it, for Cyurω, witnessing her husband's exclusion from the Venetian patriciate was apparently devastating. Indeed, it is only here—and not during his description of Urania's affair and its aftermath—that Bembo describes her emotions, writing bitterly of her sadness over his ruined reputation. Of course, this probably reflects Bembo's own preoccupation with his reputation. But she also may have publicly wrangled with the patrician men who so viciously mocked Bembo for his choices. Bembo wrote about this as a sign of her support and a way in which she consoled him. That Bembo reported her great sadness on hearing how he was excluded and mocked may not only be a reflection of his own memories and priorities. Cyurω was devoted to securing her family's future among the patriciate in Venice. She fought for Domenico's enrollment into the *Libro d'Oro*. She viewed Bembo's imperial career like a patrician woman: she saw it not as an opportunity to return to her homeland but as an opportunity to secure dowries for her daughters. As we shall see, her anxieties over her family's future would have terrible repercussions. It was Bembo's social exclusion and the inevitable consequences this would have for her family, rather than the traumatic events on Skiathos, that were perhaps the most emotionally fraught part of this experience. Cyurω's family never fully recovered from the events on Skiathos. Bembo's career in Venice was over. They would spend the next few years in Bembo's family home in a quiet corner of the Cannaregio, their travels in the Mediterranean at an end.

"Thirty-eight years, two months, thirty days, and ten hours"

Five or six years after their dramatic return from the Aegean, Cyurω fell ill and died in Venice in 1536. In perhaps the most extraordinary passage of his letter, Bembo movingly describes Cyurω's final illness and death:

> My Cyurω desired that our two daughters should be married, and so I desired and wished for the same. But the law is: you must be able to provide your daughters with a dowry of 4,000 ducats. . . . But Cyurω knew that our small savings and property didn't exceed 2,000 ducats, and she was worn down with anxiety (*macerabat*) about these poor things. Added to our griefs, our youngest son Modestino, who was learning to be a grammatician, poet, and arithmetician and who was on track to surpass all his peers, now hates books so much that he seems to be afraid to open them, nor does he study any other virtuous things. And, following my marriage with my Cyurω, our other son Domenico was made Venetian by laws of the Great Council, obtaining—as well as nobility—arrogance or pride. He scornfully rejected my Cyurω his mother; he reproached her birth, homeland, family, and lack of dowry (*nationem, patriam, genus et indotatam*) many times, and more in this way. Consider that: do you know how she suffered from the idleness and abuse of her son? How she longed for his friendship and welcome? These sicknesses of the mind were added to the sickness of her body, and after fifteen days of a continuous fever without abating heat, she died.
>
> With my Cyurω, but who was not mine anymore, the priests of Santa Maria dei Miracoli washed and dressed her in the same devout garments of Saint Clare—just as my Cyurω requested in her final testament—and I watched over the body in the house vigilantly for twenty four hours, whence she was taken to her tomb in San Cancian. . . . I have described to you this account of my truth and of my life companion, who lived with me for thirty-eight years, two months, thirty days, and ten hours (*quae mecum vixit annos XXXVIII menses II. dies XXX. horas X*).
>
> After this was done, the sorrow, weeping, crying out and mourning did not cease in the house, but pain upon pain and grief upon grief were increased and heaped upon us: my daughter Angela died twelve days after her mother, so that in the space of twenty-seven days I have been robbed of my dearest wife and my sweetest daughter by cruel fate and upended nature. The Latin doctors did not know their disease, indeed the doctors tried to cure them with dialectics and syllogisms, as Greek

medicine is of good authority and reputation. And so now you understand what state I am in, and how many accumulated sorrows have put your Giovanni Bembo into a spin.[51]

Just as she had been before the family went to Skiathos, Cyurω was concerned with her children's social futures in her adopted city. Two of her daughters had specific opportunities to marry patrician young men, and yet the family could not afford two steep dowries. Their son Modestino, once a promising scholar, had given up his studies. As we saw in chapter 1, a humanist education was an essential stage for all young patrician men. But finally, and most painfully, Domenico—the now-grown son for whom Bembo and Cyurω had fought so hard—scorned and rejected his mother. He insulted her "birth, homeland, family, and lack of dowry": a complex patchwork of identities and social status that meant that Domenico repudiated her entirely.[52] Bembo implored Andrea to imagine Cyurω's suffering at her son's rejection, and it is all too easy to picture Cyurω, who had tangled with the elite of the city to have Domenico accepted despite her own identity, finally being rejected on the grounds of her different vectors of belonging.

Bembo's evocative language describing her illness and death conveys a sense of the physical implications of these family cares. When he describes Cyurω's feelings about their inability to provide dowries, he writes that she was "worn down with anxiety," using the vivid word *macerabat*, which suggests a sense of physical erosion due to anxiety. After Domenico finally rejects her, she both suffered and waited for him to accept her again. These "sicknesses of the mind" compounded physical illness, which led to her death. Indeed, the sense that emerges from Bembo's letter is that the emotional and physical were truly one and the same. It was Cyurω's devotion to her children's futures among the elite of Venice—in marriage, in school, and in political life—that wore her down.

In the final weeks of her life, Domenico deployed Cyurω's Corfiote identities and her inability to participate in patrician society against her. Despite her marriage, her children, and her role as the governor's wife, Cyurω could not escape her origins on Corfu: even to her own Venetian son, she was an outsider. This may have been particularly distressing for a woman who had tried in meaningful ways to behave like a Venetian patrician woman on behalf of her children. And yet Domenico's insults also suggest that Cyurω's Greekness—in both her ethnic origins and her religious belief—was undisguised, even as her actions spoke of belonging to the Venetian patrician class. She was unmistakably Corfiote, and worse, labeled as a former servant. Even as she planned her daughters' marriages and dowries, they were unable to participate in this exchange of family wealth that was so central to the integration of patrician society.[53] If Bembo's letter has led us to see the ways in which she negotiated with the Venetian patriciate and adopted patrician women's practices, flickering through his letter is her difference. It was her unavoidable difference that was at stake in Domenico's rejection, and led to her illness.

And this difference seems to have been deliberately elided after her death. Cyurω's funeral was presided over by the priests of Santa Maria dei Miracoli. She was buried in the Bembo family's parish church, San Cancian, according to Latin rite. Her body was dressed in the garments of the Poor Clare nuns of San Cancian: in death, she wished to be costumed as an Italian Catholic, raising provocative questions about whether and how her religious attachments may have evolved across the course of her lifetime.[54] Her funeral procession was attended by Bembo's Venetian patrician friends and patrons, just as the baptisms of her children had been: Bembo wrote that "Lorenzo Loredan, the son of Doge Loredan . . . Giovanni Querini, of the Council of Ten, and other noble and true men" participated in Cyurω's funeral procession.[55] Cyurω had been a central part of Bembo's scholarly family, caring for his students and overseeing her children's humanist educations, and her death was a final moment at which this humanist network of scholarly friends participated in family life. And, Bembo's poignant account of their life together—thirty-eight years, two months, thirty days, and ten hours—was itself a Roman tomb monument convention, learned during his years of collecting ancient epigraphy around the Mediterranean. Cyurω was buried and commemorated as a Venetian patrician woman, by elite men, in the rhetorical trappings of humanist convention, her body dressed in the garments of devout Catholic nuns. Ultimately, in the pageantry of a Renaissance Venetian death and burial, Cyurω's differences and unacceptable belongings were concealed.

Conclusion

Nationem, patriam, genus et indotatam: toward the end of her life Cyurω was spurned by her own son for a complex of undesirable belongings and attachments that could be condensed into just four words. But Domenico's rejection of his mother's "birth, homeland, family, and lack of dowry" points to a deep contradiction in Cyurω's story. On the one hand, Cyurω created new forms of attachment and abandoned others; her identity was not a stable composition of factors, as Domenico's insult implies. As she shed her name Κιούρω and became Bembo's Cyurω, as she had children and plotted their futures, as she crisscrossed the Mediterranean as servant, consort, and governor's wife, the ways in which she belonged to Venetian political society underwent transformations, too. And yet, Domenico's insult also suggests that underlying these transformations was her unavoidable Greekness. She assumed all of the worries and strategies of a typical Venetian patrician mother, but her behavior did not always entirely conceal her difference, and indeed in the end she could not successfully raise the dowries necessary to truly participate in patrician society. As Bembo explained to Andrea, "But she was a Greek woman, and the Greeks are not much loved." In Cyurω's story, we can see the painful tension between the possibility of transformation that the Mediterranean empire offered to women and the tenacity of identity.

The connections and mobility offered by the Mediterranean state did not mean that women like Cyurω were afforded a kind of proto-globalized identity of "diversified participation, kaleidoscopic belonging and multiplied citizenship."[56] This is contrary to the picture Eric Dursteler elaborates in his stories of early modern women for whom the Mediterranean offered almost uniformly positive opportunities for transformation.[57] But neither were identities like those identified by Domenico necessarily permanently inscribed. What emerges from Cyurω's story is a picture of hybridity, in which Cyurω did not fully belong to any one category of identity at any one time, but rather experienced her world from a perspective of unfolding transformation and social difference. For Cyurω, the Mediterranean did not present a set of multiplying opportunities for transformation and agency. Rather, the connectivity and mobility that characterized the Mediterranean empire shaped her for a life spent in-between. At certain moments—during her triumphant walk on Crete, for example—those vectors of identity happily coincided, so that she felt a sense of belonging and power as the governor's wife. At others, the fragmentation of her social and cultural attachments proved harrowing, as when Domenico finally rejected her. What is ultimately important to see in Cyurω's story is that these vectors of belonging collided either to open up possibilities for transformation and belonging or to create an unshakable, fixed identity in response to exclusion. Her story reveals the gendered fault lines of agency in a Mediterranean empire composed of social and ethnic boundaries.

It was not only Cyurω but her family too who encountered Venice and its maritime empire from the perspective of hybridity. Domenico's mixed identity was elided in the *Libro d'Oro*, he rejected the source of this mixed identity by spurning his mother, and he went on to have three successful noble marriages and a patrician son. Cyurω's eldest son, Modestino, seemed never to have been able to shake off so completely his mixed parentage in the eyes of the Venetian patriciate. Despite Cyurω's preparations for her daughters' patrician marriages, Urania's traumatic experience on Skiathos with her father's scribe proved that on the fringes of the maritime empire, intimate relationships could be the grounds for redefining social and sexual boundaries. Questions of identity and sexuality were determined within mixed imperial families and on the intimate frontiers of empire. Ways of belonging and the exercise of agency within the social and political structures of the maritime empire were defined and renegotiated within the family and within intimate relationships. Bembo's governance and scholarship did not take place within a social vacuum, but in relation to his wife and children. In this case, the relationship between Bembo's humanist scholarship and his experience of empire was constructed in a letter that was also a biography of his wife. These intimate histories, like Cyurω's and her family's, are therefore crucial to understanding the wider political culture of the empire itself.

CHAPTER 4

Becoming Istrian

Introduction

On the 30th of March, 1499, Pietro Coppo married Colotta in Isola. Colotta's father, Cado de Ugo, drew up their marriage contract in his house, with Coppo, Colotta, and Colotta's mother, Zuana, gathered round.[1] There were other witnesses, too, probably friends of Cado's, and like him, probably also Isolan noblemen. One of the two *vicedomini* of Isola—men central to the municipal administration of Isola who registered all marriages, property transactions, and testaments in their *libri d'instrumenti*—would have also been present.[2] The contract was drawn up by a notary, and the wedding would have been witnessed by the town judge, carefully setting the terms of the contract with Coppo, Colotta, Cado, and Zuana. The unique legal categories of marriage in the Istrian peninsula ensured that husband and wife held property in common as "brother and sister." This arrangement, which we will explore in detail later in the chapter, meant that Istrian families writing marriage contracts carefully delineated the property owned by the husband- and wife-to-be, as well as noting the legal consent of both of their parents, mother and father. Cado de Ugo and Zuana, Coppo and Colotta, and the town administrators and witnesses, would have been keenly aware of the need to carefully elaborate and negotiate the terms of this marriage. The futures of this Isolan noble family, and of the Venetian scribe, would be shaped by this document.

We find Coppo and Colotta's world of Isola at the cusp of the Cinquecento by sifting through the mass of bureaucratic documents that ensured the smooth operation, financing, and social organization of this town jutting into the Adriatic Sea. Marriages and dowries, property transfers and testaments, petitions, notaries, scribes, customs, and legal formula: if we wish to discover the history of Coppo and Colotta's family life in this small town of the Mediterranean empire, we must enter into its complex administrative world. Notaries scribbling away in towns up and down the eastern Adriatic coast, from Trieste to Ragusa, were part of a rich culture of municipal record keeping.[3] Like their Italian counterparts on the opposite shore of the sea, the archives of the eastern Adriatic world bear witness to this flurry of writing and record keeping. As Braudel reflected, it was only when he spent time in the archives of Dubrovnik that he started to understand the Mediterranean.[4] Coppo and his sons were themselves notaries, and their family fortunes and transformations can be tracked through this documentary culture.

In Isola, town notaries bound together the futures of families, and they set the course of their social position across generations. Their documents can tell us about the ways in which Colotta, and her natal family, became bound with Coppo in Isola. They show us how, over time, Coppo transformed from a Venetian scribe of empire to a local dignitary on the Isolan municipal council. Marriage contracts that Coppo and Colotta drew up for each of their five sons tell a story of settlement, of growth through division. These five young men married Istrian women, just as their father had done, and with the substantial property given to them by their parents, they could themselves become important figures in Isolan political society. Though of a different character, of course, than Bembo's autobiographical writing, these Istrian notaries' documents also provide glimpses of insight into Coppo and Colotta's experiences in Isola: their regrets, desires, and hopes for the future. They show how an imperial man could create a mixed colonial family. It is this colonial family's story that appears in the sheaves of documents written by our Isolan scribes.

And yet the modern history of the eastern Adriatic world, and of the Istrian peninsula in particular, means that these archives can be unpredictable and incomplete. Istria was under Venetian control until the fall of the Republic in 1797, after which it became part of the Habsburg and then Austrian empire (1797–1805, 1814–1918), before being transferred to Italy with the dissolution of Austria-Hungary in the aftermath of World War I. After World War II, Istria was once again divided: Zone A, including Trieste, came under Italian control, and Zone B became Yugoslavia. After the breakup of Yugoslavia in 1991, the peninsula was divided between the Slovene Istria and Croatian Istria, though various points along this border remain in contention to this day. Because of this complex geopolitical history—with such frequent transitions and changes that "every generation experienced several"[5]—the municipal archives of the peninsula have been frequently moved and reorganized, and have experienced losses characteristic of times of political upheaval and war.

Unfortunately, the municipal archives of Isola have suffered, too. After a fire destroyed some of the *antico archivio* of Isola in 1903, some of the archives were sent to become incorporated into the *antico archivio* of nearby Capodistria.[6] Francesco Majer's 1904 inventory of Capodistria's *antico archivio* records its contents, including Coppo's and his sons' notarial books.[7] Indeed, this manuscript is the only *vicedomino* book to survive from medieval or early modern Isola. Attilio Degrassi published some of these documents that directly related to Coppo's life in 1924.[8] Degrassi also relied on Petar Stanković's partial publication of some documents related to Coppo that he must have viewed in the Isolan *antico archivio* in the early nineteenth century, before the archive was partially destroyed and then moved to Capodistria.[9] The archive in Capodistria was sold off in bits and pieces during both world wars.[10] But the catastrophic turn came at the end of World War II when Italian authorities took what remained of this archive away from Capodistria to be deposited in Venice. These documents remain in Venice's Biblioteca Marciana. As Noel Malcolm brought to our attention, these precious sources for Venetian-Slovenian history remain "unconsulted and unconsultable."[11] Microfilms were made of some of these documents in the 1960s, including of Coppo's *vicedomino* book,[12] and these have been deposited in the Archivio di Stato in Trieste, though the poor quality of these reproductions makes reading the documents extremely difficult. So while we look to these Istrian archives and to the world of the municipal notaries for our window into Coppo and Colotta's world, it is with a keen awareness of the layers of the contested history of this region and of its continued resonances across Venice and Slovenia.

This modern history of the peninsula is not only important for approaching its archives. It is also inextricably wound into our historical and anthropological sensibility of the region across the *longue durée*. This modern history shapes the questions we ask of Istrian archives in important ways. The changing senses of political and cultural belongings, and particularly the peninsula's traumatic history of exile, mean that questions of social and geopolitical identity are central for modern anthropologists who study the region.[13] Historians know that this attentiveness to questions of identity stretches back to the early modern period and even further, when Istria was a borderland between Italy and the rest of the world: the Slavic interior, the Holy Roman

Empire, and, further to the south, the Ottoman state.[14] These questions show no sign of abating. As one anthropologist of the region has explored, the tourism industry on the Slovene Istrian coast has carved out a new regional identity in the twenty-first century as epitomized by a cosmopolitan, hyperconnected Mediterraneanism.[15] Problems of identity and hybridity are symbolized in this tension: Is Istria symbolic of a Mediterranean of national, political, and regional boundaries, as might reasonably follow from the twin traumas of war and exile? Or is the layered history of the peninsula symbolic of a Mediterranean Sea that fosters intense connectivity between polities and cultures?[16] These questions are central to historical and anthropological writing about the region.

These are also questions we will ask of Coppo, Colotta, and their family's history in sixteenth-century Isola. Were boundaries of identity (Venetian / Istrian, colonizer / subject) as meaningful as those (nobility, Italian culture) that united these families? The Istrian coast was governed by noble families who spoke Italian, littered with Venetian-style *palazzi*, and indeed so physically close to Venice that there was constant economic and cultural interaction between Istria's coastal towns and the metropole.[17] And yet it was a colony, like other colonies, administered by the Venetian Senate in the metropole. Throughout the thirteenth, fourteenth, and early fifteenth centuries, Venice slowly conquered one Istrian town after another, concluding with Albona and Pinguente in 1420.[18] There were more Venetian colonial administrators and governors of all ranks in Istria than in any other Venetian Mediterranean colony. Later, the natural resources of the peninsula, particularly the timber of Montona, were harnessed by Venice throughout the sixteenth and seventeenth centuries, and Istria even became a site of forced resettlement from Italian *terraferma*.[19] Istria's identity within the larger geopolitical structure of the Venetian empire was marked by ambiguity.[20]

We will explore how these more traditional means of gauging relationships between metropole and colony were filtered through the intimate lives of one mixed family: that of Coppo, Colotta, and their five sons and daughters-in-law. As we saw in the last chapter, Cyurω's story of movement around the Mediterranean was characterized by mobility, as stories about Mediterranean and global early modern women often are. Colotta and her sons stayed put, but in a place whose Mediterraneanness—the problem of its boundaries or connectivity—has been central to the way historians and anthropologists have understood it. By studying the documents that both memorialized their history and set the course for their future, we will track these questions of imperial, colonial, and Mediterranean identity as they unfolded between husband and wife, parents and children.

"As brother and sister"

> The one *dominum* Pietro Coppo of Venice, present, and the other *dominam* Colotta, daughter of the excellent *ser* Cado de Ugo of Isola, make and contract marriage following the customary statutes of the province of Istria, and particularly of the region of Isola, called the custom of brother and sister.[21]

With this contract, Coppo and Colotta were legally bound to the uniquely Istrian marriage pattern of "brother and sister." This pattern was specific to and widespread throughout Istria, found in the registers of notaries, in civil and criminal cases. Its laws were set out in detail in the Isolan municipal statutes, and in town statutes from communities across the peninsula. To be married as "brother and sister" meant that Istrian husbands and wives had exactly equal economic rights. Each would bring property into the marriage given by their parents, called the *dota*, and this would remain the property of the husband or wife. Property acquired by the wife during marriage would remain hers, and the husband's his, unless acquired jointly. And, all property—including that brought into the marriage through dowry—was managed by both parties. Husband or wife could not act without the consent of the other party, whether in making dowry arrangements or selling off land. Debts, too, were kept separate, so a husband's debt could not be taken on by his wife. Used by both noble families and those lower on the social stratum, the Istrian marriage pattern required clear consent and resulted in a degree of economic protection for women uncommon in other European or Mediterranean marriage legislation.[22]

Coppo and Colotta's five sons were married according to this same pattern, phrased as "ad fratrem et sororem iuxta consuetudinem terrae Insulae et totius regionis Istriae" (Antonio, 1541); or, in the vernacular, "a fra et suor segondo la usanza istriana et precipue della terra de isola" (Francesco, 1542).[23] This "custom" (*consuetudinem*, or *uzanza*) was, in the legal formula, always noted to be specifically Istrian, and particularly applied in Isola. The uniqueness of the "brother and sister" marriage organization was self-consciously styled as regional to Istria. As we will see later in the chapter, for the five Coppo sons, this was a fairly straightforward arrangement. By the 1530s when their sons began to marry, Coppo and Colotta were property owners on a large scale and could give land, vineyards, houses, and other goods to their sons, their half of what would be owned communally with their wives (or legal "sisters"). But what a marriage according to the "consuetudinem provinciae Istriae" meant for Pietro Coppo, a Venetian, is perhaps less straightforward.

What would Coppo have brought to his marriage as a Venetian, not as the son of a local noble landholder in Isola?

Coppo should have returned to Venice from his scholarly travels in southern Italy and the Mediterranean, then in his late twenties or early thirties, at the end of his protracted young adulthood. But what opportunities would have been open to Coppo on his return? If Coppo had been born legitimately, he would have closed the door on his period of education and travel and married a Venetian patrician woman. His father had eventually done so, albeit after an illegitimate relationship and a marriage to a *cittadino* woman, and married a young widow from the Contarini family. But Coppo's opportunities would have been less straightforward. His inheritance status is unclear, and so we do not know whether he would have brought any property into a potential marriage. Perhaps without property, and without hope of receiving anything from his father's final, legitimate patrician marriage, Coppo's future in Venice as a young man seeking a wife may have been uncertain.

We cannot know whether it was this uncertainty that contributed to Coppo's decision to seek a wife in Istria. But it is possible to draw a meaningful connection between Coppo's illegitimacy, his father's uneven marital fortunes, and his eventual decision to marry an Istrian noblewoman. Coppo's marriage to Colotta created an alternate set of economic possibilities and social links, ones that were perhaps more lucrative than those he would have returned home to in Venice. In 1550, Coppo drew up a marriage contract for his eldest son, Marco, who had married his Istrian wife, Lucretia, in 1533. However, when they were married, it was Lucretia's father, Anzolo da Spilimbergo, who drew up their marriage contract, "without any mention of the *dota* of the said Marco." In a passage tinged with regret, Coppo noted that he had found himself in a similar predicament upon his marriage to Colotta: "In the year of our Lord Jesus Christ 1499 on the first of January, I, Pietro Coppo, had married Colotta, daughter of Cado de Hugo and of Zuana his wife with a specified *dota*. As this was written by the same Cado, there was no mention made of my property."[24]

We do not know what property Coppo brought into the marriage, only that he did indeed own property ("miei beni") that had never been carefully delineated from Colotta's. Unfortunately, Cado's detailed elaboration of his daughter's *dota* is also unknown to us, as the marriage contract was only partially transcribed before being lost when the municipal archives of Isola were dispersed.[25] Cado's *dota* for Colotta was likely substantial: their family had been members of the municipal council for over four decades by the time of Colotta's marriage.[26] The organization of Coppo and Colotta's marriage as "brother and sister," and particularly Coppo's father-in-law's control over their marriage contract, meant that the axis of wealth, property, and power was centered on Colotta, and within her natal family. It was her patrimony, rather than his, that was recorded by the Isolan notaries, and it was her wealth that provided a set of possibilities in Isolan patrician society.

With his marriage to Colotta, Coppo strayed from the intended trajectory of Venetian male adulthood. Up until 1499, he had fulfilled every expectation: he received a humanist education, attended lectures at the Scuola, and spent the requisite few years on a scholarly pilgrimage between Pomponio Leto's Accademia and his uncle's colonial home on Crete. He had even been awarded a post in the empire as a scribe, a testament to his own intellectual ability in the face of his illegitimate status. But Coppo evidently did not wish to petition, or perhaps did not think he would be successful in petitioning, for legitimation—as Bembo and Cyurω had done on behalf of Domenico. By marrying Colotta, he veered off this well-trodden path, and so permanently altered his fortunes. Coppo was still in the so-called Golfo di Venezia, and yet a world away from Venetian society. The "brother and sister" organization of Istrian marriage, Colotta's status as a noblewoman, and her father's intervention into their marriage contract meant that he would, from 1499 on, become not only "Pietro Coppo of Venice" (as he was in their marriage contract) but also Colotta's husband. This was an identity that revealed new opportunities and possibilities for Coppo in Isola. Through his Istrian conjugal family and the notarial culture of the town, Coppo would find in Isola an authority and colonial career that would have been impossible had he stayed in Venice and followed the perhaps straitened path that lay before him there.

Citizenship and the Municipal Council

Isola and the Istrian peninsula held a complex place within the larger Venetian colonial polity. This is evident particularly in the administrative organization of Istria, within both record-keeping practices and imperial governance. Venetian Senate deliberations about Istria are contained in both Stato da Mar and Stato da Terra archival series.[27] In 1483, Marin Sanudo traveled throughout the Venetian *terraferma* and Istria with Venetian *sindaci*, the men responsible for periodically evaluating the conduct of the Venetian administrators in colonial posts. Sanudo included Istria as the "last" region of Italy in his *Itinerario per la Terraferma*, his record of the journey; his inclusion of Istria in the *Itinerario* then reflected Venetian governmental practice.[28] This ambiguity in administrative practice can be found mirrored in the term and role of the Venetian patrician governors sent to Istrian towns: they were called the usual *terraferma* term, *podestà*. Yet the Istrian *podestà* was given a far greater degree of autonomy over the municipal council of Istrian towns, a striking contrast to the much less invasive practices of the *terraferma podestà* of Vicenza and Verona.[29]

Most relevantly for Coppo and his Istrian noble circle, the political power of the Isolan council was constrained to a large extent by the Venetian *podestà*. The *podestà* in Istria unusually had the authority to reform local municipal statutes, and he even reserved the right to appoint a humanist teacher in their town.[30] Alfredo Viggiano, in his research on the administration of Venetian Istria, has found their policy was to consistently favor Venetian legal precedent over any local statutes or customs. As in other areas of the *stato da mar*, the *podestà* was given the right of *arbitrium*, or judicial discretion, a concept we will discuss in more detail in chapter 5.[31] But Istria, like Dalmatia, had historically been subject to periodic revolts by its colonized inhabitants during its history as a Venetian polity, and the structure of local administration reserved the balance of power to Venetian precedent to a much greater degree than in other colonial locales.[32] The number of men assigned to Dalmatian office holding—at the end of the fifteenth century, Marin Sanudo reported twenty *podestà* in Istria, and thirty lower-ranking governors, *castellani*, and *camerlenghi*—meant that local urban governance in Istria, and Dalmatia more generally, was infiltrated with a Venetian aristocracy who intended to replicate Venetian legal precedent in their administration.[33] The local municipal councils of the Istrian peninsulas were "in short both governed and monitored" by Venice, particularly by the Venetian patrician men who made up its colonial offices. But this did not preclude a certain "convivenza" between communal and imperial institutions, which, by virtue of the sheer Venetian administrative presence in Istria, needed to work closely together.[34]

We do not know Coppo's reasons for first traveling to Isola, but as he had been appointed *cancelliere podestarile*—or the official notary of the *podestà*—to several *terraferma* cities during the 1490s, it is very likely that he first traveled to Isola in the same capacity.[35] The story of how Coppo transformed from a *cancelliere podestarile*, one of many such Venetian administrators and bureaucrats in Istria at the turn of the century, into a powerful member of local Isolan political society is inextricable from the more intimate history of his marriage, family, and children. Six years after his marriage, in December 1505, Coppo's belonging to Istrian noble society was first put to the test. He was sent to the Doge's Palace in his native Venice to present seven *capitula* to the doge, Leonardo Loredan. Perhaps his Isolan peers saw an opportunity in Coppo, a Venetian patrician familiar with the byzantine workings of the Venetian administration. They undoubtedly perceived his humanist credentials to offer a degree of cultural capital: Coppo is referred to as "Petrus coppo orator" in the petition, turning his Venetian humanist education in Latin rhetoric and style into a political tool for the Isolan municipal council.[36]

Coppo's petition built an effective argument for the authority and autonomy of the Isolan municipal council and chancery within the framework of Venetian colonial rule. He began in the first two *capitula* by arguing that the Venetian colonial governors in Istria needed to better manage the municipal funds and the treasury, which had previously been "badly governed and executed."[37] Coppo then suggested that because of the *rettori's* bad governance, the Isolan municipal council should be accorded more authority over local affairs, particularly financial ones. He argues, tellingly, against the Venetian governors' practice of disbarring Isolans "or those whose wife is an Isolan citizen, etc." from becoming notaries or judges, or taking up other administrative positions in municipal governance.[38] It is a fascinating addition that speaks to Coppo's political ambitions as a Venetian with an Isolan wife. Coppo was successful, and Loredan ratified his petitions.[39]

In recognition for his service to the Isolan council, the council members elected Coppo "cive et consiliario," an Isolan citizen and council member, a couple of months later in February 1506, in a vote of fifty-five to eleven.[40] This was scribed by Vincenzo Adalperio, "notarius imperiali," under the authority of the Venetian *podestà*. Seven years after he had arrived in Isola and married Colotta, Coppo had been officially enrolled in Isolan political society. In 1511, Coppo was elected *cancelliere del comune* and was responsible for overseeing municipal revenue and spending. As *cancelliere*, Coppo accompanied the Venetian *podestà* and noted his orders, and most importantly, Coppo would have kept a register of the revenues and expenditures of the town.[41] In addition to acting as a *cancelliere*, Coppo also acted as a public notary in Isola in 1511. Coppo had successfully proved to the doge that the municipal council could effectively manage revenues and expenditures by highlighting the financial ineptitude (or perhaps, corruption) of the *rettori*. As Monique O'Connell has found, any such corruption would be viewed severely by the Venetian state.[42] And yet, in Istria, overrun as it was with Venetian colonial governors and administrators, local municipal organization had to take place in close consultation with the Venetian imperial bureaucracy.

Coppo climbed the ranks of municipal politics throughout his lifetime: he was appointed *vicedomino* in 1514, 1531/32, 1534/35, 1538/40, 1541, 1546, 1549, 1551, and finally in 1552/53, when he was in his eighties. In addition, he was appointed as a judge in 1533 and as chief notary in 1537.[43] But he held the office of *vicedomino* most often, and indeed the role seemed to cycle through

Coppo, Coppo's son Giovanni, and men from two other families: the Manzuoli and the Egidio, both members of the local aristocracy.[44] Darovec has discussed this as evidence of the "secure salary, prestige and possibility of additional income" at stake in being elected to this role, the "central civil servant" post in the towns of the Istrian coast.[45] The office of *vicedomino* was yet another uniquely local phenomenon to Istria and Trieste.[46] The two *vicedomini* of Isola were central to the municipal administration of Isola and held the office for one-year terms. They registered all sales and exchanges of property as well as wills in a town registry book, or *libro d'istrumenti*. They supervised all other administrative offices and notarial activity in the town, and notarial documents were kept in the town's Vicedominaria: the *vicedomino's* office.[47] As town judge, Coppo would have been one of four men who met every morning with the town's Venetian *podestà* to help him in the administration of justice. As notary, Coppo would have been responsible for scribing all of the documents overseen by the *vicedomino*, as well as for witnessing and authenticating those documents in the *vicedomino's* book.[48] In one role after another, and particularly in his frequent rotation into the office of *vicedomino*, Coppo occupied administrative roles central to local communal governance and political society.

The offices of notary, *vicedomino*, and judge were normally filled by local Isolan aristocracy. By marrying into this local aristocracy, Coppo integrated into local municipal governance as a privileged Isolan citizen rather than as a colonial official from Venice. Coppo's gradual progression through powerful and privileged Isolan roles was matched by his social authority with council members. In 1511, he successfully petitioned the council to admit the local Coletti family to its ranks. Coletti, according to the petition, was an "antiqui citadin . . . de questa comunita," a well-qualified candidate for the council.[49] Coppo himself was of course no "ancient citizen" of Isola, but he was a council member, married to Colotta de Ugo, a daughter of just such an illustrious noble Isolan family. He also may have capitalized on his humanist credentials in his bid for municipal power. The Isolan nobles Giacomo Egidio and Nicolò Manzuoli were members of the local Isolan municipal council and shared the role of *vicedomino* with Coppo. Both Egidio and Manzuoli were educated in Isola and were known locally for their humanist study, although none of their works have survived. Each of them also petitioned the doge in Venice to confirm local Isolan rights and statutes, suggesting that perhaps their Latin oratorical skills were also strategically deployed by the council.[50]

Coppo also took on a variety of public services for Isola. In 1536, he was elected by the Isolan municipal council, with Nicolò Manzuoli, to oversee a large-scale engineering project at the port at Isola. The project consisted of excavating the existing port and repairing the quay.[51] Several years later, in 1542, three countryside plots were given to him by the municipal council, in gratitude for his notarial reform of its registers of rents. By this time, Coppo had amassed a formidable resumé as a municipal administrator, and so was likely an expert candidate for this notarial reform project. Interestingly, the land was given to him because the Venetian *podestà*'s stipend had apparently bankrupted the town treasury, so Coppo could not be rewarded with a payment.[52] That Coppo's local landholding was framed as a kind of consolation prize, a second-best reward that was made unavoidable by the corruption of the Venetian *rettori*, seems to indicate that this was not the landholding pattern of a colonial settler in Istria, but rather a kind of wealth holding consistent with that of the local nobility. The Venetian mismanagement or corruption that Coppo had used to successfully petition for a degree of Isolan financial autonomy was, more than three decades later, leveraged once more to underscore the difference between the (corrupt) Venetian imperial administration and Isolan municipal governance. Coppo was again confirmed as an Isolan, as one who had been victimized by Venetian bad governance. However, given that Coppo and Colotta's *dote* to their five sons would be largely made up of land, vineyards, cultivated fields, and gardens, this gift of land may have indeed been more socially useful to Coppo and his family than cash. It would facilitate their continued participation in the Isolan "brother and sister" marital arrangements between their sons and Isolan women, embedding their family in the local aristocratic society of the town.

Finally, in 1547, Coppo, acting as *vicedomino*, oversaw the reconstruction of the Duomo di San Mauro in the town.[53] San Mauro, perched on a hill, is still one of the most prominent buildings in Isola. San Mauro was an important figure in the devotional culture and traditions of Isola, repeatedly coming to the town's rescue. In 1380, under attack from a Genoese fleet, Isola was miraculously shrouded and protected by a dense fog, while a white dove flew over the Genoese ships and tricked them into heading out into open sea, away from the besieged town. These extraordinary interventions were ascribed to San Mauro. In 1411, San Mauro was said to have saved Isola from Pippo Spano's anti-Venetian army by once again veiling the town in a dense and disorienting fog. Coppo oversaw the renovation and expansion of the fourteenth-century structure of San Mauro, the church which formed the center of this important local cult. In his notes on the commissions and expenditures related to the project, Coppo noted how much the Isolan *scuole*, or confraternities, donated to the reconstruction. Indeed, the church of one of the confraternities listed, that of San Michiel, was where Coppo expressed his wish to be buried in his testament, suggesting that he may have been a member. He listed the expenditures involved (wood, stone, columns) and noted that they had hired "il più ingegnoso Maestro di Frabica di Chiesa, che si attrovasse in Venezia molto laudato."[54] Coppo's humanist scholarship and his Venetian origins perhaps made him uniquely qualified to judge on matters of engineering and architecture.

It was Colotta, along with her family and the unique arrangement of Istrian marriage, who allowed Coppo to pursue a path of local authority and responsibility among his Isolan noble peers. As an Isolan citizen and council member, he could participate in political society in a more effective and meaningful role than ever would have been available to him in Venice, where he would have been yet one more scribe in the Venetian imperial bureaucracy. In Isola, he repeatedly and over several decades held some of the most politically and administratively important offices available to the local nobility. He and Colotta owned a great deal of land. He took on civic projects for which he was handsomely rewarded, both with property and with prestige. He was likely a member of an Isolan confraternity, an important social organization within the town, and even advocated on behalf of the "ancient" families of Isola who wished to join the municipal council. Coppo's transformation into an Isolan was, we might say, an unqualified success. And yet the transformation was not complete, as Coppo still relied on his Venetian origins at key moments during his Isolan political career. Most notably, the association between Venetianness and humanism was highlighted in Coppo's self-styling as an "orator" to the doge. He could wield his knowledge of Venetian architectural fashion by identifying and patronizing Lunardo Malafuogo, the popular church architect in Venice, for his project of reconstructing San Mauro, a church central to this local Isolan cult. And yet, as we saw with his petitioning over, and continual problems with, corrupt or perhaps simply inept Venetian financial administration, Coppo could pointedly distance himself from his *patria* when necessary.

The relationship between Coppo's Isolan citizenship and his Venetianness was flexible and could adapt to the particular social or political circumstances in which he found himself. If we return to the question with which we began, we can determine how potentially contradictory categories of identity, such as Venetian/Istrian and colonizer/subject, could profitably and dynamically interact with others that bridged Coppo and Colotta, such as nobility and Italianness. These contradictory categories of identity were not liabilities, but rather could be wielded effectively in a variety of political contexts. Coppo's proximity to the Venetian nobility, his Italian language, and his marriage to Colotta undoubtedly counted for a great deal in the eyes of the Isolan council. But it was not until Coppo utilized his Venetian humanist education and his experience in Venetian administration to undercut the Venetian governors who were bankrupting the Isolan municipal treasury that he was given Isolan citizenship and a seat on that council. Colotta and her family prepared the ground for Coppo by providing him an entrée into Isolan political society. But Coppo used that opportunity extremely effectively by deftly combining his experience in Venice and his Venetian origins to make him a more effective negotiator and administrator on behalf of the Isolans. As we saw in the previous chapter, Cyurω's transformation into a Venetian patrician wife was fraught and partial, constrained by an inability to shape the social and political structures that she encountered. Coppo, on the other hand, could leverage the opportunities presented by Colotta and his own Venetian identity to acquire a great deal of power, wealth, and prestige among the Isolans. Their vastly different experiences speak not only to the gulf in political and social dynamics between metropole and colony, colonizer and colonized, but also to the ways in which gender shaped confrontations with imperial structures in the Venetian Mediterranean.

Portable Sovereignty

In 1550, just a few months before he made his final will and testament, Coppo drew up another legal document, "scrissi de man propria," written in his own hand.[55] In it, he seemed to review his life through each of the marriages of his five sons, some which had taken place decades before. He began in 1499 with his own marriage to Colotta, and the regretfully incomplete contract that her father produced on that occasion. He then moved on to his eldest son, Marco, whose 1533 marriage contract with Lucretia, the daughter of the (perhaps originally Friulian) ser Anzolo da Spilimbergo, was similarly incomplete. The ostensible purpose of this new legal document was to carefully outline the dota that Marco brought into his marriage with Lucretia, but before doing so, Coppo continued on with his other sons. He lists the 1441 marriage of Antonio to Antonia, the daughter of ser Thoma de Marinci and Catherina, his wife. In 1442, just a year later, Francesco married Maria, daughter of ser Tonin de Perentin. In 1449, Vincenzo married Degna, the daughter of ser Almerigo de Durligo and his wife, also named Colotta. Finally, in 1550, on the first day of the new year, Coppo's son Giovanni married Anzola, the adopted daughter of dona Lucia. Only after listing each of his sons' marriages, their wives, and their wives' parents did Coppo go on to list Marco's marriage portion from all those years ago.[56]

At a time when both Colotta and Coppo were at least considering, if not yet making, their final testaments, Coppo's enumeration of his and his sons' marriages reads as an autobiographical reckoning of his five decades in Isola. Over those five decades, Coppo and Colotta's family became further and further entrenched into the social world of Isola. Lucretia, Antonia, Maria, Degna, and Anzola were all Istrian women, and their lives with the Coppo sons were firmly—and quite literally—rooted in Isolan soil. Indeed, Maria Perentin's family had been aggregated to the municipal council in 1459–60, at the same time as Colotta's family, the Ugo, had joined it.[57] Over the course of these five marriages, Coppo and Colotta consented to give their sons eight vineyards, six olive groves, four houses or parts of houses in Isola, a garden, two pieces of land to cultivate, and various unitemized movable goods, such as furniture.[58] The women they married, on the other hand, brought relatively less property into their marriages: the two wealthiest, Antonia Perentin (who married Antonio) and Degna Durligo (who married Vincenzo), brought with them two vineyards and four pastures, and a vineyard and an olive grove, respectively. Lucretia, who married Marco, may have been wealthy too, but as her *dota* was detailed in a marriage contract by her father, we cannot know what she owned. The locations of the vineyards and olive groves that Coppo and Colotta gave to their sons were all local. They are identified in the marriage contracts by their proximity to their Isolan neighbors. For instance, Antonio received a vineyard near Nicolò de Manzuoli's, Coppo's peer on the municipal council, and Francesco received an olive grove "next to the priest of Isola's land."[59] Coppo and Colotta had acquired, probably both through her family and through Coppo's career in the town, a great deal of local cultivated land, which they distributed to their sons and their daughters-in-law.

Their sons remained in Isola with their wives. Marco, the eldest, became a judge in Isola, and his son Nicolò (Coppo's grandson) also had an extensive administrative career in Istria. He was *vicedomino* of Isola in 1566/67 and 1570/71, before becoming *cancelliere* in Grado in 1579.[60] Giovanni became a notary, judge, and, following in his father's footsteps, the *vicedomino* of Isola on multiple occasions, including during his father's lifetime. For a time in the late 1540s and 1550s, Giovanni and his father exchanged the office nearly every year.[61] Indeed, Giovanni began his career within the Coppo household: he drew up his brother Francesco's marriage contract in 1542.[62] He eventually became a *sindaco* in 1560–62, transitioning to a career within Venetian imperial administration in Istria.[63] Of Francesco, Vincenzo, and Antonio, we know little, except of course that, like their brothers, they were given land and property in Isola and married local women, and so may very well have stayed there. Through their parents' property ownership, Coppo's sons too came to own swaths of valuable cultivated Isolan land within their own "brother and sister" marriages. Coppo had integrated into Isolan society. Importantly, he did so through his family, his wife's noble natal family and his children's new conjugal Isolan families.

And yet, Coppo nevertheless carried the cultural and social authority of his Venetian and thus imperial origins. As we saw in his maneuvering between the Isolan council and the Venetian doge, Coppo did not simply subsume his Venetian identity under the cloak of his new Isolan one. Even Coppo and Colotta's acquisition of so much valuable cultivated land raises questions about his ambiguous position within Isolan society. Coppo and Colotta's accumulation of swaths of cultivated land in their community came about through the fortuitous intersection of Venetian social and cultural capital, on Coppo's side, and Istrian social and economic capital, on Colotta's. Coppo's transformation into an Isolan dignitary, his property ownership, and his sons' patrimonies were possible because he still carried a degree of his imperial sovereignty with him.[64] Moreover, Coppo settled in a society whose social structure among the Isolan patriciate, and governance on the municipal council, had been modeled explicitly after Venetian patrician society and the Venetian Great Council.[65] Isolan political society and political structures were imitative of the metropole, and so were stamped with Venetian imperialism. Perhaps Coppo found Isolan political society and its organization comfortably familiar, or at least legible. Coppo was able to navigate between the parameters of Venetian cultural knowledge and Isolan social practices as needed. It is only through a history of Coppo's family—his intimate relationships and their transformations over time—that his negotiations between imperial and colonial identities become clear.

Coppo's Final Testament

These tensions borne of Coppo's divided life, between his Venetian origins and adolescence, on the one hand, and his Isolan marriage, career, and family, on the other, become more explicit when we consider his final testament, written in July 1550.[66] Coppo wrote that he decided to make his will that summer because Colotta had written hers only a few months before, perhaps around the same time that Coppo had drawn up Marco's belated marriage contract and listed the marriages of his four other sons.[67] Colotta's will does not seem to be in the approximately two hundred medieval and early modern Isolan testaments that survive in the Pokrajinski arhiv in Koper/Capodistria; although her sister Benvenuta's will of 1528 does survive, and Coppo and Colotta are listed among her beneficiaries.[68] Coppo wrote one copy of his will "in my own hand," but called one notary to copy down his words, the Isolan judge and *vicedomino* to bear witness, and another notary to copy the testament into his protocol book, to be kept in the *vicedomino's* office in the town.[69] Having been on the municipal council and involved in Isolan legal procedure for five decades, Coppo even recalled the specific statute in the municipal laws that required such an elaborate system of copying and witnessing: "following . . . the laws of Isola in the statute at c. 93."[70] Even in his final testament, made "at eighty years old and a bit," Coppo strongly identified with municipal notarial culture of Isola. Surrounded by Isolan men whose administrative municipal roles he had once filled, citing the Isolan municipal statutes, Coppo's ultimate notarial record situated him within the scribal municipal culture within which he had built his career and his family.

Coppo committed his soul to Christ, Mary, and "tutta la corte celestial," and his body to the church of the confraternity of San Michiel, to be buried in its sepulchre. Coppo had very specific ideas regarding the ritual of his funeral and burial. He requested that "none of my sons" carry his casket to the church, and that his funeral procession be undertaken "senza pompa alchuna," with no special ceremony. Most remarkably, though, Coppo added one very particular request: if he should die before "Colotta mia Consorte," he requested that she not walk along with his funeral procession to the tomb, but rather stay at home, as is customary in Venice, "come se observa a Venetia."[71] Colotta was of course Isolan, her Isolan sons would be taking part in his funeral ritual, and he would be buried in an Isolan parish church by his confraternity made up of fellow Isolan citizens. And yet she had to stay at home, because that was what Venetian wives did during their husbands' funerals. Why would Coppo make this particular request? After five decades of living in Isola, it was this Venetian idiosyncrasy, specific to the gendered expectations of funerary ritual, that became important to him as he imagined his own funeral. It is a remarkable moment, in which we can glimpse Coppo sifting through the tensions in his own transformed identity.

Coppo left nothing to Colotta in his will, presumably because under the "brother and sister" marriage conventions of Istria she would receive her half of their joint property in any case. He left one item each to his five sons, and none of them particularly substantial: to Antonio, he gave thirty lire to help him buy his home; to Francesco, a small box, covered in laurel wood; to Vincenzo, a section of a garden; to Giovanni, two ducats, to be given in four years to "mio herede," Coppo's grandchild, presumably when the child was grown. Intriguingly, Coppo appointed two executors of his will: "el Magnifico Messer Marchio fiol del Clarissimo Messer Francesco Coppo et Marco mio fiol." The first, Marchiò, was Coppo's half nephew, the son of his half brother Francesco.

The difference in Coppo's styling of Marchiò's and Francesco's names, compared with his simple rendering of his son's name, is startling. This line not only hints at a continued, affectionate relationship between Coppo and his half brother's family in Venice, but also reveals a sense of the social abyss separating the legitimate, patrician Coppo half brothers and Pietro Coppo's mixed family in Istria. Marco received nothing in the will, perhaps because his belated *dota*, made a few months previous, had included Coppo's bequest. Coppo and Colotta had already given their sons huge swaths of property, cultivated land and homes, at the formation of their marriages. The bequests Coppo made at the end of his life seem to be smaller, and perhaps more sentimental, gifts related to their particular circumstances: money to finally buy a home, a perhaps particularly well-crafted object, money for his still-adolescent grandchildren.[72]

And yet, as in the moment when Coppo imagined Colotta sitting at home during his funeral like a Venetian noblewoman, other bequests in the testament speak to his continued, if imagined, relationship with the metropole of his birth and adolescence. As we saw in chapter 1, Coppo left his best manuscript, a work of "cosmographia et geografia," to the monastery of Santa Maria delle Grazie in the Venetian lagoon. The manuscript was to sit on the same shelves as those composed in the hand of his beloved teacher, Marcantonio Sabellico. Coppo perceived his own *studia humanitatis*—although, as we shall see in chapter 6, sometimes devoted to his describing and mapping his adopted region of Istria—as particularly Venetian, especially at the end of his life. Coppo gained Isolan citizenship through his performance as a humanist "orator" to the doge in the metropole. And yet at the end of his life, his scholarly work and rosy memories of adolescence spent listening to Sabellico's lecture forged an imagined intellectual link back across the Golfo di Venezia to Venice itself.[73]

Perhaps Coppo's memories of his adolescent studies suffused his testament precisely because his own sons had been disappointments to him as students and humanists. After describing Sabellico and his time in his school, Coppo wrote: "Item, that for my bequest, blessing, and satisfaction, to Nicolò my grandson, son of my son Marco: all of my books, because I see he is more willing and naturally inclined towards *lettere* than any other."[74] None of his five sons, despite even Giovanni's nascent career as a notary, were particularly interested or "naturally inclined" toward the study of "letters," or the *studia humanitatis*. This may indeed have been a deep disappointment for Coppo, whose own adolescence had been spent happily learning Latin literature and history from Sabellico, one of the great personalities of late-Quattrocento

Venice. It is tempting to see a glimpse of paternal dissatisfaction in those lines, reminiscent of Giovanni Bembo's much fiercer displeasure with his son Modestino's laziness in his studies.

Bembo was prompted to make an autobiographical reckoning of his life by Cyurω's death. Coppo decided to pen his will after Colotta decided to make hers, his own legal reckoning spurred by an inevitable sign of his wife's mortality. Bembo's letter opened with a cry of anguish: "Proh dolor!" or "What sorrow!"[75] It was their wives' mortality that seemed to strike a deep chord with both men. Mourning caused Bembo to painstakingly relate even the most violent and traumatic moments of his family's intimate life. For Coppo, the "certainty" of death—a mortality that Colotta had, evidently, already come to understand—prodded him to untangle his Isolan career, property, and family from his imaginary relationship with Venice, a relationship constituted by remembered rituals and scholarly affections. Though they take very different documentary forms, both Bembo's letter and Coppo's testament are autobiographical texts—Bembo's scrawled in his personal manuscript, Coppo's written "in my own hand." In these documents, we can see how both men probed the tensions of family life and plural identities, tensions created in lifetimes spent across the Venetian empire.

Conclusion

Fernand Braudel began his famous history of the Mediterranean with a warning of the dangers of the early modern Mediterranean archives. These archives are filled with the papers of sixteenth-century men "eager to write, to talk of themselves and others." They tempt historians who might find themselves "transported into a strange one-dimensional world, a world of strong passions certainly, blind like any other living world, our own included."[76] By sifting through this "precious mass of paper" that constituted the early modern administration of Isola, we have indeed been transported into the intimate world of the Coppo family. We have drawn a family portrait of husband and wife, sons and daughters-in-law. And we have seen in their intimate family life the regular negotiations between metropole and colony that indeed at least partially gave rise to that very mass of archival paper. If Coppo and Colotta were perhaps, as Braudel might say, "blind" to the deep history of their Mediterranean, they were sharply perceptive and self-reflexive when it came to the ways in which their lives intersected with the imperial structures of their own contemporary Mediterranean world. As we will see in chapter 6, Coppo was in fact very sensitive to the ancient history of the Mediterranean, too.

As in chapter 3, we have seen in this Coppo family portrait that it was within intimate life that subjective relationships to empire were worked out. Even at the end of his life, Coppo seems to have been unsure about the relationship between his authoritative civic identity in Isola and his long-cherished memories of his adolescence in Venice, of his scholarly family and its patrician rituals. Through his five decades in Istria, Coppo's relationship to empire—his belonging to metropole and colony, Venice and Isola, past and present—was never stable. Coppo's grandfather, father, and uncles provided names for his own sons that created remembered links back to his identity as a member of the Coppo family. Illegitimate at home, he found a new kind of political enfranchisement in the empire. He could leverage his Venetian education to gain Isolan citizenship in 1506, and almost fifty years later, nostalgically send his most beautiful manuscript to sit on the shelf next to his teacher's. But these tensions are not necessarily contradictory. The only constancy to be found in this "precious mass" of paper related to Coppo and Colotta, as well as Bembo and Cyurω, is the porousness and fluidity of social and political identities within the Venetian empire, and even in Venice itself.

Coppo carried his Venetian sovereignty with him to colonial Isola, and the consequences of this unfurled complexly. A powerful landholder in the colony, he gained that land only through his marriage to Colotta. Ensuring his sons' patrimony through gifts of that cultivated land, they married local Isolan women. Coppo did not try to replicate Venetian life in the colony but neither was it possible nor desired to efface his own Venetian identity, as patrician and especially as a humanist. As a Venetian patrician man, he successfully navigated the mirrored world of Isolan patrician society. He could translate his experience in Venetian schools and patrician political society into the Isolan municipal council and its masculine political sphere. He could represent Isola in front of the doge, advocate for "ancient" Isolan families, reform notarial practices, and oversee civic projects because the Isolan municipal council and its patrician society was a familiar one. In one sense, then, Coppo did not have to set out to remake colonial society in the image of his own Venetian metropole. It was already so. Coppo and Colotta's story in Isola provides, then, a stark contrast to Bembo and Cyurω's in Venice. The intersection of gender and social identity within empire had powerful consequences for these men and women's abilities to negotiate its political and social structures. But for both families, it was within intimate life that one's relationship to empire—to its politics, its shifting social structures, its metropolitan and colonial cultures—was determined.

Chapter 5

Colonial Governance and Mythology on Skiathos

Introduction

In the first two chapters of this book, we examined Bembo's and Coppo's natal families and their education as humanists, and the ways in which their humanist inquiry was extended into the Mediterranean world. In these chapters, I have suggested first that humanism and family life must be seen as intertwined, and second that Venetian humanism might productively be studied within the context of its Mediterranean dimensions, particularly focusing on Bembo's and Coppo's uses of cartography and epigraphy to elaborate this. In the third and fourth chapters, we tracked their marriages to women who were technically their own colonial subjects, and how with Cyurω and Colotta, these men formed families across imperial boundaries. In the fifth and sixth chapters—first, in our examination of Bembo's time on Skiathos, and second, in Coppo's scholarly life in Isola—we will see how these three themes of humanism, family, and empire coalesced in the Mediterranean world.

In this chapter, we will see through Bembo's multiple kinds of writing about the Mediterranean world how humanism shaped his understanding of the space of empire and of his own role as governor. This chapter relies extensively on books that Bembo owned, annotated, and, in the instance of his personal miscellany manuscript, wrote himself. This chapter particularly examines Bembo's lengthy autobiographical letter and its relationship to his copy of the

Isolario, the printed encyclopedia of Aegean islands that Bembo brought with him to Skiathos. While on Skiathos, and on his journey home during a stop in Crete, Bembo extensively annotated this volume.[1] Focusing on these annotations and on the intertextual relationship between these and the letter, this chapter reveals how Bembo's humanistic training—and particularly, the Mediterranean dimensions of Venetian humanism that we examined in chapter 2—shaped his perceptions of the empire and of his own purpose within the empire as a governor.

In the second half of the chapter, we return to the dark episode on Skiathos. The Bembo family faced a serious scandal on the island with consequences that rippled outward from Urania, through her family, and to Bembo's governance over the island. In the aftermath of the scandal, how did Bembo characterize his own actions, and how did he represent them to his friend Andrea in his lengthy letter? Bembo's use of classical literature and mythology reveals how deeply the classical tradition informed his own behavior and sense of himself. In this moment, the effects of a humanist education, the act of governing, and the concerns of family spectacularly clashed. While unique, this dark episode of violence and scandal allows us to probe deeply into how humanism, empire, and family matters became interrelated in the Mediterranean world. It is an extreme example that reveals that for Bembo, as desperately as he wished for a shining *cursus honorum* within the patriciate, the pressures of his mixed family would shape his identity and actions and constrain his career. While the case studied here is unique, it suggests that we might look more critically at the ways in which family matters—those concerning marriage, childbirth, and the raising of children—rippled outward to influence governance and imperial political culture.

Skiathos

Bembo was elected as *rettore* of Skiathos and Skopelos in 1525, a term that lasted two years.[2] These brief two years, and Bembo's accounting for them a decade later, are the focus of this chapter. The two islands of Skiathos and Skopelos are in the northern Aegean, part of the Sporades archipelago northeast of the island of Euboea (called Negroponte by the Venetians). These small islands were part of what Fernand Braudel memorably described as "Venice's stationary fleet"[3] and were under the city's direct control from 1453 until 1537: from the fall of Constantinople to the Ottomans (after which the Venetian state assumed direct control of the islands from the patrician Ghisi family) until the third Ottoman-Venetian war of 1537–40, in which the Venetians lost the

Cyclades (except Tinos), the Sporades, and parts of the Morea.[4] The inhabitants of Skiathos and Skopelos were primarily farmers and fishermen and were involved in Aegean shipping.[5] Close to Euboea, a major island lost to the Ottomans in 1470, Skiathos and Skopelos were not particularly economically important to the Venetian state, but rather strategically important. They were close to the Greek mainland and became a crucial connection to the continent once Euboea ceased to provide that geographical link.[6]

Perhaps the strongest link between the Sporades, Euboea, and mainland Greece was piracy and corsairing.[7] Raids took place throughout the region, not only by Ottoman pirates but also by the inhabitants of Skiathos: most likely by Greek Orthodox who "moved throughout the eastern Mediterranean not as Greeks but as . . . Venetian subjects."[8] Machiel Kiel has uncovered a set of Ottoman documents from the first decades of the sixteenth century that suggests that some of the inhabitants of Skiathos were particularly fierce pirates who attacked the Ottoman-controlled mainland coastline across from Euboea.[9] In the 1520s, Venice organized civil militias consisting of island peasantry throughout the *stato da mar*, to defend against raiding.[10] Locals were ordered to muster at strategic high elevation points on the islands, and told to send smoke signals to warn inhabitants of incoming pirate ships.[11] Although systematic fortification of the important Venetian islands did not begin until the mid-sixteenth century after the devastating raids of the late 1530s,[12] Bembo himself remarked on the ravaged state of Skopelos upon his arrival there in 1525: "[Skopelos] had a bishop, but after Euboea was captured by the Turks this [post] was destroyed; and upon my arrival, the island was deserted. However I established a refuge on the island, and sixty families with sixty equally good men cultivated it: they were strong men, and daring against pirates."[13] When he arrived on Skiathos in 1525, then, Bembo was determined to repopulate and cultivate the islands, and to defend them against—or, perhaps to participate in the vibrant economy supported by—piracy in the archipelago.[14]

Elected to the post by the Great Council, Bembo would have been given a manuscript *commissione*, or book containing his responsibilities as administrator on Skiathos and Skopelos. Although this *commissione* does not survive, comparison with similar *commissioni*, as well as Monique O'Connell's study of the role of the *rettori* within the Venetian colonies, gives a detailed picture of what would have been expected of Bembo.[15] Where Venice directly ruled a small island—as in the Sporades—the *rettore* would have been responsible in two primary spheres of governance: civil and military. The *rettore* was expected to regulate local finances and markets, was in charge of administering justice on the island, and was also expected to defend the island, both from external aggressors and in terms of public order (especially in the case of small islands such as Skopelos and Skiathos, which were assigned only one official Venetian administrator). As O'Connell has shown, this involved maintaining a careful equilibrium between "reserving power to [Venice], protecting its representatives' prerogatives, and keeping its subjects contented."[16]

The post of *rettore* was, perhaps more than any other in the Venetian government, one that was beset by conflicts between the conciliar nature of Venetian governance and the literal isolation of the individual filling the post. Elected by his peers and answerable to them in the case of misdeed while in office, the *rettore* also was the sole governor responsible locally for maintaining peace, administering justice, and protecting his subjects. Bembo commented bitterly on this balance between the pressures of his local role on Skiathos and his place within the larger picture of the *stato da mar*. "Everyday, the Turkish pirates drove [away the sheep], and they were capturing and seizing the waters and the land of the island, because the commanders of the Venetian triremes—either from Corcyra, or from Zante, or from Crete—were playing with their wealth, and squandering it drunkenly on whores."[17]

Isolated in the tiny islands of the northern Sporades, Bembo relied on the naval protection of the state to meet the expectations of his job—a resource that he viewed as being squandered, as wealthy naval fleet commanders sailing from more central (and economically important) ports in the Venetian polity abandoned their jobs defending the seas. As mentioned in many of the *commissioni*, Venice, primarily through its *rettori*, was meant to provide "peace and justice" to its colonial subjects, who in turn were expected to provide "profit and honor" to Venice.[18] When Bembo first arrived in the Cyclades, he appears to have done this: he provided refuge for the islands' inhabitants, who in turn cultivated the land. The ongoing battle against piracy was one in which the colonial state's obligation to provide peace and the subjects' obligation to provide profit neatly coincided. As Bembo's invective against the corrupt "ductores" of the Venetian fleet suggests, he perceived defense from piracy as a collaborative effort between the state and its colonial subjects.

Mapping the Venetian Aegean in the *Isolario*

Bembo brought with him to the Aegean a printed copy of Bartolomeo dalli Sonetti's *Isolario*.[19] Over the course of his years in the Mediterranean empire, he would annotate it extensively, even making up poems about islands that dalli Sonetti himself had left out.[20] We can glimpse Bembo's perceptions of his own role as governor in the Aegean in his annotations to his copy of the *Isolario*, and especially in the intertextual relationship between these annotations and his autobiographical letter. Bembo had his copy bound in fine stamped leather, sketched in it, and wrote all over its pages of sonnets and island maps. Like the more typical humanist Latin commonplace books that were filled with passages organized by thematic heading, the *Isolario* served as a kind of geographical commonplace book for Bembo, as an encyclopedic container for copying passages from classical authors on the Aegean island world. His primary classical sources were Stephanus of Byzantium's *De urbibus*, Pliny's *Naturalis historia*, and Herodotus, Thucydides, Virgil, Ovid, Strabo, Pomponius Mela, and Ptolemy.[21] We can guess, therefore, that Bembo owned or at least borrowed copies of these texts, extending our picture of his mobile library that traveled with him to the Aegean. Bembo extracted the pertinent passages from these authors and copied them onto the upper margin of the sonnet page for the relevant island. He also recorded the Venetian history of the islands.

For example, next to the sonnet on Naxos (Nicsia), Bembo recorded a passage from Pliny in Latin, as well as a long history of the island in the vernacular:

> And the said island is the principal one and the seat of the Signor Duke of the Archipelago, whose name is Signor Zuane Crispo, who came into Venice with an armed galley with men from his islands, that is to say, with 80 men from Souda; with 50 men from Milos; 40 men from Santorini; and the rest were 280 men from Naxos, on the fifth of June 1523. Six years into his stay on the island of Cervi,[22] Crispo was hunting alone with two other gentlemen, when he disappeared. That is to say, he was kidnapped on horseback by a Turkish corsair. And his gentlemen and subjects ransomed him that same hour from the corsair for *ducati*. For some reason, the Turk took offense, so that he did not return the said signor, and now I am looking for him to apprehend and hang him.[23]

Bembo's vendetta against Ottoman piracy was given its own Venetian history here, one that related how a Venetian patrician from the Archipelago was captured and ransomed by pirates. Bembo conceived of protecting his islands from piracy not only as part of his job as *rettore* but also as a responsibility that was part of a larger Venetian history in the Aegean. The conflicted nature of collective Venetian governance in the *stato da mar* comes through in Bembo's writing: in the Sonetti *Isolario*, expressing solidarity with his aristocratic peer who was ransomed; in the autobiographical letter, blaming them for abandoning him without the resources to defend Skiathos.

Bembo's anxiety about the military defense of the Sporades is also evident throughout his annotations to the *Isolario*. On the blank folios in the beginning and end of the codex, Bembo kept extensive lists detailing how many gal-leys were available from each island, how many men would be needed to fill each position to man the galleys, how many men could be conscripted from each island, which islands belonged to Venice, and which Venetian family was responsible for each. Bembo also noted next to the titles of the sonnets of Venetian-occupied islands, "Fa homini da facti," followed by the number of people resident on the island. This phrase refers to the military recruits from each island who could be mobilized for military service at short notice.[24] This kind of military preparation would have been an important responsibility within Bembo's role as *rettore*, given that the smaller posts on Skiathos and Skopelos would not have warranted a castellan or captain.[25] Bembo's copy of the *Isolario* was thus not only a place to record and preserve classical informa-tion about the Aegean Islands, but a place to quantitatively measure Venetian maritime resources. The encyclopedic structure of the book worked for both projects: it provided a neat way to organize both kinds of information, each relative to specific islands.[26] That Bembo chose to record both passages from Pliny and estimates of Venetian reserves against piracy indicates the complete absence of categorical boundaries between the two: for Bembo, the *Isolario* offered a storage system for information that he considered to be of vital importance for the survival of the Aegean. His need to preserve the classical past of these islands was bound up in his need to protect them, so that the reserves of Venetian humanist scholarship were accounted for alongside the material reserves of Venetian administration.

Bembo transferred the composite practice of commonplacing, in which often disparate passages could be easily compared thematically, into the pages of the *Isolario*. This is evident in a comparison between Bembo's annotations to dalli Sonetti's sonnet and map "Per Sciati e Scopolo," and the passage on Skiathos translated above from Bembo's autobiographical letter (figure 7). In the *Isolario*, Bembo copied the dimensions of the islands from Ptolemy's *Geo-graphia*; he wrote a Greek extract from Stephanus of Byzantium across the top of the page; he scribbled a reference to Philip of Macedonia and his battle with the Athenians in the Sporades; and he labeled the islands on the map with Greek and Latin toponymy, including ancient toponyms.[27] Dalli Sonetti's head-ing, "Per Sciati e Scopolo," was taken by Bembo as a thematic heading in a kind of unusual geographic commonplace book. Bembo then used that common-place book to compose his own original work: as we see in the passage on Skiathos excerpted below from the autobiographical letter, all of the informa-tion that Bembo copied into his *Isolario*—Ptolemy's geographical information, ancient toponymy, passages from Stephanus and Livy—was composed into a passage that tells compellingly of Bembo's perceptions of his responsibilities

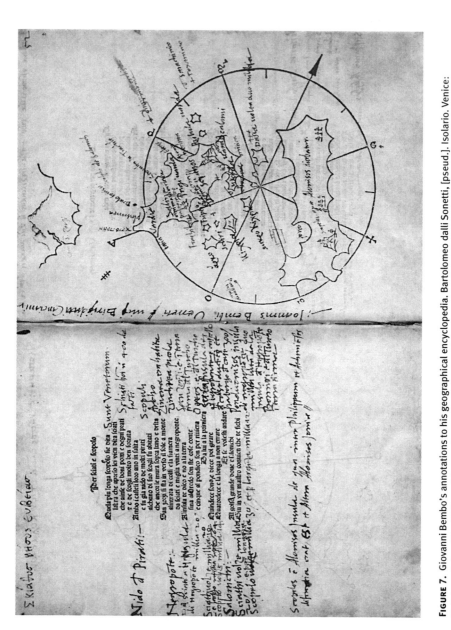

FIGURE 7. Giovanni Bembo's annotations to his geographical encyclopedia. Bartolomeo dalli Sonetti, [pseud.]. Isolario. Venice: Guilelmus Anima Mia, Tridinensis?, not after 1485. Modena, Biblioteca Estense Universitaria, Alfa E.5.15.

By kind permission of the Ministero dei beni e delle attività culturali e del turismo.

on the islands. Classical information was atomized, decontextualized, compiled, but then recomposed into autobiography.

Through composition, Bembo created a kind of textual intersubjectivity with classical authors and classical landscapes, atomizing them to recombine them with his own experience. Bembo easily switched to classical passages—and to Latin—to formulate his responsibility for Skiathos in his autobiographical letter. He wrote of the islands,

> Of this island Skiathos, Titus Livy said in the second book on the Macedonian wars: "Nor did Philip—for he had by now reached Macedonia—carry on less vigorously his preparations for the war. He sent his son Perseus, who was still a boy, with guardians from among his friends to guide his youth, with part of the troops to hold the passes which lead to Pelagonia. He destroyed Skiathos and Peparethus, cities not unknown to fame, to prevent their becoming prize and prey to the fleet of the enemy."[28] Skiathos retains its ancient name. Stephanus, author of *De Urbibus*, says: "Perparethus is one of the Cylades."[29] This island Peparethus is now called "Diadromi" by sailors, and is called "Prepathora" by the Skiathans. Its length is 30 *mille passuum*, its circumference 60 *mille passuum*, its width 7 *mille passuum*, Skiathos's circumference is 20 *mille passuum*, its width VII *mille passuum*. Stephanus says: "The island Skiathos belongs to Euboea." The distance from Skiathos to Euboea is 20 *mille passuum*. Skopelos island is at a distance to Skiathos of five *mille passuum*, whose length is 30 *mille passuum*, the true width 12 *mille passuum*.[30]

In the autobiographical letter, Bembo presented his responsibility for the Venetian presence on Skiathos as not limited to its subjects, its trade, its vulnerability to pirates. Its antique existence, the very fact that Livy, Stephanus, and Ptolemy wrote about the island, became part of Bembo's conception of his own contemporary role on the islands. The Ptolemaic dimensions of the islands, their toponymy, and their ancient history became part of a set of information that Bembo perceived as intimately related to their governance. Both kinds of information worked for the same end: a more complete and organized collection of knowledge about the space he was governing. Livy's histories as detailed in this passage were not simply historical for Bembo, but a present past through which he conceived of his own role as protector and governor. When Livy's histories are read alongside Bembo's Venetian vernacular histories and lists of Venetian resources, we can begin to understand the constant intersubjective, intertextual relationship between the classical Aegean and the contemporary, between ancient authors and lived experience, that became a way for Bembo to formulate his ideas about governance.

Scandal on Skiathos

We saw in chapter 3 that after the Bembo family arrived on Skiathos, a family scandal loomed. Urania began an affair with Bembo's scribe, and the ensuing scandal had severe consequences for Urania, Cyurω, and Bembo himself. But the scandal allows us to see more clearly how the concerns of family were related to those of empire for Bembo. His brief tenure on Skiathos and its disastrous consequences for his family allow us to perceive how the relationship between empire and family was intended to work, and how this relationship broke down, in Bembo's decision making as governor and in the aftermath of the scandal.

Bembo castrated the scribe as part of his responsibility as *rettore* to administer justice on the island, and indeed infanticide was a serious crime that Bembo sought to punish severely. The administration of justice was a crucial field in which the relationship between the metropole (embodied in the governor) and the colony was negotiated. The legal concept of *arbitrium* was central to the *rettore's* administration of justice in the colony. This concept left the ultimate provision of justice up to the highly discretionary and flexible decision making of the *rettore* himself.[31] While Bembo did serve in the Venetian judiciary, and so probably had a greater familiarity with Venetian law than many governors, in general Venetian *rettori* did not receive any formal legal training, so this process was a question of individual adherence to a wider imperial ideology or ideal. The exercise of *arbitrium* has been a significant component of scholarly debate on Venice's relationship to its *terraferma* colonies, as legal justice has proved a constructive arena to test the nature of Venetian colonization. Gaetano Cozzi, in particular, has elaborated a vision of *arbitrium* on the mainland that worked to effectively integrate the ruling metropole and subject colonies, a system in which the Venetian governor could ensure that local laws were agreeable to Venetian interests while at the same time leaving relatively undisturbed the primacy of local legal systems.[32]

Bembo, alone on Skiathos, did not conform to a Venetian ideal of justice in the crafting of relationships between colonial societies and metropolitan power. But he nevertheless saw the castration as an expression of imperial justice. When he sent his friend Andrea Anesi the letter in 1536, Andrea was too ill to respond; but Andrea's son Leonardo did write back to Bembo, who copied the response into his miscellany, underneath the draft of his autobiographical letter. Acknowledging that Bembo wished for his father's opinion on his decision to castrate the scribe during his "Regimento" on Skiathos, Leonardo conveys that "in [my father's] opinion, your judgement was very much worthy of praise" but that Andrea recognizes that many others have rebuked him for his judgment.[33] The "iuditio" of Leonardo's letter was a kind of vernacular expression of the Venetian colonial practice of *arbitrium*, indicating not only that Bembo's castration of the scribe was conceived as just, but that Bembo could reflect on that decision as flexible: a decision that, in retrospect, could have been right or wrong.

Bembo's "iuditio" must also be understood as particularly gendered, as an instance in which paternal masculinity within the realm of the family intersected with paternalistic colonial rule. As Lucien Faggion has explored for the Venetian aristocrats in the colonial *terraferma* of the sixteenth century, family identity was founded on "honor, pure bloodlines and solidarity," and so any offense against that family's honor was taken seriously by the *terraferma* judicial system.[34] For Bembo on Skiathos, the honor of the family equally played a crucial role in the process of justice. Just as he was the head of his household and so responsible for accounting for the actions of those within it, Bembo was also responsible for the affairs of Skiathos; shame within the realm of his family meant a stain on his colonial rule. If he could not control his daughter and his scribe, his control of the island was placed in doubt, too. For Bembo, castrating the scribe in the piazza meant that he could reassert himself both as the paternal head of his family and as the paternalistic colonial governor.[35] Finally, there is plenty of evidence pertaining to early modern European women that suggests that prosecution of the crime of abortion often resulted in the execution of the mother.[36] Perhaps Bembo feared the repercussions of Urania's complicity in the first aborted pregnancy, and so he chose the course of justice that would protect his family.

These are speculations, however. Bembo defends his decision to castrate the scribe in one provocative line in his autobiographical letter, and his defense has little to do with the law. Rather, he framed his decision using a narrative from Greek mythology: "Whoever is disgraced by my judgement and speaks ill of it: would he confess to allow the bull—King Minos' scribe—to debase Pasiphaë, that king's wife and queen?"[37] In Greek myth, King Minos was the king of Crete, married to the lovely queen Pasiphaë. Minos asked Poseidon for a sign of good favor, and the god sent the king a pure white bull to sacrifice. When Minos decided not to sacrifice that bull but another bull, Poseidon flew into a rage. He cursed Pasiphaë with a dangerous, lustful desire for the pure white bull. Pasiphaë climbed inside a wooden bull in order to mate with the bull. Pasiphaë then gave birth to the horrible half-man, half-bull Minotaur, who King Minos famously imprisoned in a labyrinth. This myth was told in some of the most popular classical literature available in the Renaissance, in Virgil's *Eclogues* and in Ovid's *Ars Amatoria*.[38]

Bembo's use of this particular myth in his own defense is provocative. Bembo wrote that his daughter's lover was no better than a base animal, and perhaps this particular characterization is not surprising. But in his daughter, he saw the curse of unrestrained lust, her sexual crime no better than bestiality. In Renaissance Italy, the myth of Pasiphaë was used to describe a female sexuality that was extraordinarily transgressive (as in, for example, Giulio Romano's contemporary painting of the myth at the Palazzo del Te in Mantua). And Bembo saw himself as acting as King Minos. In the myth, Minos could imprison the grotesque offspring that was evidence of his wife's bestiality. For Bembo, his only recourse was to castrate the scribe. The castration itself reveals Bembo's perception of the scribe as an unthinking animal that needed to be physically punished. The scribe's transgressions were outside the boundaries of spiritual, moral, or legal redress. Both in writing and in the physical act of castrating the scribe, Greek myth loomed in Bembo's understanding of himself and of his judgment. By framing his daughter's sexuality as just as transgressive as Pasiphaë's, Bembo was able to defend his own decision to castrate her partner. On Skiathos in 1526, the world of classical literature, colonial governance, and family life clashed spectacularly for Giovanni Bembo. Bembo was a humanist, and so he perceived himself, as both a father and a governor, through the framework of classical literature and myth. Indeed, at the center of Bembo's experience of governance was a thorny problem of sexuality, gender, and transgression. For Bembo and his family, the problems within intimate relationships were not simply domestic or private, but central to his own governance and performance of power on the island.

Fama

In a passage that directly follows Bembo's description of the castration, he wrote about the way in which the *fama* of his judgment to punish the scribe traveled throughout the Venetian empire.

> The *fama* of the judgement of the castration wandered through Greece, Thessaly, Thrace, and even through the Hellespont. By getting over the Cynaean Rocks and Symplegades islands, it made its way into the Black Sea, around the shores of Chalcedon, which is now called Scutari, by Paphlagonia and Sinope, once conquered by Lucullus, the Roman, and the country of Diogenes, and fills the ears of the Galatians and the Cappadocians, near Trapezus which was once owned by us Venetians, and into the market and the house and the castle given to us by the emperor of Trapezus. That castle was fortified by us, and the walls built, and the

great flag of San Marco of Venice was raised here. Indeed, a Venetian rector was chosen for this castle. His titles were Orator, Bailiff, and Rector, Orator to the empire of Trapezus, Bailiff for the merchants, Rector who was responsible for judging not only cases regarding money, but indeed for punishing criminal cases. Under the command of the Rector sat two elected counselors of Trapezus. . . . In the Venetian castle at Trapezus, the Venetians had scribes, interpreters, secretaries, and other ministers, all on public stipends, and the same Rector yearly had five hundred ducats. . . . Eight and sometimes ten cargo and trade triremes sailed in the Black Sea, in this part of Trapezus, some going to Tana and some to other places. They sailed very quickly through the famous Black Sea, in the region of Medea, to the place where the Lazei now live, where the Colchis and Phasis rivers and where the people called Cercetas live (they are now called Mengreli and Cerchasi). Having finally left the Meotide swamp, the river empties into the deep-flowing Tanis, which flows 18 *millia passuum* to the city of Tana. This city of Tana was Venetian, then Usbech's, and then owned by Zanibech, the emperor of the Tartars. The kingdom of this emperor was Astraca or Citracha, the emporium and the capital of the emperor, where the city Citra was located above the Volga river or the Rha which flows into the Caspian Sea. In our language, we call this whole kingdom Gaza. And often Tana was overthrown, plundered and burned by the Tartars. . . . In the year 1334, Tana was plundered of four hundred thousand and many Venetians were killed. . . . In the year 1400, Doge Michele Steno sent Pietro Loredan to Tana as Counselor and Rector, whose annual salary was 800 ducats. He had an allied Admiral, five servants, five horses. Indeed, Tana had two noble Venetian counselors. . . . In their arsenal they have 20 crossbows, 50 rifles, heavy artillery fire, bows with their arrows and oblong shields. Indeed, there is an interpreter of the language of the Tartars and of the Schytarum, and three scribes, and other arms. . . . And this *fama*, by running, by sailing, by flying, has covered all of these regions with the judgement of the testicles.[39]

Fama was a complicated word in premodern Europe, encompassing a range of meanings: from rumor, to gossip, to talk, as well as fame and its opposite, infamy. *Fama* "intersected with . . . honor, shame, status, and witnessing, and it glossed the essential nexus of performance, talk, reputation, and speech regulation."[40] Because of the affiliation in this passage between Bembo's colonial justice and *fama*, certainly one valence of the word is a legal one: referring to the kind of public talk that was reported in court contexts. Of course, this meaning had a double edge for Bembo, who felt keenly judged himself by his Venetian peers for his judgment on Skiathos.

A second meaning of *fama*, which Bembo replicates here, is that associated with Virgil's language in Book 4 of the *Aeneid*, used to describe the way that the *fama* of Dido's affair with Aeneas spread:

> Straightaway Rumor flies through Libya's great cities,
> Rumor, swiftest of all the evils in the world.
> She thrives on speed, stronger for every stride,
> slight with fear at first, soon soaring into the air
> she treads the ground and hides her head in the clouds.
> She is the last, they say, our Mother Earth produced.
> Bursting in rage against the gods, she bore a sister
> for Coeus and Enceladus: Rumor, quicksilver afoot
> and swift on the wing, a monster, horrific, huge
> and under every feather on her body—what a marvel—
> an eye that never sleeps and as many tongues as eyes
> and as many raucous mouths and ears pricked up for news.
> By night she flies aloft, between the earth and sky,
> whirring across the dark, never closing her lids
> in soothing sleep. . . .
> Now Rumor is in her glory, filling Africa's ears
> with tale on tale of intrigue, bruiting her song
> of facts and falsehoods mingled . . .
> 'Here this Aeneas, born of Trojan blood,
> has arrived in Carthage, and lovely Dido deigns
> to join the man in wedlock. Even now they warm
> the winter, long as it lasts, with obscene desire,
> oblivious to their kingdoms, abject thralls of lust.'[41]

Bembo imitated the image of a flying, screeching personification of rumor, dramatically presaging the tragedy of the repercussions of Dido and Aeneas' affair, to lend his own scandal the same level of drama and sense of impending disaster. The image of *fama* filling people's ears is paralleled in Bembo's use of *implevit* to mimic Virgil's *replebat*. The classical toponymy and cadence of the first sentences of Bembo's passage, in which *fama* moves quickly from one location to another without digression, is especially close to Virgil's depiction. So in addition to the judicial and social valences of *fama*, Bembo was also interested in its resonance with one of the greatest scandals of classical literature.

Bembo's use of the personification of *fama* meant that he was able to describe the eastern Mediterranean and the Black Sea from above: he saw imaginatively the Venetian empire from the perspective of this flying figure. It is through this space of flight that we get a sense of the ways in which Bembo could conceive of information, news, and gossip spreading across the Venetian maritime empire. From his study in Venice, penning his autobiographical letter, Bembo imagined the Venetian empire as intimately connected, as a space in which an event on Skiathos had a traceable ripple effect across colonial places. Just as Virgil's *fama* had "an eye that never sleeps" on every feather, taking in the vast expanse of the Mediterranean world below, so too Bembo used the image of *fama* to picture the ways in which information moved around the space of the Venetian empire.

As the passage moves beyond this initial resonance with the *Aeneid*, however, Bembo digresses from classical toponymy and language into the Venetian history in the Black Sea region, and to that of Tana in particular.[42] As Virgil gave a geographical setting to the racing *fama*, lending the narrative a dramatic sense of rushing toward an inescapable conclusion, Bembo borrowed this same concept, but then created the opposite effect—a slowing down or halting of the narrative—by digressing into history. By doing so, he allowed the full repercussions of his decision on Skiathos to become evident: the "judgement of the testicles," as he so vividly phrased it, was his contribution to Venetian history. Bembo used a digression into historical geography to stage his own scandal, to develop the coordinates and dimensions of his term as *rettore* in the larger historical and spatial picture of the *stato da mar*. By conflating the *Aeneid* with Venetian history, Bembo also lent that history in the Black Sea the structure and gravitas of a classical Latin epic. He remade Venetian history—and indeed, his own personal history within the larger realm of the Venetian colonial past—on an epic scale. Rather than finding himself lacking in comparison with the epic history of Venetian colonization, he still saw himself as part of it. He used *nos/nostri* to describe the castles, flags, and triremes that signaled Venetian colonization. He catalogued the arsenal and the staff of the Venetian headquarters in Tana in 1400, writing himself into the Venetian past, layering his own experience in the *stato da mar* with Pietro Loredan's in 1400. In the last sentence of this passage, the *fama* of Bembo's judgment "covered" all of these regions; we have a sense that Bembo did not simply mean the Black Sea as it existed in 1536, but as it existed in Dido's time, in Virgil's, in 1334, in 1400. Bembo composed the multiple meanings of *fama*, Virgil's epic, Venetian history, and historical geography into a single autobiographical narrative. Bembo used this geographical digression to gauge the spatial and historical dimensions of his own life, within the historical temporality of the Venetian colonial world. As we have seen in Bembo's annotation practices within the *Isolario* and in his autobiographical letter, humanist compositional technique was the foundation on which Bembo built his perception of the geography and history of the colonial world, and of his role as governor within it.

It seems likely that word of Bembo's family scandal on Skiathos reached Venice sometime in the summer or early autumn of 1526. His appointment was meant to last for two years: previous elections to Skiathos were held in 1515, 1518, 1520, and 1523, indicating that two or sometimes three years was the standard length for such an appointment.[43] But Angelo Alberto was elected on 4 October 1526 to the post, when Bembo had been in the post for eighteen months at the most.[44] How did Bembo's patrician peers in Venice hear of his scandal in the months before Alberto's election? When Bembo described Cyurω's fierce defense of him in the face of gossip and mockery by his peers in Venice, how did those peers discover the scandal? Was there a real paper news trail to match Bembo's evocation of *fama* spreading across the Mediterranean empire? Undoubtedly, with Alberto's early election, the men of the Great Council had discovered the scandal and acted to rectify it. But no paper trail for the scandal exists today: it was not discussed in Senate deliberations, in the Council of Ten, or in the Collegio. Even the letters sent to the *Capi* of the Council of Ten—filled with scandals across the empire, from fraud to exile to murder—do not seem to report on the events on Skiathos.[45] It is possible that, scandalous though the events were, Skiathos was simply not an important enough colonial outpost within the empire to merit much written reporting. Even Marin Sanudo, perhaps the most outstanding gossip of Cinquecento Venice, with an extraordinarily intimate knowledge of Venetian political life, seems not to have registered Bembo's family scandal in his diaries. Bembo's use of *fama*, then, indicates the ways in which humanist writing, literature, and history were bound up for Venetian patrician governors, rather than any actually traceable routes of gossip or scandal across the empire.

Bembo's Letter: Humanism, Consolation, and Family

Bembo accounted for his two dramatic years on Skiathos in a letter that was written upon the death of his wife. Though it survives in draft form, it was sent to Andrea Anesi, and received a response from his son, Leonardo. Bembo's letter seems to have been received by Leonardo in the spirit of a consolatory work. Leonardo wrote back mostly in Italian, but crucially, not in the sentence in which he consoles Bembo with his own grief. This sentence was written half in Italian and half in Latin: "La morte di madona Cyurω vostra consorte cuius obitus nobis quam molestissumus fuit."[46] The emotional language of consolation, here "molestissimus" (most troubling or grievous), is in Latin, suggesting that Leonardo understood that Latin was the language of consolation. Leonardo Anesi, like Modestino Bembo and Coppo's sons, seems to have been a disappointment as a scholar. He wrote that his father wished him to write back to Bembo in Latin, but he did not quite manage the Latin composition beyond his expression of consolation.[47] This slip from Latin to Italian reminds us again that humanist scholarship was of course a family enterprise. Andrea Anesi seems to have wanted to make his son into a Latin scholar. Indeed, Leonardo was much happier to convey bits of altogether more practical information. He relates news of his sister, and tells Bembo of an incoming visitor to Biria, Bembo's own neighborhood in Venice. Intimate family news and gossip comfortably coexisted with the more exalted Latin of the consolation prose letter genre.

Consolation literature was an established genre of Latin humanist writing, and as such relied on common themes, motifs, commonplaces, and oratorical skill to ease the burden of grief. John McManamon has studied many of these themes that make up consolatory writing, the ideas and values that were intended to sustain the mourner: family pride, cultural efflorescence, liberal arts, eloquence, history, rhetoric, and political and academic ideals.[48] In many consolation letters of the Renaissance, authors argued that participating in political life had its own emotional rewards that could temper the pain of the death of a loved one. For example, in a collection of consolatory writings written to the Venetian patrician Jacopo Antonio Marcello upon the death of his eight-year-old son in 1461, consolatory writers addressing themselves to Marcello reminded him of his military successes and told him he had to move past his grief for the good of the Venetian Republic. In this collection, humanists such as Francesco Filelfo try to persuade Marcello to stop grieving; they chide him for weakness, for making a spectacle of himself, for being too sad.[49] In fifteenth-century Florence, the humanist Coluccio Salutati was praised by his humanist friends for leaving his wife Piera's funeral early in order to attend to the induction ceremony of some new priors, a duty of his civic office.[50] Within humanist political culture, consolatory writers waged an emotional war of words: hope, pride, and care for all aspects of civic political culture were pitted against the individual indulgence of private grief.

In his own letter, Bembo touches on some of these central themes of consolatory literature identified by McManamon—education, the liberal arts, eloquence, political ideals, learning, family lineage—but, crucially, in a sardonic manner. In the long passage in which Bembo describes his wife's final weeks and her ultimate death, he portrays the young men courting his daughters have nothing to say for themselves when they visit; they are dumb and mute, the opposite of the ideals of eloquence and rhetoric. The laziness and entitlement to political offices that Bembo writes characterize Venetian youth are a cynical take on Venetian political ideals. His angry sarcasm toward the doctors who tried to cure Cyurω and Angela with "dialectics and syllogisms"—with their fancy but useless Greek learning—overturned the academic ideals of the civic and personal utility of Latin and Greek studies. Themes of family pride and ancestry are complicated by his Greek wife and half-Greek children, and by the evident tension between his wife and his son Domenico. The family had patrician aspirations, to be sure, but Giovanni and Cyurω could not afford patrician dowries for their daughters. These civic, academic, and family ethics were ideals that Bembo did not see being put into practice in everyday Venetian society, or within his own household.[51]

Bembo was more than simply disillusioned with Venetian politics and aristocratic society. He blamed these hypocrisies for causing the anxiety that led Cyurω to illness and death. This is especially clear in the line near the bottom of the first paragraph: "These sicknesses of the mind were added to the sickness of her body, and after fifteen days of a continuous fever . . . she died."[52] In deploying some of these set tropes of humanist consolation, Bembo used them to express his cynicism about the hypocrisy of his own class and political culture as well as his grief concerning their effect on his wife. Bembo used tropes of humanist consolatory writing to reveal the gap between the ideals that they represent and everyday life in Venetian political society. Because Bembo blamed these hypocrisies for the anxieties that led to Cyurω's illness and death, his letter becomes more than the rantings of a grieving husband. By deftly combining some of the most commonplace categories of consolation literature with hypocrisy, anxiety, anger, and grief, Bembo revealed his own troubled status, on the margins of Venetian political society.

Bembo's letter, structured around that simmering tension between alienation and ambition, therefore challenges the idea that humanist literature, and consolatory writing specifically, created an oppressive system of emotional self-mastery, part of a policing of the boundaries of political society to create a uniform and coherent political community. Humanist Latin was elaborate, highly contrived, and tightly controlled. But even so, it provided a set of linguistic tools for self-inquiry, self-expression, and the creation of empathetic relationships.[53] We can see how Bembo, even within the formal and thematic constraints of humanist consolatory literature, could manipulate these to emotional effect. He approached these themes sardonically to capture the hypocrisy and empty ideals that led to Cyurω's anxiety, illness, and death.

Bembo's letter combined themes and motifs of consolatory literature with those of writing the self, and there were models in humanist literature of the kind of autobiographical self-reckoning that he undertook in his letter. For example, Petrarch's autobiographical narrative in his *Epistola ad Posteros* begins, "Possibly you will have heard something about me . . . For almost everyone speaks as he likes it, not as truth demands; for both praise and blame (*infamie*) have no measure," a phrase that seems to resonate with Bembo's own experience of having been the object of gossip (*fama*) and mocking by his aristocratic peers.[54] Petrarch's *infamie* parallels Bembo's description of his social rejection: "[the members of the Great Council] were imputing me, a good man, to make me infamous."[55] Bembo borrowed directly from Petrarch the rhetorical use of an autobiographical epistle to reckon with what men may have "heard." Indeed, Bembo owned and annotated a copy of Petrarch's Latin works, including the *Epistola ad Posteros*.[56] Particularly interesting in Bembo's edition of Petrarch is the inclusion of a *Vita Petrarche*, which, when compared with Petrarch's own autobiographical letter, may have provided a narrative model for Bembo's construction of his own life.

Bembo labeled his own letter an oratory, and this is precisely because he intended it to do the work of convincing Andrea that his decisions on Skiathos were just, and to show both the power of his words to bind his own grief to the consolatory power of humanist friendship and the power of autobiographical reckoning in the face of public *fama*.[57] The text is therefore evidence of a complicated humanist literary culture, in which autobiographical writing, oratory, epistolary writing, and consolatory literature could comfortably coexist in the same work. Bembo's letter indicates the ways in which concerns about family, emotional life, friendship, and reputation were interwoven in humanist writing. These concerns were not unimportant or "domestic," but indeed at the heart of how a patrician governor conceived of himself and of his role within the political society of Venice and its empire.

Conclusion

Bembo evidently did not govern based on abstract or rigid principles he may have found in his *commissione* or in humanist treatises describing ideal political thought and action. Bembo read examples of great political figures of the classical past (he seemed particularly taken with his predecessor Philip of Macedonia's rule of Skiathos, for instance), and yet these examples were not taken straightforwardly as models from which to govern. This might suggest to us that the relationship between humanism and the practical politics of governance could be much more complex than a simple equivalence between reading and doing, writing and practice. Humanism was central to Bembo's perception of the space and history of the Mediterranean empire, and indeed provided the literature and language with which he could elaborate his own place within that empire. But humanist political thought—at least, Bembo's political thought as a humanist—was much messier and more improvisational than perhaps contemporary historians of political thought might recognize. He governed idiosyncratically, based on a potentially volatile mix of contemporary information, classical knowledge and literature, and his own personal experience. In cases such as Bembo's, in which we can rely on his extensive first-person writing, it becomes possible to begin to untangle these factors in order to see how they were related.

The history of humanism has been studied by historians of political thought and by intellectual historians, and this has meant that our understanding of the politics of humanism is based on a particular set of texts: mostly treatises and orations, texts that abstractly theorize about political life. But in Bembo's scrappy annotations to his *Isolario* in his personal manuscript, and in his self-reflective letter, these secondary or minor humanist sources reveal a kind of humanist political culture: a term that we might productively contrast with that of humanist political thought. Classical literature was of course deeply important to Bembo and to men like him, and the improvisational and imaginative ways in which they used the classical past to govern must equally be part of our understanding of the politics of humanism. This also suggests that we might reconsider our picture of who, exactly, participated in Renaissance Italian politics. The Venetian empire was largely governed by men like Bembo: patrician, of course, but also relatively mediocre scholars and governors. Bembo never made a great success out of his scholarship, but that does not mean it is irrelevant to our understanding of the social history of humanism. I would argue that it is these mediocre scholars and their families who can point us toward more productive insights about the nature of Renaissance humanism. They demonstrate that in their individual, even idiosyncratic uses of humanism in the Mediterranean state, mediocre scholar-governors did not straightforwardly use scholarship to justify or promote a widely held Venetian imperial history or ideology. Rather, they drew on a variety of kinds of evidence (textual and material), authority (of both Venetian and local Mediterranean actors), and scholarship practices to imagine, map, and understand the space, history, and scope of the empire as they experienced it.

Finally, Bembo's story on Skiathos and the way he relates it can also tell us something about the ways in which we might better write about the history of empire. At the very heart of Bembo's short experience of governance was a complicated, difficult problem of sexuality, gender, and transgression. It was a problem that was, at its core, about bodies: pregnant bodies, terminated pregnancy, castrated or mutilated bodies. This is not imperial politics as most historians of empire understand the word *politics*. And yet men like Bembo, and their families, were the Venetian empire. The problems of intimate relationships were not just domestic, cordoned off from a political sphere of action, but central to the ways empire worked during the early modern period. Bembo's story forces us to place intimate relationships, gender, sexuality, and the body at the center of our analysis of imperial history. Though undoubtedly an extreme example, just like the reevaluations of humanism outlined here, this troubles our understanding of who governed and how governance happened. As we will see in the final chapter, Coppo's scholarship and family life in Istria allowed him to imagine a different kind of empire from his study in Isola, and an alternative relationship to his native city of Venice.

Chapter 6

On the Borders of Italy

Introduction

Although Coppo's life became firmly rooted in Isola, across the Adriatic from the lively intellectual scene of Venice, he continued to practice the humanist scholarship he had learned as an adolescent in his native city. As Coppo moved away from the Scuola of Sabellico and the Accademia of Leto, his scholarship became geographical: composed of geographical descriptions, maritime itineraries, and his own woodcut maps, Coppo created a body of work from his study in Isola that looked outward to the wider Mediterranean world. As we saw in chapter 4, Coppo's identity as a Venetian humanist played a part in his integration into Isolan political society. But even while he worked assiduously in the municipal council and chancery of Isola, Coppo dedicated his work as a scholar to probing the geographical and historical relationship between his adopted region of Istria and the rest of the Mediterranean empire. His many woodcut maps and geographical texts allow us to track Coppo's own investigation into the history and geography of Istria, and the ways in which he came to see the peninsula not as a composite element of the Venetian empire but as the "last region" of Italy: an inheritance of ancient Roman Imperial history in the region. Through classical literature, contemporary humanist writing, and, most importantly, his own witnessing of Istrian Roman material culture, Coppo wove an alternative history for Istria than that imposed by the Venetian empire.

Coppo's spatial and historical scholarship on Istria reimagined the ways in which Istria related to its immediate Mediterranean surroundings. As we shall see throughout this chapter, Coppo built on a long literary tradition of imagining Istria as a kind of borderland of Italy, as an Italian bulwark against the barbarian civilizations just over the Alps. But Coppo was also the first to map Istria as a discrete region. Because Istria was disconnected from Italy by the Alps, Coppo imagined Istria as entirely unique and autonomous. Though Istria was the inheritor of a Roman-built environment, and so perhaps glorified by continued association, Coppo was the first author to both depict and write about Istria as having a regional—not only Roman, Venetian, or Italian—identity. In this chapter, we will look closely at the kinds of humanist writing about Roman history and ruins that Coppo responded to in his own scholarship on Istria. We will also see that Coppo was not alone in this scholarly project: other Venetian and Dalmatian humanist authors, including his own teacher Sabellico, were interested in creating through their scholarship a particular regional identity for the northeastern Adriatic world of Friuli, Istria, and Dalmatia. These links not only were literary but grounded on the deeply affective ties begun at home in Sabellico's lecture room at San Marco.

Coppo wrote prolifically from his *studio* in Isola. His first work, written in 1520, was *De toto orbe*, a geographical encyclopedia divided into four books: the first on cosmography and basic geography, the second on Europe, the third on Africa, and the fourth on Asia. The book exists in its most complete form in a manuscript now at the Biblioteca Comunale in Bologna, which contains twenty-two colored maps.[1] This manuscript is bound in a fine sixteenth-century stamped leather-covered board with clasps, and contains a later bookplate of the Cornaro family. Another copy of *De toto orbe* exists in a manuscript now in Paris, although this codex contains only text. This same manuscript also contains a summary of the encyclopedia, *De summa totius orbis*, in both Latin and Italian.[2] The *Summa* also exists in two more manuscripts: one in Piran and a second in Venice.[3] The former contains fifteen printed maps and has been produced as a facsimile.[4] Aside from the geographical encyclopedia and its summary text and maps, Coppo also wrote two works that were eventually printed. The first, the *Portolano*, was printed in Venice by Augustino di Bindoni in 1528. The text is primarily the list-format sailing directions, with some digressions into humanistic geography, and contains seven miniature woodcut maps illustrating the setting of the navigation guidelines. The *Portolano* text also survives in a manuscript copy, in the Paris manuscript that contains the *De toto orbe* and the *Summa*.

The second was Coppo's chorographic description of the Istrian peninsula, illustrated with one regional map. This was titled *Pietro Coppo Del Sito de*

Listria and was printed in 1540 by Francesco Bindoni and Mapheo Pasini. Of all of Coppo's works, the Istrian chorography was the best known in Coppo's lifetime, and the one that seems to have most interested his readers. Coppo's *Del Sito de Listria* was imitated by several Dalmatian humanist writers; the chorographic map was used to produce part of what some scholars have called the first printed nautical chart, in Giovanni da Vavassore's *La vera descrittione del Mare Adriatico* (Venice, 1541).[5] Indeed, in Abraham Ortelius's *Theatrum orbis terrarum* (Antwerp, 1570), he titles his own map of the Istrian peninsula, "Histriae tabula a Petro Coppo descr[ipsit]." Coppo's chorographic work was itself modeled on, and became the model for, a particular mode of writing, describing, and mapping this "ultima region de Italia," Venetian Istria.[6] It is the *Del Sito de Listria* that will be the focus of this chapter.

A Ruined World: Adriatic Chorography

Before turning to Coppo's own chorography, we can look to the similar chorographic work of other Venetian and Dalmatian humanists producing geographical and historical scholarship about the region around the turn of the sixteenth century. These works can all be considered as chorographies, though they take very different forms—prose, verse, itinerary—and so are not only geographically related but also generically related. In Ptolemy's *Geographia*, chorography was explained and defined as a pictorial "impression" of a particular geographical region.[7] Ptolemy primarily referred to the visual representation of a geographic region: for him, chorography was a regional visual description that focused on creating an artistic impression of landscape, classical history, and major sites of physical antique remains. Ptolemy defined chorography with an analogy to anatomy: "geography is concerned with the depiction of an entire head, chorography with individual features such as an eye or an ear."[8] Chorography was an important genre of mapping and writing not only for Coppo but also for this group of Venetian and Dalmatian humanist writers who were particularly interested in the northeastern borderlands of the Venetian empire, from Friuli to Dalmatia.

This Adriatic chorographic scholarship built on a Roman project of archaeological writing and scholarship in which Coppo also participated. The Veneto-Dalmatian chorographies examined here—Sabellico's *De vetustate Aquileiae* (Padua, between 1481 and 1483), Iliya Crijević's *De Epidauro* (manuscript, written c. 1505), and Marin Sanudo's *Itinerario* (manuscript, written in 1483)— are part of a literary tradition founded on three Roman texts of the Quattrocento: Pomponio Leto's *De antiquitatibus* (Rome, 1510) and Biondo Flavio's *Roma instaurata* (Rome, 1446) and *Italia illustrata* (Rome, 1474).[9] Sabellico and Coppo, who studied with Leto in Rome and Naples, respectively, had been directly exposed to his antiquarian Accademia on the Quirinal, his lectures on Roman archaeology and epigraphy, and his famous walking tours of Roman ruins, as we saw in chapter 2. Flavio's "philological reconstruction of the ancient city" of Rome was influential throughout the later Quattrocento and Cinquecento, providing a textual model of antiquarianism, reconstruction, and reconciliation between past and present that had far-reaching implications not only in the literary world, but in the development of Renaissance archaeology and antiquarianism.[10]

Sabellico not only studied under Leto at his Accademia but published a *Vita* of his teacher that was included in two editions of Leto's *Romanae historiae compendium* (1499 and 1500) and in Sabellico's own *Opera* (1502).[11] Sabellico thus assumed partial responsibility for his teacher's legacy, not only in the construction of the *Vita* but in his own literary production. His *De vetustate Aquileiae*, in particular, borrowed heavily from Leto's archaeological regional study of Rome, transplanted to the ancient cities of Aquileia, Udine, and surrounding Friuli. In the first edition of the text (Padua, 1481–83), Sabellico provides at the beginning of the book a list of the authors from whom he "excerpted" his history: Pliny, Ptolemy, Strabo, Pomponius Mela, Plutarch, and others. Indeed, Ruth Chavasse has noted that this edition "resembles more miscellaneous collections such as letter, epigram, and exempla collections": after the list of sources, Sabellico prints a letter from the (otherwise unknown) humanist "Cynthius" to Sabellico; a letter from Giorgio Merula, a humanist scholar based in Venice, to Sabellico congratulating him on the publication of the book; and Sabellico's own dedicatory letter to the Venetian governor of Udine, Giovanni Emo, before the text finally begins.[12] As the composite construction of Leto's text emphasized his role as an eyewitness or even collector of Roman antiquity, the layout of Sabellico's book situated him not only in relation to the classical authors from whom he constructed his text, but also in relation to the world of Venetian humanists and governors for whom his work was intended.

Called a "Chorographia" by Sabellico, *De vetustate Aquileiae* elaborates the classical and contemporary history of the region of Friuli primarily through the many wars set in the region, and through its antiquities. In the dedicatory letter to Emo, Sabellico writes that Emo himself "emulated" ancient Romans, and compares him to the Athenian statesman Phocion, constructing a parallel between his own interest in the antique history of Friuli and the modern governance of the region. In Book III, Sabellico relates the legend of Antenor, the great Trojan counselor to Priam: Virgil's story about Antenor fleeing the Greek army "to make his passage through the Illyrian gulfs, and safe through the inlands where the Liburians rule [. . . where] he erected a city for his people, a Trojan home called Padua," was considered a critical element of ancient Aquileian and Dalmatian history, proof that the Friulani were descended from Trojans.[13] Indeed, the first book of the text draws heavily on classical geography, especially from Pliny and Strabo, to establish not only the topography but the antiquity of the region. The following books are structured according to the wars that took place in Aquileia and its surroundings: wars with the Goths, wars with the Lombards, "domestic" wars, and the very recent Ottoman incursion into Friuli.

Following the establishment of Friuli's antiquity in the dedicatory letter and the initial book, the descriptions of the wars set in Friuli are violent impressions of the ruination and ravaging of the region's landscape. The destruction of the region at the hands of the Goths is paralleled both with the fall of Rome and with Sabellico's eyewitness account of the ravaging of Tarcento during the Turkish incursion in 1478. First Sabellico writes of Rome as a place "direpta solitudinis," "ruinae plena," comparing the tragedy of the fall of Rome to the death of Priam, the king of Troy, on the altar of Zeus, as it was graphically related in Book II of the *Aeneid*: "And at one time, not long after, Rome was captured—the emperor having disgracefully lost the people's splendid empire—and Rome was laid to waste, like a wilderness: and was full of only the ruins of Augustus; just as Priam himself was wretchedly murdered on the altar of Jupiter."[14]

Much like Leto's project to reconstruct imperial Rome through archaeological and topographical history that we explored in chapter 2, Sabellico's account wove together a comparison between Rome and Troy in order to assert later in the same passage that it was Antenor and the Trojans who constructed Aquileia. "Aquileia is as ancient as Rome: and equally so is Padua: and Concordia: indeed, these were at one time Trojan: they venerate Antenor, and dare to affirm their [Trojan] founding."[15] Having established the historical and geographical connection between Troy, Rome, and the construction of Aquileia, Sabellico then moved to discuss Aquileia's own destruction at the hands of the Gauls. Like Priam and Rome before, Aquileia suffered the same ravaging at the hands of barbarians. The use of the word "cineres," the charred ruins of a burned city, provided a thematic link to Sabellico's own eyewitness historical account of the Turkish incursion at Tarcento.

Sabellico compared the scene at Tarcento to the Greek myth of the fall of Phaeton, in which Helios's son was granted his sun chariot for the day and nearly incinerated the earth. Sabellico lamented the devastation of the country-side, its country villas, and the cultivated fields. Calling the Turks "barbarians," Sabellico's vivid imagery of a fertile countryside set ablaze, "buried under smoke and ash," recalls the "cineres" of Rome and Aquileia after barbarian invasion.

> The news of this defeat instilled such terror in the whole country that even those who lived in the cities hardly believed that they would remain safe. A mass exodus from the countryside began, and kept going during the night which followed the day of the battle. The next day, late in the morning, suddenly around Udine, in various places, clouds of smoke be-gan to rise up; and they realized that the enemy had reached [them]. A moment later, as if the barbarians had convened together, all of the farms that lay between the rivers Isonzo and Tagliamento were burned by the hand of the enemy. At that time I was in Tarcento: I moved there from Udine, on account of the plague. And when I had heard of the defeat at the Isonzo, I took refuge with many others, in the castle that borders [Tarcento]. From that vantage point, one can view a vast area on the en-tire country. From there, crying, I witnessed the heart-wrenching devastation of the country. It was so horrible to watch such a well cultivated and pleasant countryside buried under the smoke and the ash; but it was much more horrible and dreadful at sunset and through-out the rest of the night, waiting to see that one strip of flames, which unfolded from the river Isonzo to the Tagliamento: so it seemed like there was nothing there in the middle that had not been invaded by fire. . . . I would dare to claim that never, in any age, have mortals could have seen a fire so terrible; unless one wishes to believe the stories of poets, who invented the extraordinary tales about Phaeton.[16]

Where Leto was interested in recovering classical Rome through comparing tex-tual scholarship with the visual evidence of the city, Sabellico, through his im-pressionistic style, leaves the battle at Tarcento still smoldering at the very end of his text. Sabellico's textual archaeology and history of the region is open-ended, concluded with a ravaged landscape open for present intervention. Sabellico's vantage point above Tarcento—weeping from the tower of a nearby castle—not only indicates to the reader his firsthand experience of the battle, but presents a narrative trope common in chorographic writing and its regional articulations of space. The dizzying heights and spectacular descent in the myth of Phaeton, too, parallel Sabellico's own sense of chorographic space. Sabellico's narrative perspective, his bird's-eye view of the scene, allows the "universal" perspective of the regional landscape required in chorographic writing.

Iliya Crijević (1463–1520), a Ragusan humanist, also studied with Leto in Rome and was even crowned *poeta laureatus* there in 1484, before returning to Ragusa (present-day Dubrovnik). Although Crijević seems to have been a prolific writer, he published only four epigrams and a prose epistle during his lifetime.[17] Crijević may have had difficulty printing his work in Dalmatia: a printing house was not opened in Ragusa until the eighteenth century.[18] Crijević produced an unfinished, unpublished *epyllion* (a short narrative poem containing epic themes) titled *De Epidauro*, which related the destruction of the ancient city of Epidaurus. Crijević told how the inhabitants of Epidaurus had to flee their sacked city, and resettled in Ragusa. Epidaurus, or present-day Cavtat on the Adriatic coast fifteen miles south of Dubrovnik, was founded by Greeks and came under Roman rule in the third century BC. Its sack in the seventh century by "barbarians" meant that the classical city was ruined; but it also allowed Crijević to posit a glorious lineage for Ragusans, who were thus descended from the Greco-Roman culture of Cavtat. The poem opens with a description of the now-desolate rocks of Epidaurus:

> The stone is Socolitanum, a castle,
> deserted at the foot of a mountain. The mountain
> rises into the air from a deep source, the highest peak
> broken off: horrible rocks, a vast and terrible vision.
> I behold from above, from a watchtower: from up here,
> every perspective is surrounded by roughest stone,
> by craggy rocks torn from [the mountainside],
> by fragile cliffs, and by high mountains.
> In the back, it bends around in the shape
> of a theatre, which you would not expect to be rocky.
> But, sloping from the stony root of the mountain
> all the way to its summit, vast, horrible rocks watch over;
> and you see everything covered up by great rocks,
> ruins covered, and everywhere laid waste on all sides.[19]

Like Sabellico's description of watching Tarcento burn, Crijević's poem adopted a bird's-eye vantage point for telling of Epidaurus's ruin. This viewpoint is particularly well suited to the descriptive language of the chorography and allows Crijević to take an objective all-encompassing cartographic view of the ruined, forbidding Dalmatian landscape. Toward the end of the poem, Crijević celebrates the construction of Ragusa and its population:

You will now become a double, Epidaurus,
And the other will be celestial and great,
a sparkling world, a new, starry constellation
which will begin to shine: a fresh, new earth on high.
Now [your] citizens will renew the peaks of the mountain
which slipped away [and you will better be restored].
And they will build you, restored from earlier times, on [other] shores.[20]

Although Crijević shared Leto's interest in ruination and the physical remains of the classical past, Crijević—unlike Sabellico—ended his poem on a note of reconstruction and reconciliation. The terror of the sack and of the flight to Ragusa was redeemed by the classical heritage that fifteenth-century Ragusans could now claim, providing an antique foundation for classical poets and humanist scholars like Crijević himself. As Sabellico imported Leto's interest and style of writing about antiquarianism and ruin to the Friuli region of the Venetian *terraferma*, so too did Crijević bring Leto's mode of scholarship to bear on his own Dalmatian local history.

Although better known to Venetian historians as a diarist, the patrician Marin Sanudo (1466–1536) also wrote *Itinerario per la terraferma veneziana* in 1483, the result of his travels with Venetian *sindici* through the mainland empire, including Istria. Sanudo attended public lectures in philosophy at the school at Rialto, and studied rhetoric, history, and poetry at the school of San Marco. He was also affiliated with Aldus Manutius's humanist circle.[21] His *Itinerario* is the most overtly classical of any of his later texts, although the *Commentari della guerra di Ferrara*, written in 1484, is similar in genre to the "eyewitness" style of regional histories produced by Coriolanus and Alvise Cippico and Marcantonio Sabellico at the end of the fifteenth century. The *Itinerario*, much like Sabellico's work on Aquileia and Leto's and Flavio's works on Rome, is a kind of composite text assembled from epigrams, poems, inscriptions, lists, sketches, and prose. Writing mostly in the vernacular, Sanudo often slips in lines of Latin text and includes many Latin inscriptions. Interestingly, in his travels through the *terraferma*, Sanudo included classical Roman epigraphy alongside very recent inscriptions commemorating the deeds and patronage of Venetian governors, apparently making no distinction between the two. For example, Sanudo was as interested in recording the dedicatory inscription to Alvise Sagredo, the Venetian podestà of Piran, on the church of San Giorgio there as he was in recording the ancient Roman inscriptions on the triumphal Arch of the Sergii in the neighboring city of Pola.[22]

Sanudo's descriptions of the Istrian landscape are, like Leto's and Biondo's writing on Rome, drawn equally from classical authorities and eyewitness account, with a particular emphasis on the Venetian history in the region (perhaps inevitably, given that Sanudo's tour was determined by the route of the *sindici*). Sanudo repeatedly alternates between the contemporary Venetian political affairs of Istria (especially in listing which Venetian patrician was currently filling which administrative office) and the classical past of the region, recorded in his epigraphical documentation. In his entry on Aquileia, for instance, Sanudo begins by describing and then listing the ancient marble churches of the city; he then describes its Roman ruins, including "le vestigie di uno theatro" and the "aqueduto mal conditionato et roto," before recording an epigraph from the monastery of Santa Maria outside the city walls. Sanudo then transcribed the passage from the *Aeneid* in which Virgil describes Antenor's flight to the Illyrian shores, before ending the Aquileia text with a description of the Ottoman ruin of one of the churches and relating his journey by boat through the gulf of Trieste.[23] Part travel journal, commonplace book, sylloge, and history text, Sanudo's *Itinerario* is an example of the ways that composite and comparative philological methods of humanist scholarship that Flavio and Leto piloted in Rome could be displaced to a different geographical region and used for different aims. Although Sanudo, like Flavio in the Italian peninsula and Cyriac d'Ancona in the Mediterranean, recorded for textual posterity the ruins of the classical *terraferma*, he pursued an intrinsically Venetian project. Documenting the Venetian presence there in the same humanistic, scholarly style as the classical past, Sanudo constructed an image of the Venetian presence in Istria as a perpetuation of the Roman history of the region: a project that was indicated above all in Sanudo's mirroring of Roman classical epigraphy with inscriptions commemorating Venetian podestàs' contributions to Istrian urban architecture.

One of Sabellico's correspondents and friends, Palladio Fosco, connected with Coppo through Sabellico's literary circle. Fosco was a Paduan humanist who tried unsuccessfully to obtain Sabellico's former teaching position in Udine in 1483, when Sabellico left for Venice. The letters in which Sabellico assures Fosco of his support for this position were published in Sabellico's *Opera*.[24] While in Padua, Fosco became acquainted with a circle of Dalmatian humanists studying at the university there, including Alvise Cippico from Trogir. Sabellico had been a longtime friend of Alvise's father, Coriolanus Cippico: he had praised Coriolanus Cippico's command of rhetoric, saying that his skill was completely unexpected, as he was native to Dalmatia.[25] In the *Opera*, Sabellico published a long epistolary *consolatio* he penned for Coriolanus when his house in Trogir burned to the ground and his wife was killed.[26] Fosco had read the *consolatio* and wrote to Sabellico praising his "doctissimum libellum."[27] Fosco became friends with Coriolanus's son, Alvise, writing an elegy for him upon Alvise's election to the bishopric of Famagusta on Cyprus in 1489.[28]

When Fosco failed to obtain the teaching post in Udine, it was through his Dalmatian friends in Padua that he was led to teach first at Zara (1493–1516) and then, at the end of his life, at Capodistria. Fosco was one of many Italian humanist teachers who traveled and taught in Dalmatia and Istria (conversely, Dalmatian teachers often left for posts in Italy and central European courts).[29] Fosco even produced his major scholarly work, a commentary on the poems of Catullus, from a fifteenth-century manuscript copy of Catullus owned by the Cippico family.[30] Fosco also penned an epigram for Coppo's *De toto orbe*, which survives in the Bolognese codex:

> Reader, if you are seeking venerable volumes,
> these are the ones that Coppo constructed with his wonderful genius.
> Here he tells of the heavens, he depicts the earth and
> the sea; he omits nothing of the entire world.
> He delights many learned eyes and ears equally.
> Who, I ask, will not read this very beautiful work?[31]

Fosco's delight in Coppo's atlas—and in Coppo's ability to describe in both text and image the entire world—may have influenced his own choice of genre. Fosco produced a now-lost atlas of islands, titled *De insulis*, which his Roman editor intended eventually to publish. But it was Sabellico's and Coppo's use of the chorographic genre that influenced Fosco's second printed work, a regional description of the Dalmatian coastal cities titled *De situ orae Illyrici* (printed posthumously by his editor in Rome, in 1540).[32] Following the chorographic text in this volume are several epigrams and short poems, including an elegy for his friend Alvise Cippico. Fosco also included an epigram for Iliya Crijević.[33] Around the figure of Marcantonio Sabellico, a wider network of Venetian, Paduan, and Dalmatian humanist figures emerges: one that moved between humanistic centers within the Venetian colonial world, who were connected through schools and dedications, an interest in geographical writing, and, though more difficult to trace, perhaps affective bonds, too.

Sabellico, Fosco, and the Cippico family were also linked through the use of particular genres in their written scholarship. Coriolanus Cippico (c. 1425–93), from Trau, served on a Venetian naval galley in a skirmish against the Turks, under the general Pietro Mocenigo. His account of the battle, titled *Petri Mocenici imperatoris gestorum libri tres* (Venice, 1477), was the kind of journalistic genre that Sabellico found so compelling in his description of the Turkish incursion into Friuli: as Cippico himself wrote, he accounted for everything "in words truer than the prophecies of Apollo's oracle."[34] Sabellico even incorporated it "almost word for word" into his history of Venice.[35] Alvise modeled his own eyewitness "history" of the Venetian war against Ferrara, composed as a verse epistle to the doge Giovanni Mocenigo (Pietro's brother) in 1482, after the same genre used by both his father and by Sabellico in his *De vetustate Aquileiae*. And Fosco, although the extent of his literary production is largely unknown, also seems to have written a similar contemporary military history: in a sixteenth-century manuscript now in the Biblioteca del Seminario in Padua, a text titled "Palladius Fuscus Patavinus, de bello . . . inter Venetos et Turcos" seems to indicate his interest in the genre.[36] The eyewitness historical style was a kind of generic calling card of Sabellico's intellectual circle. These friendships worked both on a personal level between scholars and in geographical writing, creating a particular literary affiliation between Istria and Friuli, and Venetian intellectual culture.

The relationships between Sabellico, Coppo, Fosco, and Coriolanus and Alvise Cippico—relationships of patronage, teacher and student, literary exchange, and genre imitation—indicate that in this highly mobile world of Adriatic scholarship, affective intellectual networks were sustained across the empire. These connections also mapped onto the social world of Venetian governance. Coppo and the native Istrians Giacomo Egidio and Nicolò Manzuoli were all members of the local Isolan municipal council. Both Egidio and Manzuoli were educated in Isola and were known locally for their humanist study, although none of their works have survived. Each of them also petitioned the doge in Venice to confirm local Isolan rights and statutes.[37] Humanist friendships between scholars and administrators often formed in the schools of Venice and Dalmatia; once these men were sent to teach or govern in other Mediterranean cities, their friendships took on literary form, in dedicatory letters, epigrams, and bequests, and through a shared, communal use of literary imagery and genre.

Del Sito de Listria

Coppo's own chorography, the *Del Sito de Listria*, was written in the 1520s but not published in Venice until 1540. Like Sabellico and Crijević, Coppo was able to adapt Leto's Roman antiquarianism for these northeastern Italian borderlands. In his dedication of the chorography, Coppo explicitly linked it to his time in Sabellico's schoolroom in Venice. Dedicated to Coppo's friend Giuseppe Faustino, in recognition of the fact that "our most youthful age was spent in the learned school of the most cultured Sabellico,"[38] Coppo wrote in the dedicatory letter that he decided to write the book "in volgar lengua" for the benefit of Faustino's friend, who is "very eager to learn in the vernacular, so that he completely understands; and for other people, who are not so learned (as you yourself are most learned in Latin)."[39] Whether or not Faustino did indeed have a friend who specifically requested a *volgare* version of Coppo's chorography, it seems that Coppo was aware that a vernacular text might find a larger reading audience than a Latin geography (although he does not hesitate to mention that he has "already written and drawn the provinces and places of the entire earth in Latin.")[40] Coppo then introduced the chorography in the dedicatory letter by writing that he traveled extensively throughout the Istrian peninsula to research the book.

Although Coppo lived in Istria for decades and perhaps even traveled along the coastline in a boat as he claimed, he relied equally on classical sources to describe the topography and history of the peninsula. Coppo began with Pliny's description of the size of the region. He then related the legend that the Argonauts carried their galley above their shoulders to the region near the river Istro: like Virgil's description of Antenor, the story of the Argonauts at Istria gave the region its own mythological Greek history. Coppo then described the Greek history of the region in greater detail. "Before the aforesaid Argonauts came, as I said, that part was already inhabited by the pastoral Indigenous Aboriginal people. This was just like the rest of Italy, at the time of Janus (or Faun), and Saturn, who came from Greece: and they found coarse people, living following the nature of animals, and fruits produced of an uncultivated earth. After this, they came to live more humanely, and domesticated the earth through cultivating it. And they inhabited it under the cultivation of god and law."[41] The Argonauts and other Greek settlers of Istria found "gente rude," whose primary characteristic seems to have been, for Coppo, their inability to cultivate the earth. The Greeks brought civilization to Istria, in the form of agriculture, law, and religion. After the Greeks, the Romans built up the peninsula: "In many places in Istria one finds many worthy antiquities and vestiges of antique land. These demonstrate that it was already inhabited by powerful and worthy men."[42] The ruins of Istria, then, come to stand as evidence for Coppo not only of the antiquity of the landscape but of its noble history: if the men who lived in Istria were capable of building the amphitheaters, aqueducts, and fortified walls that still dotted the peninsula, then surely this was proof that classical men were "potenti et degni."

Like Leto and the other Veneto-Dalmatian chorographic writers who followed him, Coppo was primarily interested in the antiquities and "vestigii" of this classical past, weaving this interest into a narrative of barbarian destruction. His description of the destruction of Rome and the founding of Aquileia by displaced Romans is a narrative that we have seen not only in Sabellico's work on Friuli but also in a modified form in Crijević's work on the origins of Ragusa. Coppo wrote,

> And after Rome was destroyed by Brennus, the most bellicose captain
> of the French, they passed from France to Italy with three hundred thou-
> sand of the most ferocious soldiers, in order to find a new home and
> place to live . . . because there were too many living in France. Rome
> was burned and everything there was left destroyed by Brennus; he then
> went to Dalmatia, Hungary, and was successful in Greece: putting each
> land to fire and sword with terrible cruelty, without any pity. Istria was
> the first to be despoiled of all sustenance and good things. After some
> years Totila, King of the Goths, with many of his men, again came into
> Italy. They destroyed many cities: Florence was deserted and left with-
> out a name for many years in this way, from the Goths' furor. It is said
> that they even destroyed Rome, dominator of the world from East to
> West: and Florence, and other famous cities. Many of the powerful and
> rich of these great Romans came to the said city of Aquileia with their
> riches, and they made the city the greatest. And [they came] to this land
> of Istria, and especially to Pola: and with their riches, they made these
> notable buildings. And so their ancestors were great Romans, of whom
> nothing remains but some wonderful traces.[43]

As in Sabellico's account of Friulian history, Coppo's history of Istria contains a series of sacks of the region. By comparing the Istrian devastation to that of Rome and of Florence, and then relating how great Romans came to settle in the Istrian peninsula, Coppo appropriated some of the classical authority of those cities for his own adopted region.

Coppo and other Venetian-Dalmatian authors thus expressed a desire to uncover the physical and literary remains of the classical past in Istria. As we saw in detail in chapter 2, the Mediterranean contact with the physical rem-nants of the classical past transformed the practice of Venetian humanism. Es-pecially in their archaeological focus on Roman ruins, these authors wove a narrative of contemporary Istria as having emerged from a glorious classical history. The reoccurring theme of a classical aristocratic population fleeing one burning city to found a still greater one, and especially Coppo's clear sense of teleological progression from indigenous people, to Greeks, to Romans, indi-cates the ways in which history was used to imagine the potentiality of the present. The tropes and themes of renewal and permanence articulated a sense of optimism about the ability of humanist scholarship to contribute creatively and lastingly to history, where the Roman ruins were left collaboratively open to humanists' intervention. In his study of Renaissance archaeology, Leonard

Barkan has similarly explored Michelangelo's aesthetic of incompleteness, or of the "openness" of the ruin or unfinished work to the "collaborative force" of the contemporary artist. Imitation, according to Barkan, does not seek to attain the perfection of the elusive complete classical sculpture, because completeness was not necessarily an aesthetic or stylistic aim for every artist or writer. Rather, the creativity of intertextuality, the possibility of collaboration offered by fragmentariness, and the hermeneutic instability of heterogeneous composition were real aesthetic aims.[44] In the chorographic writing of Coppo and his peers, the architectural description of Roman ruins was a kind of imitative practice in itself, in which the fragmentariness of the ruined landscape allowed a creative space within textual practice to revise the past. In Venetian chorographic writing about the ruined Adriatic landscape, the textual or architectural model is both ancient and contemporary, part of the composition of fragments that is continually open to creative intervention by contemporary writers. The textual description of the ruined built environment of Istria, dotted with crumbling amphitheaters and triumphal arches, saw the condition of ruin as a place from which they could begin to revise and reassess notions of Istrian colonial identity.

The Borderlands of Empire

Pomponio Leto provided one model of thinking through ruins: one that took a philological approach to the ruined built environment, and that Sabellico, Coppo, and Crijević successfully adapted to the northeastern Adriatic. But another Roman author, Biondo Flavio, played an equally important role as a model of archaeological humanist writing for Pietro Coppo. Perhaps even more widely read than Flavio's *Roma instaurata*, a text we explored in chapter 2, was his *Italia illustrata*, a text that Sanudo references by name in his discussion of Pola.[45] Written between 1447 and 1453, *Italia illustrata* was conceived as an expansion of *Roma instaurata*, in which Flavio moved his project of humanist reconstruction to all of the regions of Italy. Modeled after Livy's and Pliny's histories, Flavio's *Italia illustrate* opens:

> And because the barbarians confounded everything . . . we as a result are in a great part ignorant of the very location of the regions of Italy, of the cities, towns, lakes and mountains, whose names appear so frequently in the ancient authors. . . . I wanted to discover if, through the practical experience of the history of Italy I have gained, I shall be able to apply the names of current coinage to the appropriate places and

peoples of Italian antiquity, to settle the authenticity of the new no-
menclature, to revive and record the names that have been obliterated,
and in a word to bring some light to bear upon the murkiness of Italian
history.[46]

This "obscuritatem," Flavio wrote, is due to the destruction of Italy by barbarian tribes who so disrupted the landscape and the continuity of Italian classical history that "we are [now] ignorant" of the toponymy of Italy. Most
importantly for those Istrian writers, Flavio included Istria in his descriptions,
justifying his decision by writing, "Let us now make a start on the region of
Istria, not indeed a new addition to Italy, since it was reckoned to be part of
the country before the age of Augustus, but the last of the provinces to be
added to it."[47] Flavio returned to the Roman classical conception of the
boundaries of Italy, although by adding it at the end of the book, he affirmed
that Istria was indeed the "last" and most liminal of the classical regions of
Italy.

As Flavio and Leto had discussed for Roman history, and Sabellico for the
history of Friuli, Flavio was especially interested in his section on "Histria" in
the long history of "barbarorum incursionibus" into the region. This was most
problematic for Flavio in the history of the Italian and Slavic language in the
region. Flavio claimed that St. Jerome—the translator of the Latin Vulgate,
and so a particularly important saint for humanist scholars—brought writing
and the Latin divine office to the Slavic people in Dalmatia.[48] The writing and
"letters" that Flavio mentioned Jerome to have brought to Dalmatia were those
of the Slavic alphabet, a history that has been sometimes marshaled to argue
for the Slavic character of Istria.[49] But Flavio vigorously denied this interpretation that the Istrians were Slavic rather than Italian, writing,

> Now to those who stubbornly insist that St. Jerome appears to have been
> a foreigner, since he used in his own country an idiom wholly alien to
> any Italic language, and wanted his fellow Istrians to use it, and taught
> them to do so, I counter that Calabria and the land of the Bruttii is a
> bigger and better part of Italy than Istria: yet in these indisputably Ital-
> ian regions the use of the Greek tongue has always flourished, and still
> does today. Not only this, but around Asti, Turin, Ivrea, and that whole
> region of Italy at the foot of the Alps, over which Gallic people have long
> held sway, the people use (or abuse) a foreign tongue rather than their
> native Italian. The case is similar with the famous and civilized Italian
> cities of Vicenza and Verona: though far from Germany, there are many
> villages and towns subject to those cities whose people regularly speak
> German rather than Italian.[50]

Flavio wrote that even southern Italian regions in which Greek is a "living" language are still considered to be Italian, and that the northern Italian towns bordering the Alps, and those clustering around Verona and Vicenza in the Venetian *terraferma*, contain people who speak various Germanic dialects and yet are nevertheless Italian. So too is Istria an Italian region, although it contains a multilingual and multiethnic population who speak both Italian and Slavic dialects. Flavio thus elided the problem of having to excise St. Jerome from his history of Istria, rather accommodating him and Slavic culture by allowing for linguistic diversity under the broader aegis of Italian identity. However, Flavio quickly put aside his discussion of language to relate the sackings and destruction of the region: first by barbarians, then by the Visigoths, and then during battles between the Venetians and the Genoese. Even if he was willing to admit that Slavic languages are spoken in Istria, the dialect, and the region itself, was identified with a vulnerability to barbarian destruction.[51]

Following Flavio's example, Coppo also wrote about the complications of mixed languages. However, rather than focusing on the coexistence of Slavic and Italian, Coppo wrote scathingly about the historical formation of the *volgare*: "The Langobards completely destroyed and annihilated the Latin language, and burned all the Latin books they could find, in order that they could speak their barbarian language and so that they could rule. And it was from the combination of the corrupt words of the Barbarians and from Latin that the *volgare* was born."[52] Coppo presented a much more conflicted regional linguistic picture than Flavio. Writing himself in the *volgare*, Coppo wrote scornfully of the formation of that very language as emerging from the "vocaboli corotti" of the Langobardic "barbarians." Coppo, however, chose to illustrate this linguistic history of the Italian vernacular as part of his larger narrative of the corruption, devastation, and decay of the entirety of the Italian peninsula during the various barbarian invasions. This was a history that characterized all of Italy: indeed, it was central to the formation of the Italian language. If Istria so demonstrably suffered from the same barbarian sackings, then it too could be considered as part of an Italian geographical and historical identity. Rather than directing his impassioned discussion of the *volgare* at contemporary Italian writers who were engaging in the linguistic debate raging in intellectual circles in the metropole at this time, Coppo was interested in building the evidence of Istria's inclusion in the total devastation wrought by the barbarians to the Italian peninsula. This, as we have seen, was an important element not only in Flavio's project but in the writings of Leto on Rome, Sabellico on Friuli, and Crijević on Ragusa.

Istria was not only a region characterized by its prolific physical evidence of Roman occupation. It also was a liminal space that needed to be justified as a part of Italy. In the opening passage, in which Flavio justified including Istria in his geography, he wrote, "se inter ceteras oras ultimo additam inchoemas." Flavio's sentence emphasizes Istria's remoteness and liminality: "But we shall commence with the farthest [Istria], annexed between other shores." Istria not only was the "last" region of Italy but was bounded by "ceteras oras": lands that were not Italian.[53] The preoccupation in many of these texts, including Flavio's, with barbarian invasions was not only a means of conveying the destruction of the region but a way of conceiving of the dangerous porousness of Istria at the boundaries of the civilized world. This is especially evident in Flavio's closing paragraph to his book on Istria: "But now the breadth of our country of Italy, 450 miles from the river Var to the Arsa, reaches its boundary and concludes at this stretch of the Alps which was thrown up by nature to protect her against foreigners, in fresh commemoration of the glorious Doctor of the Church, St. Jerome. May he protect her, and me his devotee, from all adversaries, as I in turn have shown that he was born on these frontiers of Italy."[54] The image of Istria as a borderland and bulwark against the barbarians is emphatically clear in Flavio's writing. Flavio also crafted an image of himself as having authored a convincing argument not only for including Istria into Italy but even for being part of a campaign to protect it against barbarian invasion. By proving in the text that Jerome was indeed born in Istria, Flavio concluded that Jerome must then in gratitude protect his own homeland. Flavio's reconstructive project here is based not on physical antiquity but on a kind of literary, humanistic devotion to both Italy and Jerome.

Pietro Coppo derived his interest in Istria as a borderland from Flavio's *Italia illustrata*. He described Istria in the opening dedicatory letter as "questa ultima region de Italia," mirroring Flavio's description of the region as a borderland. Sanudo also wrote that Istria "è ultima region de l'Italia fine et termine" and referenced Flavio's claim that this geographical distinction dates to the time of Caesar Augustus.[55] This was a literary trope that stretched back as far as Dante:

> Sì come ad Arli, ove Rodano stagna,
> sì com' a Pola, presso del Carnaro
> ch'Italia chiude e suoi termini bagna,
> fanno i sepolcri tutt'il loco varo.[56]

Dante's passage intertwined Istria's place at the "confines" of Italy with its Roman heritage, its landscape marked by broken, ruined Roman tombs. In the last passage of his chorography, Coppo makes a similar geographical distinction. "There are two large mountains close to the Alps: they separate Italy from the barbarous nations. One, between Maistro and the north, is called Monte Caldiera, above the Gulf of Trieste. The other is between Grego and the east above the Carner, called Monte Mazor. And this is the site of Istria."[57] In Coppo's formulation, two great peaks cleaving to the Alps separate Italy from the "barbarous nations": mountains that form part of a boundary overlooking Trieste, Friuli, and the Istrian peninsula. The mountains embody the tension in Coppo's conception of the Istrian peninsula as both particularly vulnerable to and protected from barbarian attack. They are a natural but unpredictable boundary separating Italy—and, notably, Istria too—from the uncivilized world of northern Europe; but the history that Coppo elaborated in the preceding text would seem to indicate the fallibility of that natural border.

The same idea of a mountainous border region that hemmed in Istria with the rest of Italy is represented in Coppo's maps: both in his regional map of Istria in the chorography and in his maps of the Adriatic included in his *De toto orbe* atlas. Particularly in the first map of the Italian peninsula and Adriatic Sea in the atlas, Coppo depicted a forbidding, continuous mountain range that encircles northern Italy, before forming a border (contiguous with the physical border of the folio) above Friuli, Istria, and the Illyrian coast of Dalmatia.[58] In the second map, the border of the mountain range has grown even wider but ends at the eastern edge of Istria. In this map, Istria is the same deep yellow as the rest of the Italian peninsula and is edged with a dense depiction of the Alps; the rest of the Dalmatian Adriatic coast is a light yellow and lacks mountainous borders. Dalmatia seems to be both protected and unprotected, but certainly not part of Italy; this perhaps reflects Dalmatia's inclusion in the Venetian, rather than the Italian, geopolitical world.[59] This distinction is emphasized in the map of the Adriatic, Dalmatia, and Hungary. Here, Coppo again depicted the mountain range barrier that separates Italy, Istria, and the Adriatic coastline from the interior. But this map is intended to describe the toponymy and rivers of the inland space: Italy itself is left almost entirely blank, with only Venice depicted on the northern Adriatic shore (figure 8).[60] There is thus a sense in this map that Istria and the Dalmatian coast are identified with the Venetian metropole while the eastern interior and indeed the rest of the Italian peninsula are part of different geographical spheres.

In the woodcut map of Istria included in the Piran codex of Coppo's *Summa*, he used the depiction of mountains to even greater effect.[61] Here, in a large-scale regional chorographic depiction of the Istrian peninsula, the entire area north of the peninsula itself is covered in a very dense cover of mountains. Prominently marked in capital letters in the center of the peninsula is Montona, a large forest directly governed by the Venetian state. The mountains with their dense forests and Montona itself were of central importance to

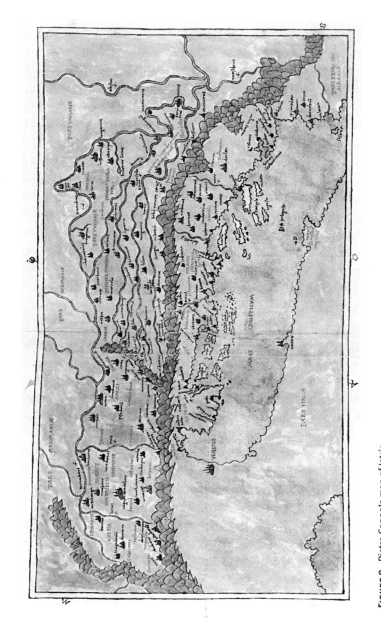

FIGURE 8. Pietro Coppo's map of Istria.

By kind permission of the Biblioteca dell'Archiginnasio, Bologna.

Venice, as crucial supplies of timber (used for building the piers on which the city rested, as well as its galleys) were sourced from Istria.[62] Regulated by Venetian governors from inland fortified towns like Raspo, and sent downstream to the coastal port cities, the timber resources of Istria are suggested in the map by the elaborate mountain ranges, the centrality of Montona, and the density of coastal towns controlling the estuaries. Istria's identity as an important site of natural resources is conveyed by the chorographic map, even in the absence of a representation of its geographical proximity to the metropole. The map thus ultimately shows Istria as its own autonomous local space: rich in resources but bounded by mountain ranges and by the border of the page, unmoored from larger geopolitical structures.[63]

By copying the ruined architecture, inscriptions, and histories of barbarian incursions into their own compositions, Coppo and his peers opened those ruined landscapes for historical revision. The present geopolitical identity of Istria was thus opened for revision, too. The physical and textual incompleteness of Istria—indicated, for these scholars, by its eroded Roman monuments and the destruction of its texts by barbarians—allowed them creative space to imagine a new kind of Istrian history. As Coppo explained, this history had a strong sense of progression and culmination in the flight of Roman patricians from their sacked city and their resettlement in Istria, Aquileia, and Friuli. Istria represented the threat posed by the absence of civilization: its ruined landscape and linguistic diversity were testimony to what happened when the mountain boundaries were breached. Istrian chorography became a compelling genre for humanists, as it symbolized the aims of the entire humanist reconstructive project for antiquity, in a style of writing that intimately connected the physical, eyewitness remains of the past, and its texts.

That these humanist writers emphasized the antiquity, the *Romanità*, and the Italian geographical identity of Istria does not emerge only from their interest in humanist scholarship. The geopolitical ambiguity of the region—whether it was to be defined as part of the Venetian mainland or maritime empire—could be effectively resolved by revising Istrian history to reconcile it with the present. This was a period when Venice itself was politically and culturally attending more and more to the rest of mainland Italy; it was in this context that the humanists working in Istria promoted their own region's affiliations with Roman conceptions of Italian identity.[64] Indeed, as Thomas Dandelet has argued, a particularly imperial form of humanist political thought, modeled on the texts and political figures of Imperial Rome, became increasingly important in these decades in which the Spanish and French presence in Italy deepened.[65] That many of the texts examined here were produced in imitation of Roman antiquarianism, whether through textual traditions or personal friendships, seems to indicate that in a very important sense, Venetian conceptions of political space competed intensely with their sense of the space of ancient Rome and its imperial colonies. Coppo, a Venetian imperial scribe who became deeply integrated into Isolan society, could construct classical geographical and political identities for himself and for his adopted homeland of Istria, in the face of a complex set of allegiances and administrative practices associated with Venice.

Conclusion

The writings produced by the circle of humanist scholars around the figure of Pietro Coppo indicate how a particular genre, chorography, came to be associated with Veneto-Dalmatian scholarship about the region of Istria. These men involved in administering and writing about the Venetian colonial world in the eastern Adriatic established a tradition of chorographic scholarship, built on the archaeological, epigraphical, and regional historical texts produced in Rome in the second half of the Quattrocento. These texts, with their emphasis on the description and recovery of the built environment of the classical city, appealed to the Veneto-Dalmatian humanists living in Istria. Istrian scholars would have seen in their own landscape the kinds of ruins and physical evidence of antiquity that Leto and Flavio so imaginatively reconstructed. But Coppo and his peers also saw in Istrian ruins, and in Roman archaeological scholarship, an opportunity to adapt the geopolitical and historical identity of Istria in the face of contemporary political and personal ambiguities in identity. The complex sets of political allegiances and administrative practices that characterized Coppo's family life in Isola, and indeed the history of Istria under Venetian domination more generally, could be accommodated into a local sense of identity and history by affiliating the region with that of the imperial Roman colony, and its related texts, inscriptions, and built environments.[66]

However, it would be a mistake to see these writers' interests in Roman ruins and antiquarian scholarship as the manifestation of a straightforward desire to write an entirely Roman past for Istria and Friuli, to the exclusion of Venetian history and heritage in the region. As we have seen in Coppo's will, he maintained his desire to be considered part of Venetian intellectual society at his death. Sanudo's *Itinerario* employed humanistic methods of documenting the physical world to record both classical and Venetian inscriptions, Roman buildings, and the deeds of Venetian colonial governors. Venetian and Dalmatian humanists and governors maintained relationships with each other and, crucially, with the metropole, through bequests, dedications, and the use of particular genres. The imperial relationships that these men imagined did not link only to ancient Rome, just as they did not link only to contemporary Venice. The history, heritage, and geographical identities elaborated in the texts and maps were part of a distinctive strand of humanist writing: one that adapted Roman ruins and Roman history to the geopolitical configurations of the contemporary Venetian empire. The physical remains of Roman history did not allude to Rome-the-metropole but rather to the Roman Imperial history within their colonies. For Coppo and his peers, humanist chorographic writing provided an intellectual framework for imagining the history and geopolitical space of the colonies, and its focus was the connections, links, and networks between metropole and colony, the space of the threshold between the *Serenissima Repubblica* and the *stato da mar*.

For Coppo, it is tempting to imagine that this alternative geographical and historical identity that he elaborated for Istria was linked to his own personal history in the region. He subjectively experienced this threshold space between Venice and its empire. Excluded from patrician society, he found in Venetian humanism the social links and intellectual abilities that allowed him to launch a career in the empire. And yet he did not return to Venice to pursue what he had started, either politically or socially. He instead created an entirely new life as an Isolan. Indeed, Coppo seems to have found an alternative intellectual approach alongside his new subjective perspective. From his study in Isola and from his perspective as Colotta's husband, as an Istrian landowner, and as a local dignitary, the Venetian empire looked different—so did his place within it.

Conclusion

Writing Empire from the Margins

Both Bembo and Coppo inhabited the margins of Venetian political and intellectual society. Their marginal condition was particularly meaningful in Venice, where perhaps to a greater degree than any other early modern city, the boundaries of the cultural, political, and social elite were coterminous. These boundaries mapped very closely onto the list of names in the *Libro d'Oro*, the book of patrician membership, which, as we have seen, proved contentious for both Coppo's and Bembo's families. Bembo was a member of the patriciate and enjoyed all of the benefits of membership, until he had children with a Corfiote woman. Coppo was never a member, the only person in his household to be disenfranchised while his father, half brothers, and stepmother all were impeccably patrician. Rather than fighting for his legitimacy, he pursued a family life and career in the empire, integrating himself into a different kind of patrician community. As humanists, Bembo and Coppo participated in the institutions and scholarship of the main academic circles of Venice but were never prominent writers, teachers, or editors. As governors, they held minor posts within the Venetian empire, until their trajectories of office holding veered widely off-course with their marriages to unsuitable women. Through the specular histories of Bembo and Coppo, we have seen what it meant to live on the margins of patrician political society and culture in early modern Venice and in its empire.

As we saw particularly in chapters 1 and 2, Bembo and Coppo were "secondary" or minor humanists, affiliated to the elite intellectual circles of Sabellico, Brugnolo, Egnazio, Aldus, and Leto, but not at their heart. These minor humanists and the secondary audiences of humanism have only very recently become the subjects of intellectual histories.[1] This historiographical legacy has meant that not only Bembo and Coppo but many men (and women) like them wrote texts that are not now considered to be representative of the dominant cultural center of humanist practice in Venice. Bembo has been remembered as a member of Aldus's circle; Coppo, within Istrian historiography and the history of cartography as the first to map the peninsula.[2] But they, and many others like them, have been effectively excluded from the history of humanism.

In this respect, this book has contributed to our understanding of secondary or minor humanistic texts—letters, marginalia, geographical writing, even vernacular literature—that should be used to expand our current understanding of who participated in humanism and what kinds of media they used to do so. These sources reveal the kind of private writing previously thought to be nonexistent in Venice.[3] Many of the sources from which we have previously constructed social histories of humanism were aimed at wider publics. Funeral orations, treatises, and textual scholarship were written to be read aloud or circulated in manuscript, even within relatively small scholarly communities. But private scholarship, the Greek and Latin excerpts found in the margins of Bembo's vernacular geographical encyclopedia, or the homemade woodcut maps of Crete in the single beloved copy of Coppo's atlas are evidence of the different forms and media of humanism, typically overlooked in histories of both humanism and of private writing.

By attending to a greater diversity of personal humanist writings and mappings, and to their intertextuality, we have also gained an unusual insight into the emotional tenor of lifelong humanist practice. Bembo's and Coppo's humanism was deeply scholarly, forged in the vibrant intellectual communities of the Scuola, at the printing presses of Venice, through friendships with teachers and brilliant fellow students. But it was also intensely personal, a scholarly practice that developed and changed over the course of their lifetimes as they encountered the scholars and material culture of the Mediterranean world. Their humanist practice developed to describe and interrogate their new lives in the empire. The span of Bembo's and Coppo's scholarship across their lifetimes, and the density and variety of these sources, has meant that we have been able to sense the emotional depths of humanist practice for the first time.

For future research, these kinds of sources may be used to explore the relationship between humanism and political culture in Venice and elsewhere. As we saw in chapters 5 and 6, Bembo's and Coppo's humanist reading and writing were at the crux of their perception of the political space of the Venetian empire. A majority of the patrician men who filled the offices of the empire had received some form of a classical, humanistic education, and as we saw, this humanist education had important implications for the way in which these men would perceive the Mediterranean world. There was a literary culture in Renaissance Venice that was rooted in humanist scholarship, but that was concerned chiefly with documenting the past and present of the Mediterranean: in epigraphical albums, archaeological scholarship, and geographical writing and mapping. Venetian humanism, particularly in its Mediterranean dimensions, was the political culture of the governing elite in Venice and in its maritime state—even if we must look for this political culture in the margins of manuscripts and in secondary humanistic texts, rather than in political treatises or orations.

On the geographical margins of empire, these men elaborated distinctive geographies and histories of the Venetian maritime state. In their writings and their uses of geography and cartography, Bembo and Coppo sketched what their empire looked like from the political, social, and even physical margins: intellectual historians must consider what happened to humanism outside of its geographical and social center of gravity. For Bembo and Coppo, translating their humanist education to the Mediterranean was intensely personal and subjective. It involved a deepening interest in geography. It relied on a jumbled mixture of manuscript and print; of Latin, Greek, and the vernacular; of classical history and Venetian maritime history and legends. As we saw in chapter 2, Venetian humanism was deeply tied to the Mediterranean physical landscape and material culture. The ways in which early modern empire was written from the margins of intellectual and political life may provide a new perspective on the relationships between literary culture and colonial governance, both in the *stato da mar* and perhaps beyond it.

These men were also themselves marginal within the bureaucratic office-holding structure of Venetian governance, both at home in the city and in the empire. Bembo's post in Skiathos was unimportant within the larger scheme of imperial governance. Coppo's imperial career began auspiciously enough, until he began working for the colony instead of the empire. They formed families there with women who were their own colonial subjects: cementing even further their in-between status within the Venetian state. Bembo and Coppo were failures according to the patriciate's own ideal of itself as "homogeneous and harmonious," in which the link between these ideas of the purity of the aristocracy and their political accord was particularly important.[4]

These families were mixed and thus excluded—or, after much strife, only partially included—from the documentary repositories of patrician social life. Bembo and Coppo were part of a minority of men who married women from outside Venice. But a vast majority of the men who governed the Venetian empire were also husbands and fathers, making up more traditional patrician families. Thanks to the work of Stanley Chojnacki and others, we know a great deal about the importance of family connections maintained through marriage contracts, dowries, and testaments. Social historians of the Venetian patrician family have long understood how important marriage and reproduction were to the political coherence of the patriciate, and the central roles that women and children played in those relationships.[5] In the context of the empire, Monique O'Connell has explored the ways in which Venetian men relied on their family relationships to consolidate their office-holding and trading strategies.[6]

But we know much less about the history of imperial women and families. Cyurω and Colotta, Urania and Angela, the Coppo boys' five Istrian wives: these are only a very small number of the women of the Venetian Mediterranean whose experiences have largely been effaced from our histories of its empire. By reading their husbands' and fathers' writings with careful attention to the particularities of early modern life-writing—its formal diversity and retrospective intertextuality, especially—we have been able to gain fresh insight into the worlds of these women in Venice, the Greek islands, and the Istrian coast. The historical project of recovery of women's lives in early modern empire is an important one. But this kind of analysis must sit alongside a deeper consideration of gender, the body, and interior experience, too. Who were the Venetian "men of empire" as fathers, husbands, brothers? How did family concerns about marriage, sexuality, and childbearing shape experiences of empire, and what was the place more widely of intimate relationships within the wider political culture of the empire? Bembo's and Coppo's mixed marriages have offered a particularly useful perspective from which to explore the intersections of gender, ethnicity, and social identity as they unfolded across the early modern Mediterranean. This book has offered one view of what a history of the Venetian empire might look like if we took seriously these questions of gender and the family. But much of the intimate life in the Venetian Mediterranean world remains to be explored. This, in my view, is potentially the most exciting path for future research.

One of the implications of this book's consideration of women's interior lives and experiences has been to level a critique at the primacy of agency in gender history, and in the history of "border crossing" or "global" women, in particular.[7] As Lynn Thomas has argued, the question of agency, its nature and extent, often becomes an argument in itself, an ending to a conversation about gender and power, rather than a conceptual tool.[8] Certainly, we have analyzed and interrogated the ways in which Cyurω and Colotta were able to shape their circumstances. We have seen where senses of belonging intersected to create moments of possibility, as during Cyurω's triumphal return to the Greek islands during her walk on Crete, or when Colotta's economic and social influence reached its culmination in the marriages of her five sons. And we have seen the frustrations and even despair when these women could not shape their circumstances, most dramatically on Cyurω's final conflict with Domenico and her ensuing illness and death. But I have also tried to show throughout the book the ways in which the interior lives and experiences of these women exceeded the boundaries of the dynamic of power and limitation that we understand as female agency. For Cyurω and Colotta, as well as for their husbands, I have been interested above all in their desires, needs, emotions, and perceptions of self-regard as they changed and evolved over the course of their lifetimes. These are the features of human experience that, in Thomas's words, may "exceed rational calculation," and so are often neglected in gender histories.[9] In the final section of the book, it is to the collective dimensions of the interior lives of Bembo, Coppo, Cyurω, and Colotta that I turn next.

Myth and Reality

In their scholarship, careers, and family choices, Bembo and Coppo failed to meet the high standards required to fully belong to the inner circles of patrician life, instead remaining on its margins. Coppo was disadvantaged from the start, of course, but nevertheless turned from a promising career within the Venetian imperial bureaucracy to start a different kind of career in Isola. On the margins of the patriciate, Bembo and Coppo (and particularly Cyurω and their children) felt the full weight of what it meant to fail to fulfill the expectations of the patriciate class. Probably the most well-known expression of those expectations is the "myth of Venice," a much-discussed, much-critiqued elaboration of political and social ideals related to the stability, peace, and justice that supposedly differentiated the Venetian republic from all other polities in late medieval and early modern Europe. In this epilogue, I wish to draw out some provisional ideas for a new approach to the myth of Venice, based on the tensions between myth and reality, ideal and failure, which have characterized the Bembo and Coppo family stories throughout this book.

The patriciate was the keystone of the myth of Venice as it was elaborated in the fifteenth and sixteenth centuries. The patriciate was intended to be a bulwark of defense against historical change, the source of Venice's ability to politically withstand the transformations wrought by the external forces of history. As Gasparo Contarini wrote in his *De magistratibus et Republica Venetorum*, Venice alone was able to stop "the movable wheel of fortune."[10] And it was the patriciate—not only with its political institutions but with its social ones, particularly those related to marriage and reproduction—that was responsible for this defense. As discussed in chapter 3, Francesco Barbaro wrote in his *De re uxoria*, "While other things are uncertain, shifting, and transitory, this legacy of nobility is fixed with secure roots, can withstand any force, and will never be destroyed."[11] Borrowing from Thucydides and from the ancient example of Sparta, Barbaro saw the patriciate as a physical embodiment of this resistance to change. "So we may call those born thus honorably 'the walls of the city.'"[12] Venice, the city famously without walls, at the mercy of the lagoon and the Adriatic tides, battled against the forces of transformation through the physical stability and endurance of its patriciate class and their institutions.

The myth of Venice was predicated on a deep resistance to change, and the patriciate was meant to embody the conservative, stable defense to any such transformative threats. And indeed, we have seen the psychic costs of transformation within the social world and political culture defined by this mythology, in the family stories described in these pages. We have tracked our subjects' lives across multiple transformational trajectories: transitions from adolescence to adulthood; of social mobility; of intersections of gender, ethnic, and class identities; of evolving emotional histories, political subjectivities, and methods of private writing. Giovanni Bembo ended his life seemingly angry and isolated, parceling out blame in his autobiographical letter. According to Bembo, Cyurω ended her life anxious and ill over the futures of her children. Domenico Bembo succeeded in accessing the elite inner realm of the patriciate, marrying patrician women three times over. He achieved greater upward social mobility than his father, and yet seemed to have done so by alienating his natal family. On the margins of the empire, Urania Bembo suffered through the violent ordeal of her sexual scandal and abortion. For the Bembo family, the emotional consequences of the belief in the myth and their failure to live up to its mark were dark indeed.

Pietro Coppo, particularly if we rely on his final testament, seems to have reached an uneasy emotional equilibrium between his imperfect origins in Venice and his new life in Istria, as he reached both backward to his life in Venice fifty years before and forward to his family's colonial legacy as landholders in Isola. Coppo transformed from a marginal figure in Venetian political society and intellectual life to a central figure in Isolan municipal politics, highly regarded in Isola for his intellectual pursuits. Colotta and indeed her and Coppo's five sons were also central to Isolan life, as Colotta was a member of the local nobility and the sons benefited from their parents' central status through land and careers in Istrian municipal administration. Coppo transformed from a figure on the margins of the very large imperial and social structures of Venice to the center of political society in the tiny seaside town of Isola—even while his ability to make this transformation was conditioned by his belonging to Venetian intellectual society. While he achieved political and economic success in Isola, the emotional consequences of this transformation were profoundly ambivalent.

Of course, in their family lives and political choices, Bembo and Coppo were not alone in failing to live up to the impossibly high expectations put on the members of the Venetian political class. As James Grubb has written in his well-known article on the myth of Venice, social and political historians have documented the many ways in which Venetian patrician men failed to live up to their own mythologies. We now have revisionist histories of the patriciate that understand them as corrupt, violent, and petty—in short, subject to the same shortcomings as the rest of humanity.[13] But as Grubb argued, what is important is that "Venetians evidently believed and acted on their myths,"[14] even while failing to live up to them. Venetian historians have taken up this question of belief, focusing on the ways in which the myth of Venice was reflected back to Venetians themselves.[15] The myth has been deconstructed through empirical critiques of patrician behavior, motivations, and intentions; more recently, Filippo de Vivo has shown how Venetians and their skeptics began to critically reexamine and revise aspects of Venetian mythology.[16]

But how did Venetians internalize these myths, how did mythology shape their actions, and what were the emotional costs of failure? Historians have largely ignored the psychic and emotional significance of this mythology, and its consequences for the men and women who lived under its influence. If, as Grubb writes, the importance of the myth is that Venetians believed in it and acted on it, we must discover the interior dimensions of that belief and those actions. In our parallel family histories, we have seen intensely personal reckonings between myth and reality. We have seen how Venetian men and their families fought for, combatted, and reconciled themselves with the pervasive mythologies of the Venetian state and its patrician governing class, as they repeatedly failed to live up to its impossible ideals. These negotiations were emotional and had implications for their most intimate family lives, on marriage, reproduction, and the childhoods of their sons and daughters.[17] Piecing together their education, intellectual work, family histories, and private writing alongside their political activity, the book has shown how the ideals of an imperial political society acted on the interior lives of the early modern men, women, and children who navigated between empire and metropole.

The myth of Venice, then, was not only an important component of European political history and theory. It was also intensely important in the private sphere, for the people whose lives were shaped by a deep belief in its ideals. The myth of Venice was a fantasy, a collective articulation of, and participation in, a set of powerful desires, beliefs, and illusions.[18] To my mind, studying the myth of Venice not only as a political phenomenon but as a cultural, subjective, and interior one is now an urgent task for historians of Venice. For Bembo, a deep belief in the collective fantasy of his own class led to destruction, violence, and alienation. Coppo ultimately rejected the fantasy of patrician belonging, even while at the very end of his life he seemed rather more ambivalent about this choice. The interior dimensions of this fantasy drove the people who believed in it in meaningful ways. They did not always act rationally or according to objective interests, but then the collective fantasy to which they subscribed was not rational or objective, either. The stories in this book, then, reveal to us how the sometimes unfathomable desires and illusions of fantasy could shape the lives of early modern Venetian men and women.

Appendix I

Giovanni Bembo describes Cyurω's final illness and death, and the death of his daughter Angela.[1]

Cupiebat Cyurω mea, ut duae filiae nostrae coniugarentur, et ego quoque cupiebam et optabam. Sed lex est: posse dotare filiam quatuor millibus ducatis. . . . Sed quia mea Cyurω sciebat peculium nostrum et censum non excedere duo millia ducatorum, hanc ob rem paupercula sese macerabat. Accedebat dolori misellae, quod Modestinus filius noster qui, dum parvus esset, grammaticen, poeticen et Arithmeticen ita discebat, ut omnibus aequalibus anteiret, postea vero, quam ex ephebis excessit, ita libros odit ut aperire eos metuere videatur, nec studet alicui rei, quae ad virtutem frugemue pertineat. Et quia alter filius Dominicus ob matrimonium meum cum mea Cyurω secundum civitatis leges factum Venetam Maioris Consilii nobilitatem sive arrogantiam et superbiam adeptus est, dedignabatur meam Cyurω, suam esse matrem et saepe obiiciebat nationem, patriam, genus et indotatam esse, pluraque alia eiusmodi. Cogita tu et animo tuo versa, quomodo illa filiorum et ignaviam et convitia tanta pateretur? Quae gratiam ab illis gratam expectabat? His morbis animi adcessit etiam morbus corporis, quo die quinto decimo continentibus et continuis febribus sine remissione ardentibus mortua est.

Quum meam Cyurω, sed non amplius meam, sacerdotes ipsae Sanctae Mariae miraculorum laverunt et illa induta fuit ab ipsis religiosis vestimentis Sanctae Clarae—sic enim se mea Cyurω sepeliri iusserat ultimis suis elogiis—domi cadaver a vigilibus seruatum quatuor et viginti horas, inde exportatum in aedem Sancti Canciani. . . . Hoc tibi meae verum et sociae meae vitae curriculum descripsi, quae mecum vixit annos XXXVIII menses II dies XXX horas X.

His absolutis, ne curae, lachrymae, ploratus et moesti clamores domi cessarent, sed dolor dolore luctusque luctu cumulate augeretur, Angela filia mea XII die post matris obitum mortua est, ita ut intra vigesimum septimum diem fata crudelia et praepostera natura me uxore charissima dulcissimaque filia privarint. Quarum morbos non cognitos a medicis latini enim medici mederi conabantur Dialectica suisque Syllogismis, medici autem graeci auctoritate et existimatione. Itaque intelligis, in quo nunc statu et quot moeroribus coacervatis tuus Joannes Bembus versetur.

APPENDIX II

Giovanni Bembo describes how the rumor of his scandal on Skiathos spread.[1]

Testicularii huius iudicii fama no modo vagata et per Graetiam Thessaliam Thratiam, verum per Hellespontum et Cyaneis Symplegadibusque insulis superatis Pontum Euxinum penetravit, et praetereundo oram Calcedoniorum, quae nunc Scutari dicitur, per Paphlagoniam Sinopem a Lucullo Romano iam subactam Diogenisque patriam Gallatiorum Cappadocumque aures implevit, apud quod nos Veneti Trapezum habuimus et forum et domus et castrum nobis ab imperatore Trapezi datum, quod castrum a nobis fuit corroboratum et muris munitum et vexillum S. Marci Veneti in illo tantum erigebatur. Rector autem illius castri creabatur Venetiis. Illius tituli erant Orator, Baiules et Rector Orator ad Imperatorem Trapezi, Baiulus propter mercatores, Rector autem quia non solum causas pecuniarias iudicabat, verum etiam maleficios puniebat. Penes hunc Rectorem sedebant duo Consiliarii electi Trapezi. . . . In castro Venetico Trapezi Veneti habebant scribas, interpretes, praecones et alios ministros, publico stipendio solutos ipseque Rector quotannis habebat ducator quingentos. . . . Octo et interdum decem onerariae nundinariaeque triremes navigabant in Pontum Euxinum, earum partim Trapezum, partim Tanam et partim ad alia loca. Ipsa fama Pontum, regionem Medeae, etiam velociter pertransivit, ubi nunc habitant Lazei, Colchosque et Phasida fluvium et Cercetas populos, Mengreli nunc et Cerchasi dictos, profecta tandem paludem Meotidem ingressa permenso amne Tanais 18 millia passuum Tanam civitatem pervenit. Quae civitas Tana

Venetorum fuit ipsamque ab Usbech et postea a Zanibech imperatoribus Tartarorum habuere. Quorum imperatorum regnum erat usque Astracam sive Citracham, emperium et regiam imperatorum, quae civitas Citracam sita est super fluvio Volga Edil sive Rha ubi fluit in mare Caspium. Nostri autem totum regnum appellabant Gazan. Et saepe Tana diruta, depredata et combusta a Tartaris. . . . Praeda autem anni 1334 fuit quatercentena millia ducatorum et plurimi Veneti interfecti. . . . Michael Stenus Dux anno 1400 Tanam misit Petrum Lauredanum Consulem et Rectorem, cuius salarium quotannis erant ducati DCCC. Habebat socium Admiratum, quinque famulos, quinque equos. Tanae etiam erant Consiliarii duo nobiles Veneti . . . Habebant XX ballistarios et armamentarium, sclopetos 50, bombardas, ballistas cum suis sagittis et scuta oblonga. Erat etiam ibi interpres linguae Tartatorum et Schytarum et Praecones tres et aliquot Bastonerii. . . . Ea ipsa fama modo currens modo navigans modo volans has omnes regiones hoc testiculari iudicio complevit.

Notes

Introduction

1. "Fata crudelia et praepostera natura." Unless otherwise noted, all translations are my own. Bembo's autobiographical letter is included in his personal miscellany manuscript: BSM, CLM 10801. The autobiographical letter (not the entire manuscript) was edited by Theodor Mommsen. Giovanni Bembo, "Autobiographie des Venezianers Giovanni Bembo (1536)," ed. Theodor Mommsen, *Sitzungsberichten der Kaiserlichen Akademie der Wissenschaften* (1861): 581–609. In his autobiographical letter, Bembo rendered his wife's name in a mixture of Latin and Greek letters, and I have reproduced his spelling here. I discuss her name at greater length in chapter 3.

2. "Proh dolor! Cyurω mea obiit tertio calendas Nouembris hora decima noctis. Quae septimum decimum agebat annum et ego vigesimum quartum quando isthic Corcyrae sociati sumus." Bembo, "Autobiographie des Venezianers Giovanni Bembo (1536)," 584.

3. "ita libros odit ut aperire eos metuere videatur, nec studet aliqui rei, quae ad virtutem frugemue pertineat." Ibid., 604.

4. Archival documentation relating to Coppo's life in Istria, including his will, is partially published in Pietro Coppo, "Di Pietro Coppo e delle sue opere: documenti inediti e l'opusculo *Del Sito De Listria* ristampato dall' edizione del 1540," ed. Attilio Degrassi, *L'Archeografo triestino: raccolta di opuscoli notizie per Trieste e per L'Istria*, 3rd ser., 11 (1924): 319–87. Coppo's testament, 370–73. Degrassi's article was republished in *Scritti Vari di Antichità* (Trieste, 1971), 4: 367–423. Citations throughout refer to the original 1924 publication.

5. Coppo, "Di Pietro Coppo e delle sue opere": marriage contracts for Antonio, 359–60; Francesco, 360–62; Vincenzo, 366–67; Giovanni, 367–68; Marco, 368–70.

6. Ibid., 411.

7. Margaret King, *Venetian Humanism in an Age of Patrician Dominance* (Princeton, NJ: Princeton University Press, 1986); and King, "The Venetian Intellectual World," in *A Companion to Venetian History, 1400–1797*, ed. Eric R. Dursteler (Leiden: Brill, 2013): 571–614.

8. Patricia Fortini Brown, *Venice and Antiquity: The Venetian Sense of the Past* (New Haven, CT: Yale University Press, 1996) remains the best account of the Venetian uses of the physical remains of antiquity.

9. Bembo edited a philological volume: *In hoc volumine haec continentur: Marci Antonii Sabellici annotationes veteres et recentes: ex Plinio: Livio: & pluribus authoribus* (Venice: Iacobum Pentium de Leuco, 1502); and Pietro Coppo, *Del Sito de Listria* (Venice: Francesco Bindoni and Maffeo Pasini, 1540).

10. Bartolomeo dalli Sonetti [pseud.], *Isolario* (Venice: Guilelmus Anima Mia, Tridinensis?, not after 1485). BEst, Alfa E. 5. 15.

11. For Venice and its empire (overviews; local studies can be found in the bibliography): Monique O'Connell, *Men of Empire: Power and Negotiation in Venice's Maritime State* (Baltimore: Johns Hopkins University Press, 2009); Benjamin Arbel, "Venice's Maritime Empire in the Early Modern Period," in *A Companion to Venetian History, 1400–1797*, ed. Eric R. Dursteler (Leiden: Brill, 2013), 125–253; Michel Balard, ed., *État et colonisation au Moyen Âge et à la Renaissance* (Lyon: La Manufacture, 1989); and Bernard Doumerc, "Il dominio del mar," in *Storia di Venezia: Il Rinascimento. Politica e cultura*, ed. Alberto Tenenti and Ugo Tucci (Rome: Enciclopedia Italiana, 1996), 4: 113–80.

12. King, *Venetian Humanism*; and King, "The Venetian Intellectual World."

13. For example, Eric R. Dursteler, *Venetians in Constantinople: Nation, Identity, and Coexistence in the Early Modern Mediterranean* (Baltimore: Johns Hopkins University Press, 2006); Sally McKee, *Uncommon Dominion: Venetian Crete and the Myth of Ethnic Purity* (Philadelphia: University of Pennsylvania Press, 2000); and E. Natalie Rothman, *Brokering Empire: Trans-Imperial Subjects between Venice and Istanbul* (Ithaca, NY: Cornell University Press, 2011).

14. For early modern "imperial humanism," see Thomas J. Dandelet, *The Renaissance of Empire in Early Modern Europe* (Cambridge: Cambridge University Press, 2014. For Venice specifically, see David S. Chambers, *The Imperial Age of Venice* (London: Thames & Hudson, 1970).

15. On social boundaries, regulations, and mobility in early modern Venice: Victor Crescenzi, *Esse de Maiori Consilio: Legittimità civile e legittimazione politica nella Repubblica di Venezia (sec. XIII–XVI)* (Rome: Istituto Palazzo Borromini, 1996); Anna Bellavitis, *Identité, mariage, mobilité sociale. Citoyennes et citoyens à Venise au XVᵉ siécle* (Rome: École française de Rome, 2001); and more generally, Claudio Donati, *L'idea di nobiltà in Italia: secoli XIV–XVIII* (Rome: Laterza, 1988). Alexander Cowan offers an analysis of this literature in his introduction to *Marriage, Manners and Mobility in Early Modern Venice* (Aldershot: Ashgate, 2007).

16. O'Connell, *Men of Empire*. For a Florentine parallel, see William J. Connell, "The Humanist Citizen as Provincial Governor," in *Florentine Tuscany: Structures and Practices of Power*, ed. W. J. Connell and Andrea Zorzi (Cambridge: Cambridge University Press, 2000): 144–64.

17. Like Monique O'Connell's work, these social histories of the Venetian patriciate are foundational for the analysis undertaken here. Among the works I refer to most frequently are Donald Queller, *The Venetian Patriciate: Reality versus Myth* (Urbana: University of Illinois Press, 1986); Dennis Romano, *Patricians and Popolani: The Social Foundations of the Venetian Renaissance State* (Baltimore: Johns Hopkins University Press, 1987); and Stanley Chojnacki, *Women and Men in Renaissance Venice: Twelve Essays on Patrician Society* (Baltimore: Johns Hopkins University Press, 2000). Also see Dorit Raines, *L'invention du mythe aristocratique: l'image de soi du patriciat vénitien au temps de la Sérénissime*, 2 vols. (Venice: Istituto Veneto di Scienze, Lettere ed Arti, 2006).

18. Yuen-Gen Liang, *Family and Empire: The Fernández de Córdoba and the Spanish Realm* (Philadelphia: University of Pennsylvania Press, 2011).

19. Anthony Grafton, *Defenders of the Text: The Traditions of Scholarship in an Age of Science, 1450–1800* (Cambridge, MA: Harvard University Press, 1991), 50; and Martin Lowry, *The World of Aldus Manutius: Business and Scholarship in Renaissance Venice* (Oxford: Blackwell, 1979), 51.

20. Biondo Flavio, Pietro Coppo, Giovanni Baptisa Goineo, Leando Alberti, and Ludovico Vergerio, "Corografie dell'Istria," in *Archeografo Triestino*, ed. Pietro Kandler, 1st ser., 2 (1830): 13–100.

21. BSM, CLM 10801.

22. Bembo's copy of Petrarch's Latin works, *Librorum Francisci Petrarche impressorum annotatio* (Venice: Simon Bevilacqua, 1503) is BL, 11421. k. 13; his annotated Lucretius, *De rerum natura* (Venice: Theodorus de Ragazonibus, 1495) is BTriv, Inc. c. 54; and his manuscript collection of Cicero's texts is BAV, Vat. Pal. Lat. 1476. His annotated copy of a Greek grammar textbook is *Institutiones Graecae grammatices* (Venice: Aldus Manutius, 1497), BNM, Incun. D 393 D 150. His annotated *Isolario*, or geographical encyclopedia of islands, is BEst, Alfa E. 5. 15.

23. Giovanni Bembo, ed., *In haec volumine continentur: Marci Antonii Sabellici annotationes* (Venice: Iacobum Pentium de Leuco, 1502).

24. *De toto orbe* survives in its most complete form in a manuscript: BCA, Ms. A. 117. On this manuscript, see Roberto Almagià, "The Atlas of Pietro Coppo, 1520," *Imago Mundi* 7 (1950): 48–50. Another copy of the *De toto orbe*, which contains only text, is BnF, Fond. Lat. 9663. The Paris manuscript also contains a copy of Coppo's second geographical work, a summary of the encyclopedia called the *De summa totius orbius*, in both Latin and Italian. The *Summa* exists in two further recensions: one held in Piran, Sergej Mašera Maritime Museum, available in facsimile: Luciano Lago and Claudio Rossit, eds., *Pietro Coppo, Le "Tabulae" (1524–1526)* (Trieste, Italy: Lint, 1986); and BNM, Ms. Lat. X 146 (=3331). The copy of the *Summa* in Piran contains fifteen printed maps. Coppo also authored and created maps for his *Portolano* (Venice: Augustino di Bindoni, 1528); and for *Del Sito de Listria* (Venice: Francesco Bindoni and Maffeo Pasini, 1540).

25. James S. Grubb, "Memory and Identity: Why Venetians Didn't Keep *Ricordanze*," *Renaissance Studies* 8, no. 4 (1994): 375–87. Also see Grubb, *Family Memoirs from Venice (15th to 17th Centuries)* (Rome: Viella, 2009).

26. Adam Smyth, *Autobiography in Early Modern England* (Cambridge: Cambridge University Press, 2010). Linda Colley discusses the use of a wide range of archival material, including maps, to construct the inner life of one early modern woman in *The Ordeal of Elizabeth Marsh: A Woman in World History* (London: Harper Press, 2007), xxx.

27. Smyth, *Autobiography in Early Modern England*, 11.

28. Barbara Taylor, "Separations of Soul: Solitude, Biography, History," *American Historical Review* 114, no. 3 (2009): 651.

29. Barbara Taylor, "Historical Subjectivity," in *History and Psyche: Culture, Psychoanalysis, and the Past*, ed. Sally Alexander and Barbara Taylor (Basingstoke: Palgrave Macmillan, 2012), 195–97; and Joan Wallach Scott, *The Fantasy of Feminist History* (Durham, NC: Duke University Press, 2011).

30. Lyndal Roper, *Oedipus and the Devil: Witchcraft, Religion and Sexuality in Early Modern Germany* (London: Routledge, 1994), 5.

31. On the social history of humanism in Venice, see King, *Venetian Humanism*; other works include Patricia H. Labalme, *Bernardo Guistiniani: A Venetian of the Quattrocento* (Rome: Edizioni di storia e letteratura, 1969); Felix Gilbert, "Humanism in Venice," in *Florence and Venice: Comparisons and Relations*, ed. Sergio Bertelli, Nicolai Rubinstein, and Craig Hugh Smith (Florence: La Nuova Italia, 1979), 1: 13–26; Vittore Branca, "Ermolao Barbaro and the Late Quattrocento Venetian Humanism," in *Renaissance Venice*, ed. J. R. Hale (London: Faber and Faber, 1973), 218–43; Branca, ed., *La sapienza civile: studi sull'umanesimo a Venezia* (Florence: L. S. Olschki, 1998); and Branca, *Lauro Quirini Umanista* (Florence: L. S. Olschki, 1977).

32. The exceptions to this are Gadi Algazi, "Scholars in Households: Refiguring the Learned Habitus, 1480–1550," *Science in Context* 16, nos. 1–2 (2003): 9–42; and Rosa Salzberg, "Masculine Republics: Establishing Authority in the Early Modern Venetian Printshop," in *Governing Masculinities in the Early Modern Period: Regulating Selves and Others*, ed. Susan Broomhall and Jacqueline Van Gent (Farnham: Ashgate, 2011), 47–65.

33. King, *Venetian Humanism*, 219, 244. Also see Clémence Revest's work on the use of Ciceronian oratory in conjunction with Venetian governance on the *terraferma*: "Les discours de Gasparino Barzizza et la diffusion du style cicéronien dans la première moitié du XVe siècle. Premiers aperçus," *Mélanges de l'Ecole française de Rome* 128, no. 1 (2016): 47–72.

34. Fortini Brown, *Venice and Antiquity*, 145–80.

35. Deno John Geanakoplos, *Greek Scholars in Venice: Studies in the Dissemination of Greek Learning from Byzantium to Western Europe* (Cambridge, MA: Harvard University Press, 1962).

36. David Holton, ed., *Literature and Society in Renaissance Crete* (Cambridge: Cambridge University Press, 1991); and Benjamin Arbel, Evelien Chayes, and Harald Hendrix, eds., *Cyprus and the Renaissance (1450–1650)* (Turnhout: Brepols, 2013). Also see Gilles Grivaud, *Entrelacs chiprois. Essai sur les lettres et la vie intellectuelle dans le royaume de Chypre (1191–1570)* (Nicosia: Moufflon Publications, 2009); and Alexandre Embiricos, *La renaissance crétoise*, vol. 1 (Paris: Société d'édition "Les belles lettres," 1960–67). For the Cretan built environment, see Maria Georgopoulou, *Venice's Mediterranean Colonies: Architecture and Urbanism* (Cambridge: Cambridge University Press, 2001).

37. Francesco Semi, "Umanesimo e libertà degli istriani," in *L'Umanesimo in Istria*, ed. Vittore Branca and Sante Graciotti (Florence: L. S. Olschki, 1983), 1–6.

38. Nancy Bisaha, *Creating East and West: Renaissance Humanists and the Ottoman Turks* (Philadelphia: University of Pennsylvania Press, 2004), 7.

39. Bisaha, *Creating East and West*; Kate Fleet, "Italian Perceptions of the Turks in the Fourteenth and Fifteenth Centuries," *Journal of Mediterranean Studies* 5, no. 2 (1995): 159–72; Margaret Meserve, "News from Negroponte: Politics, Popular Opinion, and Information Exchange in the First Decade of the Italian Press," *Renaissance Quarterly* 59, no. 2 (2006): 440–80; and Bronwen Wilson, *The World in Venice: Print, the City, and Early Modern Identity* (Toronto: University of Toronto Press, 2005).

40. Erin Maglaque, "The Literary Culture of the Venetian Mediterranean," *Italian Studies* 73, no. 1 (forthcoming).

41. Mary Beard, "Officers and Gentlemen? Roman Britain and the British Empire," in *From Plunder to Preservation: Britain and the Heritage of the Roman Empire, c. 1800–1940*,

ed. Astrid Swenson and Peter Mandler (Oxford: Oxford University Press, 2013), 49–62, is a parallel to my study of the role of a classical education in forming aristocratic governors' attitudes toward the history of their empire.

42. The book aims to answer Christopher Celenza's call for a more inclusive analysis of Latin literature by Renaissance intellectual historians. *The Lost Italian Renaissance: Humanists, Historians, and Latin's Legacy* (Baltimore: Johns Hopkins University Press, 2004). Also see Brian Maxson, *The Humanist World of Renaissance Florence, 1400–1480* (Cambridge: Cambridge University Press, 2014).

43. Paul O. Kristeller outlines his definition of humanism in *Renaissance Thought and Its Sources*, ed. Michael Mooney (New York: Columbia University Press, 1979), 21–30. He expands on his definition in "The Humanist Movement," in *Renaissance Thought: The Classic, Scholastic, and Humanistic Strains* (New York: Harper & Row, 1961), 10. The legacy of Kristeller's definition is outlined in Charles Nauert, "Renaissance Humanism: An Emergent Consensus and Its Critics," *Indiana Social Studies Quarterly* 33 (1980): 5–20.

44. Paul O. Kristeller, *Iter Italicum: A Finding List of Uncatalogued or Incompletely Catalogued Humanistic Manuscripts of the Renaissance*, 6 vols. (London: Warburg Institute, 1963–96).

45. For more on humanism outside Italy, see David Rundle, ed., *Humanism in Fifteenth-Century Europe* (Oxford: Society for the Study of Medieval Languages and Literature, 2012).

46. Dandelet, *The Renaissance of Empire*. Also see Cary J. Nederman, "Humanism and Empire: Aeneas Sylvius Piccolomini, Cicero and the Imperial Ideal," *Historical Journal* 36, no. 3 (1993): 499–515.

47. See the collected essays in James Hankins, ed., *Renaissance Civic Humanism: Reappraisals and Reflections* (Cambridge: Cambridge University Press, 2000).

48. For King's selection criteria, see *Venetian Humanism*, 257–66.

49. King, *Venetian Humanism*; Branca, *La sapienza civile* and "Ermolao Barbaro and the Late Quattrocento Venetian Humanism," in Hale, *Renaissance Venice*; Manlio Pastore Stocchi, "Scuola e cultura umanistica fra due secoli," in *Storia della cultura veneta*, vol. 3, *Dal primo Quattrocento al concilio di Trento*, ed. Girolamo Arnaldi and Manlio Pastore Stocchi (Vicenza: Neri Pozza, 1980–81), 92–121; also see Franco Gaeta's chapter in the same volume, "Storiografia, coscienza nazionale e politica culturale nella Venezia del Rinascimento," 1–91.

50. O'Connell, *Men of Empire*, 120. For scandal and gossip in the political culture of Venice, see Elizabeth Horodowich, "The Gossiping Tongue: Oral Networks, Public Life and Political Culture in Early Modern Venice," *Renaissance Studies* 19, no. 1 (2005): 23–45; and Filippo de Vivo, *Information and Communication in Venice: Rethinking Early Modern Politics* (Oxford: Oxford University Press, 2007).

51. Christiane Klapisch-Zuber and David Herlihy, *Tuscans and Their Families: A Study of the Florentine Catasto of 1427* (New Haven, CT: Yale University Press, 1985); and Klapisch-Zuber, *Women, Family, and Ritual in Renaissance Italy* (Chicago: University of Chicago Press, 1985). Also see F. W. Kent, *Household and Lineage in Renaissance Florence: The Family Life of the Capponi, Ginori, and Rucellai* (Princeton, NJ: Princeton University Press, 1977).

52. The work of Stanley Chojnacki was pioneering in this regard; his articles have been collected in *Women and Men in Renaissance Venice*. Also see Monica Chojnacka,

Working Women of Early Modern Venice (Baltimore: Johns Hopkins University Press, 2001); Cowan, *Marriage, Manners, and Mobility*; Joanne M. Ferraro, *Marriage Wars in Late Renaissance Venice* (Oxford: Oxford University Press, 2001); and Guido Ruggiero, *The Boundaries of Eros: Sex Crime and Sexuality in Renaissance Venice* (Oxford: Oxford University Press, 1985).

53. Patricia Fortini Brown, *Private Lives in Renaissance Venice: Art, Architecture, and the Family* (New Haven, CT: Yale University Press, 2004).

54. For example, P. Renée Baernstein and John Christopoulos, "Interpreting the Body in Early Modern Italy: Pregnancy, Abortion and Adulthood," *Past and Present* 223, no. 1 (2014): 45–75; and Jutta Sperling's work, both *Convents and the Body Politic in Late Renaissance Venice* (Chicago: University of Chicago Press, 1999), and *Roman Charity: Queer Lactations in Early Modern Visual Culture* (New York: Columbia University Press, 2017).

55. For Venice, see James C. Davis, *A Venetian Family and Its Fortune, 1500–1900: The Donà and the Conservation of Their Wealth* (Philadelphia: American Philosophical Society, 1975); for Florence, see Richard A. Goldthwaite, *Private Wealth in Renaissance Florence* (Princeton, NJ: Princeton University Press, 1968).

56. The classic article on the Venetian *fraterna* is Frederic C. Lane, "Family Partnerships and Joint Ventures in the Venetian Republic," *Journal of Economic History* 4, no. 2 (1944): 178–96.

57. O'Connell, *Men of Empire*; Liang, *Family and Empire*.

58. "The importance of individual and family histories alongside broader political developments for the relation between the personal and the political remains critical, even when trying to understand the configurations of global power." Catherine Hall, "Making Colonial Subjects: Education in the Age of Empire," *History of Education* 37, no. 6 (2008), 774. The study of "intimate frontiers" of empire was pioneered by Ann Laura Stoler in "Tense and Tender Ties: The Politics of Comparison in North American History and (Post)Colonial Studies," *Journal of American History* 88, no. 3 (2001): 829–65.

59. For example, Susanah Shaw Romney, *New Netherland Connections: Intimate Networks and Atlantic Ties in Seventeenth-Century America* (Chapel Hill: University of North Carolina Press, 2014); and Ann Twinam, *Public Lives, Private Secrets: Gender, Honor, Sexuality and Illegitimacy in Colonial Spanish America* (Stanford, CA: Stanford University Press, 1999).

60. Grafton, *Defenders of the Text*, 50.

61. BEst, Alfa E. 5. 15.

62. Esme Cleall, Laura Ishiguro, and Emily J. Manktelow, "Imperial Relations: Histories of Family in the British Empire," *Journal of Colonialism and Colonial History* 14, no. 1 (2013): n.p.

63. "Quamvic Graeca esset, non multum tamen Graecos amabat." Bembo, "Autobiographie des Venezianers Giovanni Bembo (1536)," 595.

64. This is in contrast to microhistorical writing, which often attributes a much more constant experience of agency for its subjects. See John Brewer, "Microhistory and the Histories of Everyday Life," *Cultural and Social History* 7, no. 1 (2010): 99; and Brad S. Gregory, "Is Small Beautiful? Microhistory and the History of Everyday Life," *History and Theory* 38, no. 1 (1999): 102–3.

1. Venetian Families

1. Chojnacki, "Political Adulthood," in *Women and Men in Renaissance Venice*, 231. This is the figure given by Marin Sanudo.

2. Such as Labalme, *Bernardo Guistiniani*; or Branca, "Ermolao Barbaro and the Late Quattrocento Venetian Humanism," in Hale, *Renaissance Venice*.

3. Maxson, *The Humanist World of Renaissance Florence*; and Sarah G. Ross, *Everyday Renaissances: The Quest for Cultural Legitimacy in Venice* (Cambridge, MA: Harvard University Press, 2016). Also important is Patrick Baker's study of humanists' self-perceptions and the relationships between them: *Italian Renaissance Humanism in the Mirror* (Cambridge: Cambridge University Press, 2015).

4. On this hyperelite group, see Chojnacki, "In Search of the Venetian Patriciate: Families and Factions in the Fourteenth Century," in Hale, *Renaissance Venice* 47–90; and Gaetano Cozzi, "Authority and Law in Renaissance Venice," in Hale, *Renaissance Venice*, 293–345. For further bibliography on the elite within the patriciate, see King, *Venetian Humanism*, 277, n. 19.

5. On Gian Matteo, see Patricia Fortini Brown, "Becoming a Man of Empire: The Construction of Patrician Identity in a Republic of Equals," in *Architecture, Art, and Identity in Venice and Its Territories, 1450–1750*, ed. Nebahat Avcioğlu and Emma Jones (Farnham: Ashgate, 2013), 231–49; Renard Gluzman, "Resurrection of a Sunken Ship: The Remarkable Salvage of the Venetian *Marciliana* That Saved Cattaro from Barbarossa," *Archivio Veneto*, 6th ser., no. 8 (2014): 29–78; and Lorenzo Calvelli, "Archaeology in the Service of the Dominante: Giovanni Matteo Bembo and the Antiquities of Cyprus," in Arbel, Chayes, and Hendrix, *Cyprus and the Renaissance*, 19–66.

6. On the Ca' Bembo as a *casa da statio*, see Fortini Brown, *Private Lives in Renaissance Venice*, 191.

7. ASV, Dieci savi alle decime in Rialto, Condizioni di decima della città, 1514, b. 27, S. Cancian 17.

8. Francesco Galantino, *Storia di Soncino, con documenti* (Milan: Bernardoni, 1869), 1: 354, n. 3.

9. Benjamin G. Kohl, Andrea Mozzato, and Monique O'Connell, "The Rulers of Venice, 1332–1524," record nos. 45107, 53251, 31299, accessed April 26, 2017, http://rulersofvenice.org..

10. ASV, M.A. Barbaro (with additions by M. Tasca), "Bembo" (San Cancian branch), *Arbori de' patritii veneti* (1733–43).

11. Fortini Brown, "Becoming a Man of Empire," 231.

12. Bembo, "Autobiographie des Venezianers Giovanni Bembo (1536)," 593. Many thanks to Holly Hurlburt for confirming this (e-mail message to author, May 28, 2015).

13. Holly Hurlburt, *Daughter of Venice: Caterina Corner, Queen of Cyprus and Woman of the Renaissance* (New Haven, CT: Yale University Press, 2015), 72–76, 219–35.

14. Chojnacki, "Political Adulthood," in *Women and Men in Renaissance Venice*, 235.

15. ASV, Avogaria di comun, Balla d'Oro, reg. 165 (1414–1523), 23r.

16. ASV, Dieci savi alle decime in Rialto, Condizioni di decima della città, 1514, b. 27, S. Cancian 17.

17. Chojnacki, "Political Adulthood," in *Women and Men in Renaissance Venice*, 231 (figure given by Marino Sanudo).

18. Ibid.; and Cozzi, "Authority and Law," in Hale, *Renaissance Venice*, 298–300.

19. Thomas Kuehn, *Illegitimacy in Renaissance Florence* (Ann Arbor: University of Michigan Press, 2002), 13.

20. The San Paternian branch of the Coppo family tree is sketched in "Un breve trattato dell'antichissima famiglia Copa Nobile Veneta," BNM Ms. It. VII 90 (=8029), 193r. Only Pietro Coppo's half brothers, Francesco and Giacomo, are included here.

21. Based on the tax declaration made by Pietro Coppo's uncle, Nicolò Coppo. By the time of the 1514 *redecima*, Pietro Coppo had been living in Istria for over a decade. ASV, Dieci savi alle decime in Rialto, Condizioni di decima della città, 1514, b. 57, S. Paternian 4.

22. Four brothers are listed in the Coppo genealogy (Marco, Antonio, Nicolò, and Francesco); an additional three are found in the Rulers of Venice database (Jacopo, Giordano, and Girolamo).

23. ASV, Avogaria di comun, *Cronaca Matrimoni*, reg. 107, 95v.

24. James S. Grubb, "Elite Citizens," in *Venice Reconsidered*, ed. John J. Martin and Dennis Romano (Baltimore: Johns Hopkins University Press, 2000), 350–51.

25. Dennis Romano, *Housecraft and Statecraft: Domestic Service in Renaissance Venice, 1400–1600* (Baltimore: Johns Hopkins University Press, 1996), 52–53; and ibid., 348.

26. ASV, Avogaria di comun, *Cronaca Matrimoni*, reg. 107, 95v.

27. ASV, Avogaria di comun, Balla d'Oro, reg. 165 (1414–1523), 115r.

28. ASV, Notai, Testamenti, Atti Canal, b. 190, no. 256.

29. Thomas Kuehn, *Illegitimacy in Renaissance Florence*, 14.

30. BNM, Ms. It. VII 90 (=8029), 193r.

31. Kohl, Mozzato, and O'Connell, "The Rulers of Venice": for Marco, record nos. 32082, 23630, 30530, 28644, 31477, and 25138; for Nicolò, record nos. 31452, 45477, 31510, and 44854.

32. Ibid., record no. 16605.

33. Ibid., record no. 53026.

34. For family "specialization" in particular posts in the maritime empire, see O'Connell, *Men of Empire*, 50–56.

35. Kohl, Mozzato, and O'Connell, "The Rulers of Venice": for Antonio, record nos. 24934 and 31988; for Girolamo, record nos. 24928 and 53129.

36. Governors and captains of Crete were in what Monique O'Connell has called the "first tier" of maritime office holding. *Men of Empire*, 41–42.

37. The documents related to this extraordinary case have been partially published in Hippolyte Noiret, *Documents inédits pour servir à l'histoire de la domination vénitienne en Crète de 1380 à 1485* (Paris: Thorin & Fils, 1892), 541–42.

38. Jana Byars, "From Illegitimate Son to Legal Citizen: Noble Bastards in Early Modern Venice," *Sixteenth Century Journal* 42, no. 3 (2011): 643–63.

39. Ross, *Everyday Renaissances*.

40. According to Paul Grendler's data for the late sixteenth century, about half (46.8 percent) of Venetian students were educated in Latin, the majority of those independently, but others in communal and in church schools. Grendler, *Schooling in Renaissance Italy: Literacy and Learning, 1300–1600* (Baltimore: Johns Hopkins University Press, 1989), 43.

41. BAV, Vat. Pal. Lat. 1476.

42. Grendler, *Schooling in Renaissance Italy*, 408. This is not a universal view. See Anthony Grafton and Lisa Jardine, *From Humanism to the Humanities: Education and the*

Liberal Arts in Fifteenth- and Sixteenth-Century Europe (Cambridge, MA: Harvard University Press, 1986). For an overview of this debate, see Robert Black, "Italian Renaissance Education: Changing Perspectives and Continuing Controversies," *Journal of the History of Ideas* 52, no. 2 (1991): 315–34.

43. Grendler, *Schooling in Renaissance Italy*, 216–22.

44. Grafton, *Defenders of the Text*, 4.

45. Grendler, *Schooling in Renaissance Italy*, 263.

46. On humanist commonplacing, see Ann Blair, *Too Much to Know: Managing Scholarly Information before the Modern Age* (New Haven, CT: Yale University Press, 2010); and Ann Moss, *Printed Commonplace-Books and the Structuring of Renaissance Thought* (Oxford: Oxford University Press, 1996), discussion of pedagogical tradition, 53–57.

47. Maya Djikic and Keith Oatley, "The Art in Fiction: From Indirect Communication to Changes of the Self," *Psychology of Aesthetics, Creativity, and the Arts* 8, no. 4 (2014): 502–3. Also see Djikic, Oatley, Sara Zoeterman, and Jordan B. Peterson, "On Being Moved by Art: How Reading Fiction Transforms the Self," *Creativity Research Journal* 21, no. 1 (2009): 24–29.

48. Djikic and Oatley, "The Art in Fiction," 501.

49. The scope of the first chair at San Marco gradually expanded to teach grammar and rhetoric to many young noblemen, not only those *cittadini* bound for the chancellery. J. B. Ross, "Venetian Schools and Teachers Fourteenth to Early Sixteenth Century: A Survey and a Study of Giovanni Battista Egnazio," *Renaissance Quarterly* 29, no. 4 (1976): 529. On the expansion of the Venetian chairs, see Grendler, *Schooling in Renaissance Italy*, 62–63.

50. Lowry, *The World of Aldus Manutius*, 182; and Ross, "Venetian Schools and Teachers," 527.

51. Chojnacki, "Measuring Adulthood: Adolescence and Gender," in *Women and Men in Renaissance Venice*, 196–97.

52. On Brugnolo, see Ross, "Venetian Schools and Teachers," 536; Branca, "Ermolao Barbaro and the Late Quattrocento Venetian Humanism," in Hale, *Renaissance Venice*, 220; and Bruno Nardi, "Letteratura e cultura veneziana del Quattrocento," in *Saggi sulla cultura veneta del Quattro e Cinquecento*, ed. Paolo Mazzatini (Padua: Antenore, 1971), 31–33.

53. Ross, "Venetian Schools and Teachers," 543.

54. Patricia H. Labalme, "The Last Will of a Venetian Patrician (1489)," in *Philosophy and Humanism: Renaissance Essays in Honor of Paul Oskar Kristeller*, ed. Edward P. Mahoney (New York: Columbia University Press, 1976), 491; Giorgio Castellani, "Giorgio da Trebisonda, maestro di eloquenza a Vicenza e a Venezia," *Nuovo Archivio Veneto* 11, no. 1 (1896): 1, 138. For his bibliography, see King, *Venetian Humanism*, 342–43.

55. On the rivalry, see Ross, "Venetian Schools and Teachers," 537–38.

56. On the role and significance of baptismal godfathers in Renaissance Venetian political culture, see Crescenzi, *Esse de Maiori Consilio*, 77–84.

57. "Restorer of letters and producer of Latin books." Bembo, "Autobiographie des Venezianers Giovanni Bembo (1536)," 606.

58. His name is also sometimes rendered as Avramis. On his book collecting, see Basile Markesinis, "Janos Lascaris, la bibliothèque d'Avramis à Corfou et Le Paris, Gr. 854," *Scriptorium* 54 (2000): 302–6. Many thanks to Anna Gialdini for alerting me to this article.

59. Bartolomeo Zamberto, *Euclidis megarensis philosophi platonici mathematicarum disciplinarum janitoris* (Venice: Johannis Tacuinus de Tridino, 1505).

60. Bembo, "Autobiographie des Venezianers Giovanni Bembo (1536)," 605–7.

61. This was despite the Council of Ten's 1505 prohibition of noblemen standing as baptismal godfathers to the sons of their noble friends. Robert Finlay, *Politics in Renaissance Venice* (New Brunswick, NJ: Rutgers University Press, 1980), 203.

62. On Sabellico, see Baker, *Italian Renaissance Humanism in the Mirror*, 184, for an up-to-date bibliography. Ruth Chavasse, "The *studia humanitatis* and the Making of a Humanist Career: Marcantonio Sabellico's Exploitation of Humanist Literary Genres," *Renaissance Studies* 17, no. 1 (2003): 27–38; Felix Gilbert, "Biondo, Sabellico, and the Beginnings of Venetian Historiography," 276–93; and Francesco Tateo, "Marcantonio Sabellico e la svolta del classicismo quattrocentesco," 41–64, both in *Florilegium historiale: Essays Presented to Wallace K. Ferguson*, ed. John Gordon Rowe and W. H. Stockdale (Toronto: University of Toronto Press, 1971). For Sabellico's bibliography, see King, *Venetian Humanism*, 425–27.

63. Eric Cochrane, *Historians and Historiography in the Italian Renaissance* (Chicago: University of Chicago Press, 1981), 86, on the afterlife of Sabellico's histories.

64. Lowry, *The World of Aldus Manutius*, 183.

65. Ibid., 181.

66. See Gilbert, "Biondo, Sabellico, and the Beginnings of Venetian Official Historiography," 286.

67. Chavasse, "The *studia humanitatis*," 32. William J. Bouwsma contested Sabellico's popularity: "His remoteness from the attitudes of a true Venetian, and his inadequacies as a philologist" made him out of touch with "the precise scholarship now beginning to characterize Venetian humanism." *Venice and the Defense of Republican Liberty: Renaissance Values in the Age of the Counter Reformation* (Berkeley: University of California Press, 1968), 90.

68. Ruth Chavasse, "Humanism Commemorated: The Venetian Memorials to Benedetto Brugnolo and Marcantonio Sabellico," in *Florence and Italy: Renaissance Studies in Honour of Nicolai Rubinstein*, ed. Peter Denley and Caroline Elam (London: Westfield Publications in Medieval Studies, 1988), 456 (quotes Sanudo).

69. *Ioannis Quirini Nicolai Oratio in Eximii Viri Benedicti Brugnoli Laudem* (Venice: n.p., 1502), 3r: "sicq[ue] non eruditione solum ac doctrina suos erudire discipulos studebat: veram etiam a vitiis absterrere & bonis imbuere moribus nitebatur." Many thanks to Lia Costiner for photographing this text.

70. Ibid., 5v–6r: "discipulos vero ita semper benigne erudivit, ac si ex seipso procreati fuit." Also quoted in King, *Venetian Humanism*, 22.

71. Bembo, "Autobiographie des Venezianers Giovanni Bembo (1536)," 587.

72. "nell libraria de ditto monastier dove lexcelente Messer Marcantonio Sabellico conditor della Veneta Historia per la qual lhebbe ducati 200 alanno de promision lettor pubblico de studio de humanita in Venetia del qual fui suo Carissimo auditor anni tre continui lasso le sue opere composte de sua man qual mia opera habbia a star nella dita libraria appresso le sua a mia memoria." Coppo, "Di Pietro Coppo e delle sue opere," 372.

73. Chavasse, "Humanism Commemorated," 460, n. 3.

74. According to Sabellico's will, these volumes were originally intended to be removed from the "capse" in the church of Santa Maria delle Grazie and sent to Vico-

varo; this evidently was not carried out: "Item ordeno & dispono oltra ale coffe preditte che li zinque volumi de libri ornati de tuole & inminiati, quali sono nele capse, siano dali mei executori mandati a Vicovaro." Published in Apostolo Zeno, *Degl'istorici delle cose Veneziane* (Venice: Il Loviso, 1718), 1, lxx.

75. "quem non res hominum non omnis caeperat aetas scribentem capit haec Coccion urna brevis." Quoted and translated by Chavasse, "Humanism Commemorated," 458.

76. On the question of Sabellico's origins, see Francesco Tateo, "Coccio, Marcantonio, detto Marcantonio Sabellico," in *Dizionario Biografico degli Italiani*, vol. 26 (Rome: Istituto della Enciclopedia italiana, 1982).

77. "gia da Iouenil etate contratta nel litteratissimo contubernio del nostro gia humanissimo Sabelico." Coppo, "Di Pietro Coppo e delle sue opere," 377.

78. Perhaps the best-known example of teacherly affection is that between Guarino and his students. A moving eulogy to Guarino by one of his students is found in Ludovico Carbone, "Oratio habita in funere . . . Guarini Veronensis," in *Prosatori latini del Quattrocento*, ed. Eugenio Garin (Milan: Ricciardi, 1952), 382–417.

79. Jacob Burckhardt, *The Civilization of the Renaissance in Italy*, trans. S. G. C. Middlemore (1990; repr., London: Penguin Books, 2004), 178.

80. On studying humanist intellectual communities "both generationally and relationally," see Celenza, *The Lost Italian Renaissance*, 74–75.

81. Bembo, *Marci Antonii Sabellici Annotationes*.

82. Grafton, *Defenders of the Text*, 50. Brugnoli's edition is Niccolò Perotti, *Cornucopiae nuper emendatum* (Milan: Giovanni da Legnano, 1502).

83. Lowry, *The World of Aldus Manutius*, 51.

84. Ibid., 184–85.

85. Grafton, *Defenders of the Text*, 71.

86. Marcantonio Sabellico, *Marcantonio Sabellico: De Latinae Linguae Reparatione*, ed. Guglielmo Bottari (Messina: Università degli studi, Centro interdipartimentale di studi umanistici, 1999). For a detailed discussion of this text in relation to Sabellico's career and the history of humanist criticism and philology, see Baker, *Italian Renaissance Humanism in the Mirror*, 184–233.

87. Lowry, *The World of Aldus Manutius*, 51.

88. Ibid., 83. Also see Nicolas Barker, *Aldus Manutius and the Development of Greek Script & Type in the Fifteenth Century*, 2nd ed. (New York: Fordham University Press, 1992), 44, for a later partnership contract between Pierfrancesco Barbaro and Andrea Torresani, Aldus's father-in-law.

89. Bembo, "Autobiographie des Venezianers Giovanni Bembo (1536)," 606.

90. On Erasmus's stay with Aldus as an important episode in the history of humanism, see John C. Olin, "Erasmus and Aldus Manutius," in *Erasmus, Utopia, and the Jesuits: Essays on the Outreach of Humanism*, ed. John C. Olin (New York: Fordham University Press, 1994), 39–56.

91. Gadi Algazi, "Food for Thought: Hieronymus Wolf Grapples with the Scholarly Habitus," in *Egodocuments and History: Autobiographical Writing in Its Social Context since the Middle Ages*, ed. Rudolf Dekker (Hilversum: Verloren, 2002), 28.

92. Salzberg, "Masculine Republics," 53.

93. Albert Rabil Jr., *Erasmus and the New Testament: The Mind of a Christian Humanist* (San Antonio, TX: Trinity University Press, 1972), 66.

94. Olin, "Erasmus and Aldus Manutius," in Olin, *Erasmus, Utopia, and the Jesuits: Essays on the Outreach of Humanism*, 48.

95. Ross, "Venetian Schools and Teachers," 538. The unfinished work is *Marci Antonii Cocci Sabellici Exemplorum Libri Decem* (Venice: Ioan. Barthol. Astensis, 1507), and was based on the model of Valerius Maximus.

96. Bembo, "Autobiographie des Venezianers Giovanni Bembo (1536)," 595–96; *Enciclopedia Italiana* 1: Appendice (1938), "Delle Grèche, Domenico." See http://www.treccani.it/enciclopedia/domenico-delle-greche.

2. Documenting the Mediterranean World

1. BTriv, Inc. C. 54, front flyleaf (Venice: Theodorus de Ragazonibus, 4. Sept. 1495).

2. See Ada Palmer, *Reading Lucretius in the Renaissance* (Cambridge, MA: Harvard University Press, 2014), 96.

3. Fortini Brown, *Venice and Antiquity*; Deborah Howard, *Venice and the East: The Impact of the Islamic World on Venetian Architecture 1100–1500* (New Haven, CT: Yale University Press, 2000); Wilson, *The World in Venice*; and Giada Damen, "The Trade in Antiquities between Italy and the Eastern Mediterranean (ca. 1400–1600)" (PhD diss., Princeton University, 2012).

4. Important work on materiality and temporality in the Italian Renaissance has been done by Alexander Nagel and Christopher Wood, *Anachronic Renaissance* (New York: Zone Books, 2010); and Leonard Barkan, *Unearthing the Past: Archaeology and Aesthetics in the Making of Renaissance Culture* (New Haven, CT: Yale University Press, 1999).

5. On the cultural relationships between Venetian subjects and the metropole, see Nicholas Davidson, " 'As Much for Its Culture as for Its Arms': The Cultural Relations of Venice and Its Dependent Cities, 1400–1700," in *Mediterranean Urban Culture, 1400–1700*, ed. Alexander Cowan (Chicago: University of Chicago Press, 2000), 197–214; and Anastasia Stouraiti, "Collecting the Past: Greek Antiquaries and Archaeological Knowledge in the Venetian Empire," in *Re-imagining the Past: Antiquity and Modern Greek Culture*, ed. Dimitris Tziovas (Oxford: Oxford University Press, 2014), 29–46.

6. Grendler, in *Schooling in Renaissance Italy*, has compiled statistics that suggest a very small minority of students learned Latin and Greek in independent schools: only 60 of the circa 2,160 students enrolled in Latin and vernacular schools in Venice in 1587 studied Greek alongside their Latin curricula (48, table 2.3). Paul Botley has found that the Aldine press produced many more advanced scholarly Greek editions than elementary student texts, which would seem to support Grendler's data. "Learning Greek in Western Europe, 1476–1516," in *Literacy, Education and Manuscript Transmission in Byzantium and Beyond*, ed. Catherine Holmes and Judith Waring (Leiden: Brill, 2002), 210–11.

7. BNM, D 393 D 150. *Institutiones Graecae grammatices* (Venice: Aldus Manutius, 1497).

8. BSM, CLM 10801, 37r.

9. Many thanks to Spyridon Gkounis, who provided a detailed report on the Greek folios of the manuscript. He also drew my attention to the close similarities (in shared texts) between Bembo's Greek folios and BAV, Cod. Vat. Gr. 914, which contains an

extended version of the recipe texts, as well as the Libanius monody and several of Aesop's Fables. An edition of some of the recipe texts featured in the Vatican manuscript has been produced: Niki Tsironis, ed., *The Book in Byzantium: Byzantine and Post-Byzantine Bookbinding* (Athens: Greek Society of Bookbinding, National Hellenic Research Foundation, 2008), 43–62.

10. The local intellectual cultures of the early modern Mediterranean have been the focus of several important works. On Cretan literature, see David Holton, "Classical Antiquity and Cretan Renaissance Poetry," *Journal of the Hellenistic Diaspora* 27, nos. 1–2 (2001): 87–101; Holton, *Literature and Society in Renaissance Crete*; and Nikolaus M. Panagiotakes, "The Italian Background of Early Cretan Literature," *Dumbarton Oaks Papers* 49 (1995): 281–323. For Cyprus, see Arbel, Chayes, and Hendrix, *Cyprus and the Renaissance*. On Dalmatia, see Luka Špoljarić, "Power and Subversion in the Ducal Palace: Dalmatian Patrician Humanists and Congratulatory Orations to Newly Elected Doges," in *Neo-Latin Contexts in Croatia and Tyrol: Challenges, Prospects, Case Studies*, ed. Špoljarić, Neven Jovanović, Johanna Luggin, and Lav Šubarić (Vienna, forthcoming).

11. On the *incanto* and the "great galleys," see Claire Judde de Larivière, *Naviguer, commercer, gouverner: Économie maritime et pouvoirs à Venise (XVe-XVI siècles)* (Leiden: Brill, 2008); Frederic C. Lane, *Venice: A Maritime Republic* (Baltimore: Johns Hopkins University Press, 1973), esp. chap. 24, "The Peak and Passing of the Merchant Galleys"; and Doris Stöckly, *Le système de l'incanto des galées du marché a Venise (fin XIIe-milieu XVe siècle)* (Leiden: Brill, 1995).

12. Lane, *Venice: A Maritime Republic*, 338.

13. Elisabeth Crouzet-Pavan, *Venice Triumphant: The Horizons of a Myth*, trans. Lydia G. Cochrane (Baltimore: Johns Hopkins University Press, 2002), 95; and Eric Cochrane and Julius Kirschner, "Deconstructing Lane's Venice," *Journal of Modern History* 47, no. 2 (1975): 321–34.

14. Bembo, "Autobiographie des Venezianers Giovanni Bembo (1536)," 589.

15. Stöckly, *Le système de l'incanto*, 169–73.

16. Judde de Larivière, *Naviguer, commercer, gouverner*, 314. The other two patrician partners—Domenico Cappello and Sebastiano Dolfin—are not the same men as Bembo recorded as investing in their galley. Dolfin, according to Bembo, sailed on another galley in the same convoy, but Cappello does not appear anywhere in Bembo's account; the official state records leave no trace of Contarini, Mauroceno, Cornaro, or Querini, who may have sailed as companions rather than as official business partners.

17. Stöckly, *Le système de l'incanto*, 173.

18. BSM, CLM 10801, 7v.

19. Bembo, "Autobiographie des Venezianers Giovanni Bembo (1536)," 589–93.

20. Punta di Pellaro.

21. "Ibi vidi templum Solis, per cuius duas fenestras inter se adversas paruas circulares et rotundas sol aequinoctiali tempore aeque permeat." Bembo, "Autobiographie des Venezianers Giovanni Bembo (1536)," 590.

22. Ibid., 590.

23. "Vulcanias, ex quibus Hiera Vulcano sacra adhuc ardet et ignem aut fumum semper euomit." Ibid., 590.

24. "Nunc sunt villiae et magalia et horti consiti arboribus, quae gignunt fructus optimos et praecipue mala punica, e quibus illis est incolis maximus proventus." Ibid., 591.

25. Souk Ahras, Algeria.

26. "Inter navigandum vidimus tres maximos pisces immania cete in mare pariter natantes, magnitudine instar triremium nostrarum, quos pisces Cao de oio nautae nostri dicunt"; "Vidi etiam ibi duas pantheras aligatas catenis cum maximo pondere saxi pendentis e collo"; and they saw there "faeminae utuntur tunica brevi et brachis laxis." Bembo, "Autobiographie des Venezianers Giovanni Bembo (1536)," 592.

27. "In hoc navali itinere mea Cyurω plurimas ad me literas miserat in Sicilium, Africam Bethicam et in Hispanias, quibus illa coram loqui mecum videbatur, nec aliud quam literas de mea valitudine a me postulabat seu potius flagitabat." Ibid.

28. The sylloge makes up the majority of Bembo's autograph manuscript, BSM, CLM 10801, 1r–148v (approximate; excerpts of texts, letters, and sketches are interspersed throughout). On Bembo's inscriptions, see Carlo Dionisotti, *Gli umanisti e il volgare fra Quattro e Cinquecento* (Florence: Felice Le Mournier, 1968), 20–21.

29. BSM, CLM 10801, 87r, 96r.

30. Cyriac's texts and letters have been published in *Cyriacus of Ancona and Athens*, ed. and trans. Edward W. Bodnar (Brussels: Latomus, 1960); *Cyriacus of Ancona's Journeys in the Propontis and the Northern Aegean, 1444–1445*, ed. and trans. Edward W. Bodnar and Charles Mitchell (Philadelphia: American Philosophical Society, 1976); and, with some overlap with previous editions, *Cyriac of Ancona: Later Travels*, ed. and trans. Edward W. Bodnar (Cambridge, MA: Harvard University Press, 2003). The most comprehensive monograph on Cyriac is Jean Colin, *Cyriaque d'Ancône: le voyageur, le marchand, l'humaniste* (Paris: Maloine, 1967); and see the papers collected in Gianfranco Paci and Sergio Sconocchia, eds., *Ciriaco d'Ancona e la cultura antiquaria dell'umanesimo. Atti del convegno internazionale di studio* (Parma: Diabasis, 1998). Also see Franz Babinger, "Notes on Cyriac of Ancona and Some of His Friends," *Journal of the Warburg and Courtauld Institutes* 25, no. 3 (1962): 321–23; and Julian Raby, "Cyriacus of Ancona and the Ottoman Sultan Mehmed II," *Journal of the Warburg and Courtauld Institutes* 43 (1980): 242–46.

31. Cyriac of Ancona, *Cyriacus of Ancona and Athens*, 69.

32. Milan, Biblioteca Ambrosiana, Trotti MS 373, fols. 101–25. A selection of folios from the Trotti codex have been published: Fortini Brown, *Venice and Antiquity*, 86–88.

33. Cyriac of Ancona, *Cyriacus of Ancona and Athens*, 69–70.

34. Cyriac of Ancona, "Vita Viri Clarissimi et Famosissimi Kyriaci Anconitani," ed. and trans. Charles Mitchell and Edward W. Bodnar, *Transactions of the American Philosophical Society*, n.s., 86, no. 4 (1996): 132.

35. Manuscripts of Cyriacana collections include BodL, Ms. Canon Misc. 280 (see Charles Mitchell, "Ex libris Kiriaci Anconitani," *Italia Medioevale e Umanistica* 5 [1962]: 283–299); Rome, Biblioteca Casanatense Ms. 106 and Treviso Biblioteca Comunale Ms. 323 (Claudia Barsanti, "Costantinopoli e l'Egeo nei primi decenni del XV secolo: la testimonianza di Cristoforo Buondelmonti," *Rivista dell'Istituto Nazionale d'Archeologia e Storia dell'Arte* 56 [2001], 90); and Antonio Venier's manuscript held in Berlin, Staatsbibliothek Hamilton Ms. 108 (Helmut Boese, ed., *Die Lateinischen Hand-*

schriften der Sammlung Hamilton zu Berlin [Wiesbaden: Harrassowitz, 1966], 58–60). Also see Ruth Barbour, "A Thucydides Belonging to Cyriac d'Ancona," *Bodleian Library Record* 5, no. 1 (1954): 9–13; and Remigio Sabbadini, *Le scoperte dei codici latini e greci nè secoli XIV e XV* (Florence: G. C. Sansoni, 1905), 48–49.

36. Cyriac of Ancona, *Cyriac of Ancona: Later Travels*, 199–201. "in villa Graeca quoque religione sacerdotes, qui nostra aetate Dianam ipsam suis cumque candentibus nymphis, albis depositis vestibus, nudas abluentes quandoque vitreo ipso sub gurgite demergere vidisse testantur."

37. Ibid., 233.

38. Bembo, "Autobiographie des Venezianers Giovanni Bembo (1536)," 595–96.

39. Cyriac of Ancona, *Cyriac of Ancona: Later Travels*, 203.

40. Kathleen Wren Christian, *Empire without End: Antiquities Collections in Renaissance Rome, c. 1350–1527* (New Haven, CT: Yale University Press, 2010), 129.

41. Pomponio Leto, *Romanae historiae compendium* (Venice: Bernardinus Venetus, de Vitalibus, 1499).

42. "Petrus homo diligens et curiosus secum in reditu feret compendium quorundam gestorum romanorum tibique ostendet." Marcantonio Sabellico, *Opera* (Venice: Albertinus Vercellensis, 1502), 47r.

43. Marcantonio Sabellico, "Pomponii Vita M. Antonius Sabellicus. M. Antonio Mauroceno Equiti Salutem," in *Romanae historiae compendium* (Venice, 1499), sig. pi (recto)–pic (verso).

44. Roberto Weiss, *The Renaissance Discovery of Classical Antiquity* (Oxford: Blackwell, 1969), 76–77.

45. Vladimir Zabughin, *Giulio Pomponio Leto: saggio critico* (Rome: La Vita Letteraria, 1909–12), 2: 170–86.

46. Pomponio Leto, *Pomponius Lactus de Romanae urbis vetustate noviter impressus* (Rome: Giacomo Mazzochi, 1515), 10v.

47. Translation from David Karmon, *The Ruin of the Eternal City: Antiquity and Preservation in Renaissance Rome* (Oxford: Oxford University Press, 2011), 19. Also see Catharine Edwards, *Writing Rome: Textual Approaches to the City* (Cambridge: Cambridge University Press, 1996), 8.

48. Barkan, *Unearthing the Past*, 35.

49. Weiss, *The Renaissance Discovery of Classical Antiquity*, 166.

50. See Sean Roberts, *Printing a Mediterranean World: Florence, Constantinople, and the Renaissance of Geography* (Cambridge, MA: Harvard University Press, 2013), for a parallel study charting geographical writing and cartography related to the Mediterranean world at the interface of manuscript and print.

51. Buondelmonti's *Descriptio insulae Cretae* has been edited twice: first by Flaminio Corner, *Creta Sacra* (Venice: Jo. Baptistae Pasquali, 1755), 1: 77–109; and then by Marie-Anne Van Spitael, *Descriptio Insule Crete et Liber Insularum* (Heraklion: Syllogos Politistikos Anaptyxeos, 1981). On the textual problems with these editions, see Dimitrios Tsougarakis, "Some Remarks on the 'Cretica' of Cristoforo Buondelmonti," *Ariadnē* 3 (1985): 88–108.

52. On Buondelmonti, see Hilary L. Turner, "Christopher Buondelmonti and the *Isolario*," *Terrae Incognitae* 19 (1987): 11–28; and Giuseppe Ragone, "Il Liber Insularum Archipelagi di Cristoforo dei Buondelmonti: filologia del testo, filologia dell'immagine,"

in *Humanisme et culture geographique à l'epoque du Concile de Constance*, ed. Didier Marcotte (Turnhout: Brepols, 2002): 177–218. The most recent and comprehensive work on Buondelmonti's biography, writing, and the reception of the *Liber insularum* is Barsanti, "Costantinopoli e l'Egeo." A French translation of a Greek manuscript copy has been published by Émile L. J. Legrand, *Description des îles de l'archipel par Christophe Buondelmonti* (Paris: Leroux, 1897).

53. Turner, "Christopher Buondelmonti and the *Isolario*," 13.

54. Berlin, Staatsbibliothek Hamilton Ms. 108.

55. BCP, Ms. CM 289. See Barsanti, "Costantinopoli e l'Egeo," 89. The full inscription reads: "Insularum Aegei pellagi descriptio usque Costantinopollim foeliciter incipit ab expertissimo viro composita et quae perpetuae observantiae mei Thadei Quirino est ad reverendum dominum dominum Iacob[um] Zeno episcopum Paduanum comitem Saccensem virum regium et omni laude praestantissimum cui aequo offitio dono trasmissa est."

56. BNM, Ms. Lat. X 124 (=3177); Ibid., 89. See also Aubrey Diller, "The Library of Francesco and Ermolao Barbaro," *Italia Medioevale e Umanistica* 6 (1963): 253–62.

57. Van Spitael, *Descriptio Insule Crete*, 117. On this passage also see Benedetta Bessi, "Cristoforo Buondelmonti: Greek Antiquities in Florentine Humanism," *Historical Review/La Revue Historique* 9 (2012): 65.

58. Van Spitael, *Descriptio Insule Crete*, 114–15.

59. Bessi, "Cristoforo Buondelmonti: Greek Antiquities in Florentine Humanism," 66.

60. Francesco Petrarch, *Letters on Familiar Matters*, trans. and ed. Aldo S. Bernardo (1975; repr. New York: Italica Press, 2005), 1: VI.II, 293.

61. Cyriac of Ancona, *Cyriac of Ancona: Later Travels*, 179: "Dico egregiisque spectantibus accolis civibus et colonis."

62. On Venetian loggia in the *stato da mar*, see Patricia Fortini Brown, "The Venetian Loggia: Representation, Exchange, and Identity in Venice's Colonial Empire," in *Viewing Greece: Cultural and Political Agency in the Medieval and Early Modern Mediterranean*, ed. Sharon E. J. Gerstel (Turnhout: Brepols, 2016), 207–35.

63. See Coppo, *Pietro Coppo, Le "Tabulae,"* Tavola XIII.

64. BnF, Fond. Lat. 9663 (in both Latin and Italian); with maps, Slovenia, Piran, Sergej Mašera Maritime Museum; and Venice, BNM, Ms. Lat. X 146 (=3331).

65. "La isola de candia antigamente / fo habitada da cento cita. / daligreci fo dita centonipoli / fo regname huberrimo." Coppo, *Pietro Coppo, Le "Tabulae,"* 65.

66. Chambers, *The Imperial Age of Venice*.

67. Patricia Fortini Brown, "Between Observation and Appropriation: Venetian Encounters with a Fragmentary Classical Past," in *Pietre di Venezia: spolia in se, spolia in re*, ed. Monica Centanni and Luigi Sperti (Rome: L'Erma di Bretschneider, 2016), 221–40.

68. Maya Jasanoff, *Edge of Empire: Conquest and Collecting in the East, 1750–1850* (London: Fourth Estate, 2005).

69. Patricia Fortini Brown, "Ritual Geographies in Venice's Colonial Empire," in *Rituals of Politics and Culture in Early Modern Europe: Essays in Honour of Edward Muir*, ed. Mark Jurdjevic and Rolf Strøm-Olsen (Toronto: Centre for Reformation and Renaissance Studies, 2016), 43–89.

3. Gender and Identity between Venice and the Mediterranean

1. "Incedens mea Cyurω per urbem Craetae audiebat praetereuntes et ambulantes dicere: Haec est uxor et marita Rectoris insularum Sciathi et Scopuli. Ipsam alii salutabant dicentes: Ἁαίρε χυίρα ρετοῦρενα!' Quantum gaudii et laetitiae putas tunc fuisse in mea Cyurω, quando a populo a nautis a civibus et nobilibus sic se venerari videbat?" Bembo, "Autobiographie des Venezianers Giovanni Bembo (1536)," 596. Thanks to Rosemary Bancroft-Marcus for assisting with this translation.

2. For a parallel study of Greek women who married Venetian patrician men in Venice, see Ersie Burke, "Our Daughters and Our Future: Elite Greco-Venetian Marriages, 1520–1610," in *Marriage in Premodern Europe: Italy and Beyond*, ed. Jacqueline Murray (Toronto: Centre for Reformation and Renaissance Studies, 2012), 169–98. Burke concentrates primarily on noble Greek women.

3. Of a large bibliography, see Stoler, "Tense and Tender Ties"; and the collected essays in Stoler, ed., *Haunted by Empire: Geographies of Intimacy in North American History* (Durham, NC: Duke University Press, 2006). For a historiographical overview, see Cleall, Ishiguro, and Manktelow, "Imperial Relations."

4. Lawrence Grossberg, "Identity and Cultural Studies: Is That All There Is?," in *Questions of Cultural Identity*, ed. Stuart Hall and Paul du Gay (London: Sage, 1996), 91–92. Julie D. Campbell and Anne R. Larsen emphasize that for women whose lives crossed geopolitical boundaries, it becomes imperative for the historian to understand the ways that race, gender, status, and religion were interwoven. "Introduction," in *Early Modern Women and Transnational Communities of Letters* (Farnham: Ashgate, 2009), 1.

5. See Catherine Holmes's discussion of this debate, "'Shared Worlds': Religious Identities—A Question of Evidence," in *Byzantines, Latins, and Turks in the Eastern Mediterranean World after 1150*, ed. Holmes, Jonathan Harris, and Eugenia Russell (Oxford: Oxford University Press, 2012), 31–56, esp. 37.

6. Bembo, "Autobiographie des Venezianers Giovanni Bembo (1536)," 583. On the 1506 legislation, see Chojnacki, "Marriage Regulation in Venice, 1420–1535," in *Women and Men in Renaissance Venice*, 63–65.

7. BNM, Ms. It. VII, 538 (=7734), 10v.

8. Nadia Zeldes, "Jewish Settlement in Corfu in the Aftermath of the Expulsions from Spain and Southern Italy, 1492–1541," *Mediterranean Historical Review* 27, no. 2 (2012): 177–78.

9. Gerassimos Pagratis, e-mail message to author, July 7, 2015.

10. "Corfun," in Bernhard von Breydenbach, *Peregrinatio in Terram Sanctam* (Mainz: Erhard Reuwich, 1486), 16v–17r.

11. Pietro Casola, *Canon Pietro Casola's Pilgrimage to Jerusalem in the Year 1494*, trans. and ed. M. Margaret Newett (Manchester: University of Manchester Press, 1907), 185.

12. O'Connell, *Men of Empire*, 64–66. Also see Freddy Thiriet, *La Romanie Vénitienne au Moyen Âge: le développement et l'exploitation du domaine colonial vénitien* (Paris: E. de Boccard, 1959), 399–400, on Greek and Latin Corfiote nobility.

13. In Marco Barbaro's eighteenth-century patrician family genealogies, Bembo is recorded as having "Chiara Mustafa da Corfu sua garzona." Barbaro (with additions by M. Tasca), "Bembo" (San Cancian branch), ASV, *Arbori de' patritii veneti* (1733–43).

14. On the social organization of Corfu under the Venetians in the fifteenth century, see Eugenio Bacchion, *Il Dominio Veneto du Corfù (1386–1797)* (Venice: Edizioni Altino, 1956), 51–67, esp. 53–54.

15. "Quae septimum decimum agebat annum et ego vigesimum quartum quando isthic Corcyrae sociati sumus." Bembo, "Autobiographie des Venezianers Giovanni Bembo (1536)," 584.

16. ASV, Avogaria di comun, *Cronaca Matrimoni*, reg. 107, 33v.

17. Grubb, "Elite Citizens," in Martin and Romano, *Venice Reconsidered*, 346.

18. On Bembo's time as a teacher in Pesaro, see Piergiorgio Parroni, "Maestri di grammatica a Pesaro nel Quattrocento," *Res Publica Litterarum* 5, no. 1 (1982): 205–20.

19. Bembo, "Autobiographie des Venezianers Giovanni Bembo (1536)," 584–88.

20. The Giustizia Nuova was formed in 1261 to oversee the wine trade and regulations regarding the city's taverns. James Shaw, *The Justice of Venice: Authorities and Liberties in the Urban Economy, 1550–1700* (Oxford: Oxford University Press, 2006), 22.

21. "laetabatur Cyurω mea; gestiebat, sperabat et animo spem concipiebat me quoque a Maiori Consilio posse consequi aliquem honorem et magistratum in urbe vestra Corcyrea: ut ipsa in sua patria veneraretur et cognatis et amicis prodesse posset." Bembo, "Autobiographie des Venezianers Giovanni Bembo (1536)," 589.

22. Burke, "Our Daughters and Our Future," 171.

23. Ibid., 190.

24. McKee, *Uncommon Dominion*, 112.

25. "Erat tunc Cyurω mea praegnans; laetabatur se a triremium turmis κατεργάκι vocari. Aequora autem et tristis imago ponti meam Cyurω perterre faciebant et navigationem longam et periculosam formidabat circuendo Africam ad Herculis fretum et columnas usque, et postea Hispaniarum litora atque iterum Africam." Bembo, "Autobiographie des Venezianers Giovanni Bembo (1536)," 589.

26. "Cyurω mea . . . binas ad me dedit literas, admonens ut sibi literas saepe darem." Ibid., 590.

27. On classical naming practices in Venetian scholarly households, see Ross, *Everyday Renaissances*, 47–51.

28. The precise order of Domenico's and Cornelio's births is unclear. In the list of his children's baptisms, Bembo writes that Domenico was born before Cornelio; in an earlier section of his letter, he writes that Cornelio was born before Domenico.

29. Bembo, "Autobiographie des Venezianers Giovanni Bembo (1536)," 593.

30. Chojnacki, "Marriage Regulation in Venice, 1420–1535," in *Women and Men in Renaissance Venice*, 65. On marriage legislation later in the sixteenth century and the institution of the *prove di nobilità*, see Cowan, *Marriage, Manners, and Mobility*.

31. For an introduction to the text in the context of patrician social values, see King, *Venetian Humanism*, 92–98; and King, "Introduction," in *The Wealth of Wives: A Fifteenth-Century Marriage Manual*, trans. and ed. Margaret King (Toronto: Iter Academic Press, 2015), 1–63.

32. King, *The Wealth of Wives*, 80.

33. Ibid., 68–69.

34. Ibid., 68.

35. Ibid., 121.

36. "Curavit mea Cyuro filias discere literas Palladiasque artes, suere, telas, et serica pectine percurrere et eas semper exercuit omnibus in rebus domesticis quae ad bonam

matremfamilias pertinent. Quamvic Graeca esset, non multum tamen Graecos amabat." Bembo, "Autobiographie des Venezianers Giovanni Bembo (1536)," 595.

37. Ibid., 594.

38. Ibid., 594.

39. M. Barbaro, "Bembo" (San Cancian branch), ASV, *Arbori de' patritii veneti* (1733–43).

40. "quantum quia mea Cyurω sperabat ex lucro Sciathio posse filiabus dotem parare, quae tunc tres integrae erant, Polymnia Urania et Angela." Bembo, "Autobiographie des Venezianers Giovanni Bembo (1536)," 594–95. Presumably their eldest daughter, Faustina, was already married, as she was twenty-five at the time Bembo was appointed to Skiathos.

41. Chojnacki, "Introduction: Family and State, Women and Men," in *Women and Men in Renaissance Venice*, 8.

42. Chojnacki, " 'The Most Serious Duty': Motherhood, Gender, and Patrician Culture," in *Women and Men in Renaissance Venice*, 169–84.

43. Bembo, "Autobiographie des Venezianers Giovanni Bembo (1536)," 596.

44. "scriba meus stupravit filiam meam Uraniam et bis eam gravidam fecit. Fecit autem primo partu abortum artibus ipsius scribae radice maluae pice intincta. Et rursus ipse scriba conatus est ut puella secundum foetam ejiceret, sed puella prae timore noluit, quia in primo abortu mortis periculo laboraverat. In media urbe frequenti populo edicto meo a carnifice testes ipsius scribae exempti fuere, ne amplius infanticida committeret." Bembo, "Autobiographie des Venezianers Giovanni Bembo (1536)," 599.

45. O'Connell, *Men of Empire*, 91.

46. Ruggiero, *The Boundaries of Eros*, 93–96.

47. Julius R. Ruff, *Violence in Early Modern Europe* (Cambridge: Cambridge University Press, 2001), 147–53.

48. Ibid., 153. On infanticide and abortion in Renaissance Florence and Milan, respectively, see Richard C. Trexler, "Infanticide in Florence: New Sources and First Results," *History of Childhood Quarterly* 1, no. 1 (1973): 98–116; and Baernstein and Christopoulos, "Interpreting the Body." For abortion practices in late medieval rural Greece, see Sharon E. J. Gerstel, *Rural Lives and Landscapes in Late Byzantium: Art, Archaeology, and Ethnography* (Cambridge: Cambridge University Press, 2015), 88–90.

49. See Joanne M. Ferraro, *Nefarious Crimes, Contested Justice: Illicit Sex and Infanticide in the Republic of Venice, 1557–1789* (Baltimore: Johns Hopkins University Press, 2008); and Claudio Povolo, "Note per uno studio dell'infanticidio nella Repubblica di Venezia nei secoli XV–XVIII," *Atti dell'Istituto Veneto di Scienze, Lettere ed Arti* 137 (1978–79): 115–31.

50. "Quum ergo mea Cyurω intelligeret et sentiret, me sic a perditis impudicisque viris contemni, cor suum dolore magno cruciabat: me autem solabatur, ut me intra pauper meum patrimonium continerem eoque contentus viverem et magistratus et honores multis obfuisse praedicabat." Bembo, "Autobiographie des Venezianers Giovanni Bembo (1536)," 603.

51. Bembo, "Autobiographie des Venezianers Giovanni Bembo (1536)," 604–5. See Appendix I for Latin text.

52. Eric R. Dursteler, *Venetians in Constantinople: Nation, Identity, and Coexistence in the Early Modern Mediterranean* (Baltimore: Johns Hopkins University Press, 2006), 13–15 (on the concept of *natione*).

53. See Chojnacki, "Dowries and Kinsmen in Early Renaissance Venice," in *Women and Men in Renaissance Venice*, 132–52; and Donald Queller and Thomas F. Madden, "Father of the Bride: Fathers, Daughters, and Dowries in Late Medieval and Early Renaissance Venice," *Renaissance Quarterly* 46 (1993): 685–710.

54. On Florentine women's funeral dress, see Carole Collier Frick, *Dressing Renaissance Florence: Families, Fortunes, and Fine Clothing* (Baltimore: Johns Hopkins University Press, 2002), 88–89. On the pageantry of sixteenth-century Italian funerals, see Sharon Strocchia, *Death and Ritual in Renaissance Florence* (Baltimore: Johns Hopkins University Press, 1992), 179.

55. "Postea delata est procedente pompa in sacellum ipsarum sacerdotum S. Mariae miraculorum, quarum ego iam multis annis cum Laurentio Lauredano, Lauredani Ducis filio, fui procurator, et etiam nunc sum cum Hieronymo Quirino decemuiro et aliis probis et honestis viris." Bembo, "Autobiographie des Venezianers Giovanni Bembo (1536)," 605.

56. Naor Ben-Yehoyada critiques this position in "The Moral Perils of Mediterraneanism: Second Generation Immigrants Practicing Personhood between Sicily and Tunisia," *Journal of Modern Italian Studies* 16, no. 2 (2011): 388.

57. Eric R. Dursteler, *Renegade Women: Gender, Identity, and Boundaries in the Early Modern Mediterranean* (Baltimore: Johns Hopkins University Press, 2011).

4. Becoming Istrian

1. Coppo, "Di Pietro Coppo e delle sue opere," 353.

2. Luigi Morteani, "Isola ed i suoi statuti," *Atti e Memorie della Società Istriana di Archeologia e Storia Patria* 4, no. 1 (1888): 158.

3. For an overview of the notarial culture of Istria, in particular, see Darko Darovec, "Ruolo dei vicedomini Istriani nella redazione degli atti notarili in rapporto ad uffici affini dell' area Adriatica," *Acta Histriae* 18, no. 4 (2010): 789–822.

4. "J'ai eu la chance . . . d'arriver à Dubrovnik . . . Ses archives sont merveilleuses et . . . C'est là que j'ai commencé à comprendre la Méditerranée." Fernand Braudel, *Une leçon d'histoire de Fernand Braudel* (Paris: Arthaud, 1986), 6.

5. Mimi Urbanc, "Contested Slovene Istria: A Distinctive Region of Its Own or Merely Part of a Larger Supranational Region?" *Die Erde* 138, no.1 (2007): 79.

6. Darko Darovec, "Istria in the System of Adriatic Relationships," in "Città e sistema Adriatico alla fine del medioevo," ed. Michele Pietro Ghezzo, *Atti e memorie della Società dalmata di storia patria* 26 (Venice, 1997): 95.

7. Francesco Majer, *Inventario dell'Antico Archivio Municipale di Capodistria* (Koper: Cobol & Priora, 1904), 10, no. 50: "Libro d'instrumenti fatto in Isola sotto i Vicedomini." Also see Pietro Kandler, "L'Archivio di Capodistria," in *L'Istria* (Trieste: Svevo, 1852), 177, n. 38 and 39.

8. Coppo, "Di Pietro Coppo e delle sue opere."

9. Petar Stanković, *Biografia degli uomini distinti dell'Istria* (Trieste: Marenigh, 1829), 2: 84–93.

10. Salvator Žitko, e-mail message to author, June 6, 2015.

11. Noel Malcolm, *Agents of Empire: Knights, Corsairs, Jesuits and Spies in the Sixteenth-Century Mediterranean World* (London: Allen Lane, 2015), xxii.

12. AST, Antico archivio di Capodistria. The manuscript is reproduced on three microfilms (nos. 69, 70, and 71). Many thanks to the archivists at the Archivio di Stato in Trieste for helping me access and read these microfilms.

13. See, for example, Pamela Ballinger, *History in Exile: Memory and Identity at the Borders of the Balkans* (Princeton, NJ: Princeton University Press, 2002).

14. See Egidio Ivetić, *Un confine nel Mediterraneo. L'Adriatico orientale tra Italia e Slavia (1300–1900)* (Rome: Viella, 2014). On Venice's later colonization of Dalmatia and its related ethnographic writing, see Larry Wolff, *Venice and the Slavs: The Discovery of Dalmatia in the Age of Enlightenment* (Stanford, CA: Stanford University Press, 2002). For a survey of early modern Istrian history, see Ivetić, *L'Istria moderna 1500–1797: una regione confine* (Verona: Cierre Edizioni, 2010).

15. See Pamela Ballinger, "Lines in the Water, Peoples on the Map: Maritime Museums and the Representations of Cultural Boundaries in the Upper Adriatic," *Narodna umjetnost: Hrvatski časopis za etnologiju folkloristiku* 43, no. 1 (2006): 15–39.

16. See Christian Bromberger, "Towards an Anthropology of the Mediterranean," *History and Anthropology* 17, no. 1 (2006): 91–107.

17. Darovec, "Istria in the System of Adriatic Relationships," in Ghezzo, *Atti e memorie della Società dalmata di storia patria*, 85–86.

18. Ivetić, *Un confine nel Mediterraneo*, 114.

19. Karl Appuhn, *A Forest on the Sea: Environmental Expertise in Renaissance Venice* (Baltimore: Johns Hopkins University Press, 2009), 167, 169–70; and Lia De Luca, "Le immigrazioni in Istria nel Cinquecento e Seicento: un quadro d'insieme," *Ateneo Veneto* CXCIC, ser. 3 11/I–II (2012): 49–82.

20. Arbel, "Venice's Maritime Empire in the Early Modern World," 131.

21. Coppo, "Di Pietro Coppo e delle sue opere," 353.

22. On Istrian "brother and sister" marriage: Marija Mogorović Crljenko, "Women, Marriage, and Family in Istrian Communities in the Fifteenth and Sixteenth Centuries," in *Across the Religious Divide: Women, Property, and the Law in the Wider Mediterranean (ca. 1300–1800)*, ed. Jutta Sperling and Shona Kelly Wray (New York: Routledge, 2010), 137–57; and Mogorović Crljenko, "The Position of Women in 'Istrian Marriage Pattern' (15th–16th centuries)," in "Donne a Venezia: spazi di libertà e forme di potere (sec. XVI–XVIII)," *Storia di Venezia* (2008), accessed February 12, 2016, http://www .storiadivenezia.net/sito/donne/Mogorovic_Position.pdf.

23. Coppo, "Di Pietro Coppo e delle sue opere," 359 (Antonio), 361 (Francesco).

24. Coppo, "Di Pietro Coppo e delle sue opere," 368–69.

25. Ibid., 353: Degrassi relies on Stanković's earlier, partial transcription from 1829. By the time Degrassi edited these documents in 1924, the contract had been lost.

26. Morteani, "Isola ed i suoi statuti," 172. Cado de Ugo was enrolled in the municipal council in 1459–60.

27. Benjamin Arbel has argued for Istria's inclusion in a study of the *stato da mar* (while admitting the ambiguity of the case), but Monique O'Connell excluded it from her study of Venetian *rettori* because the archival evidence was held in these two different series. Arbel, "Venice's Maritime Empire in the Early Modern World," 131; and O'Connell, *Men of Empire*, 141, n. 22.

28. Marin Sanudo, *Itinerario per la Terraferma veneziana*, ed. Gian Maria Varanini (Rome: Viella, 2014), 446–64, on Istria.

29. James S. Grubb, *Firstborn of Venice: Vicenza in the Early Renaissance State* (Baltimore: Johns Hopkins University Press, 1988), 60–61. However, Grubb has found the "vitality" of these *terraferma* municipal councils to have decreased by the beginning of the Cinquecento. See Morteani, "Isola ed i suoi statuti," 155–56 on the office, 198 for the Venetian podestà of Isola during Coppo's lifetime.

30. Sandra Ivović, "Humanism in Schools: Italian Humanists as Teachers in the 15th-Century Ragusa and Dalmatian Communes," *Croatiae auctores Latini*, accessed September 24, 2013, http://www.ffzg.unizg.hr/klafil/dokuwiki/doku.php/z:humanism-eastern-adriatic. The Dalmatian municipal councils' loss of prerogatives under Venetian rule is also stressed by Neven Budak, "Urban Elites in Dalmatia in the Fourteenth and Fifteenth Centuries," in Ghezzo, "Città e sistema Adriatico," 193. A comparative study could be made with the published municipal statutes of Piran. *Statut Piranskega komuna od 13. do 17. stoletja*, ed. Miroslav Pahor and Janez Šumrada (Ljubljana: Slovenska Akademija, 1987), 1–2.

31. Alfredo Viggiano, "Note sull'amministrazione veneziana in Istria nel secolo XV," *Acta Histriae* 3 (1994): 7–8.

32. Reinhold C. Mueller, "Aspects of Venetian Sovereignty in Medieval and Renaissance Dalmatia," in *Quattrocento Adriatico: Fifteenth-Century Art of the Adriatic Rim*, ed. Charles Dempsey (Bologna: Nuova Alfa Editoriale, 1996), 30–31. On fourteenth-century rebellions in Istria, see Ivetić, *Un confine nel Mediterraneo*, 99.

33. Mueller, "Aspects of Venetian Sovereignty," 36.

34. Ivetić, *Un confine nel Mediterraneo*, 105–7.

35. Coppo, "Di Pietro Coppo e delle sue opere," 324.

36. Ibid., 354–55.

37. "pecunie tam istius civitatis quam fontici male gubernantus et exigunter." This is from the first *capitulum* of the document, which relates that the city finances and treasury are badly governed, and requests that the *rettori* begin to collect on all debts owed to the city. Ibid., 354.

38. "qui fuerit de illa terra vel loco cuius uxor fuerit civis etc." Ibid., 354.

39. In 1546, he was sent to confirm the previous privileges with a new doge, Francesco Donato. Ibid., 364.

40. Ibid., 355–56.

41. Morteani, "Isola ed i suoi statuti," 158.

42. O'Connell, *Men of Empire*, 119–23, on syndics' investigations into corruption and fraud in the maritime empire.

43. Attilio Degrassi, "Podestà e Vicedomini d'Isola," *Atti e Memorie della Società Istriana di Archeologia e Storia Patria*, n.s., 17 (Venice, 1969): 11–12.

44. Ibid.

45. Darko Darovec, *Auscultauerint cum notario: Istrian Notaries and Vicedomini at the Time of the Republic of Venice* (Venice: Cafoscarina, 2015), 94–95.

46. Darovec, "Ruolo dei Vicedomini Istriani," 790.

47. Because of the availability of archival material, more research has been completed on the office of the *vicedomino* in Trieste. Francesco Antoni, "Materiali per una ricerca sui vicedomini di Trieste," *Archeografo Triestino*, 4th ser., 51 (1991): 151–77; Delia Bloise, "I Vicedomini e i loro registri," in *Le magistrature cittadine di Trieste nel secolo XIV* (Rome: Edizioni dell'Ateneo, 1982), 45–50; and Elena Maffei, "Attività notarile in

aree bilingui: i vicedomini a Trieste e in Istria nel 1300," *Nuova Rivista Storica* 83 (1999): 489–542.

48. Morteani, "Isola ed i suoi statuti," 155–58.

49. Coppo, "Di Pietro Coppo e delle sue opere," 356–57.

50. Attilio Degrassi, "Un umanista Isolano del Cinquecento: Francesco Egidio," *Atti e memorie della Società istriana di archeologia e storia patria* 37 (1925): 235–45.

51. Coppo, "Di Pietro Coppo e delle sue opere," 357–59.

52. "et ipsas pecunias non posset habere ab ipsa camera comunis agravata in solutione rectoris et stipendiariorum raspurch, petijt habere pro dictis pecunijs terrena infrascripta." "and [Coppo] cannot have money from the city treasury, which is burdened by the payment of the *rettori* and the stipends of [the castle] Raspurch, he may seek to have in lieu of the said money the abovewritten land." Ibid., 362. The fortress Raspo (modern-day Raspor) was an important administrative and military center of Venetian Istria.

53. Ibid., 365–66.

54. "The most ingenious architect of churches, whose work is highly praised in Venice." Ibid., 365.

55. Ibid., 370.

56. Ibid., 368–69.

57. Morteani, "Isola ed i suoi statuti," 172.

58. Coppo, "Di Pietro Coppo e delle sue opere": Antonio, 359–60; Francesco, 360–62; Vincenzo, 366–67; Giovanni, 367–68; Marco, 368–70.

59. Ibid., 360.

60. Degrassi, "Podestà e Vicedomini d'Isola," 12; and Morteani, "Isola ed i suoi statuti," 179.

61. Degrassi, "Podestà e Vicedomini d'Isola," 11–12.

62. Coppo, "Di Pietro Coppo e delle sue opere," 368.

63. Giorgio Busetto, "Coppo, Pietro," in *Dizionario Biografico degli Italiani*, vol. 28 (Rome: Istituto della Enciclopedia italiana, 1983).

64. Paraphrased from Lorenzo Veracini, *Settler Colonialism: A Theoretical Overview* (Basingstoke: Palgrave Macmillan, 2010), 3.

65. Ivetić, *Un confine nel Mediterraneo*, 105–6.

66. Coppo, "Di Pietro Coppo e delle sue opere," 370–73.

67. "la preditta mia Consorte nelli mesi precedenti fece el suo testamento." Ibid., 371.

68. Some of these surviving wills have been published: *Testamenti di Isola d'Istria (dal 1391 al 1579)*, ed. Giovanni Russignan (Trieste: Società istriana di archeologia e storia patria, 1986). Benvenuta's will, 57–58, no. 22. She made her will independently of her husband Balsamino de Adalperio, who had been exiled from Isola for murder. Testaments were enrolled separately from other kinds of notarial documents, held in the Isola *vicedomino's* book, and it is perhaps for this reason that 207 of them survive in the Koper/Capodistria archive. Darovec, *Auscultauerint cum notario*, 17–18, 159–60.

69. Coppo, "Di Pietro Coppo e delle sue opere," 371.

70. "scripto secondo che vuol la leze de Isola nel statuto a c. 93." Ibid., 371.

71. Ibid., 371.

72. Ibid., 372.

73. Ibid., 372.

74. "Item lasso per rason de legato et benediction et contento a Nicholo mio nevodo fiol de Marco mio fio tutti li miei libri per chel vedo piu prompto et naturalmente Inclinato alle lettere cha alcun altro." Ibid., 372.

75. Bembo, "Autobiographie des Venezianers Giovanni Bembo (1536)," 584.

76. Fernand Braudel, *The Mediterranean and the Mediterranean World in the Age of Phillip II*, 2nd ed., trans. Siân Reynolds (London: William Collins, 1972), 21.

5. Colonial Governance and Mythology on Skiathos

1. BSM, CLM 10801; Bembo, "Autobiographie des Venezianers Giovanni Bembo (1536)"; and *Isolario* (BEst, Alfa E. 5. 15).

2. Bembo's election is recorded in BNM, Ms. It. VII 198 (=8383), 218r. His election in 1525 evidently meant that he fell between the two series of registers in the Segretario alle voci. The first series (ASV, Segretario alle voci, Reggimenti [1491–1523], reg. 8) contains records for the Skiathos post until 1523 (99r); and the next series (ASV, Segretario alle voci, Elezioni in Maggior Consiglio [1524–40], reg. 1) begins with an appointment in 1526 (156v–157r).

3. Braudel, *The Mediterranean*, 149.

4. On the Sporades before direct Venetian rule, see Raymond-Joseph Loenertz, *Les Ghisi: Dynastes vénitiens dans l'Archipel 1207–1390* (Florence: L. S. Olschki, 1975). On their Ottoman rule, see Machiel Kiel, "The Smaller Aegean Islands in the 16th–18th Centuries According to Ottoman Documents," *Hesperia Supplements*, vol. 40, *Between Venice and Istanbul: Colonial Landscapes in Early Modern Greece* (2007): 35–54.

5. Kiel, "The Smaller Aegean Islands," 35.

6. On mobility between Euboea and the mainland in a slightly earlier period, see David Jacoby, "The Demographic Evolution of Euboea under Latin Rule, 1205–1470," in *The Greek Islands and the Sea*, ed. Julian Chrystostomides, Charalambos Dendrinos, and Jonathan Harris (Camberley: Porphyrogenitus, 2004), 132–79.

7. On Euboean piracy, see Silvano Borsari, *L'Eubea veneziana* (Venice: Deputazione di storia patria per le Venezie, 2002), 88–89.

8. Molly Greene, *Catholic Pirates and Greek Merchants: A Maritime History of the Mediterranean* (Princeton, NJ: Princeton University Press, 2010), 21.

9. Kiel, "The Smaller Aegean Islands," 35.

10. Arbel, "Venice's Maritime Empire in the Early Modern World," 205.

11. Benjamin Arbel, "Colonie d'oltremare," in *Storia di Venezia dalle origini alla caduta della Serenissima*, vol. 5, *Il Rinascimento*, ed. Alberto Tenenti and Ugo Tucci (Rome: Istituto della Enciclopedia Italiana, 1996), 966.

12. Arbel, "Venice's Maritime Empire," 206–7; and "Colonie d'oltremare," 967. In the latter article, Arbel reproduces photographs of the mid-sixteenth-century fortifications on Corfu (961, 965). Also see Michael E. Mallett and John R. Hale, *The Military Organization of a Renaissance State: Venice, c. 1400–1617* (Cambridge: Cambridge University Press, 1984), 429–54.

13. "Habebat episcopum, sed eius civitas post Euboeam a Turco captam fuit diruta et insula usque ad meum adventum deserta. Ego autem constitui in ea insula tanquam asilum, et 60 familiae cum 60 paribus bonum eam coluere, viri fortes et ad propellen-

dos piratas audaces." Bembo, "Autobiographie des Venezianers Giovanni Bembo (1536)," 597.

14. Dionysios A. Zakythinos, "Corsaires et pirates dans les mers grecques au temps de la domination Turque," *L'Hellenisme Contemporain* 10–11 (1939): 695–738.

15. O'Connell, *Men of Empire*; and *Ire debeas in rettorem Caneae: la commissio del doge di Venezia al rettore di Canea, 1589*, ed. Chryssa A. Maltezou (Venice: Elleniko institouto byzantinon, 2002). For a later period, see Giovanni Tatio, *La imagine del rettore della bene ordinata città* (Venice: Giolito, 1573). On *commissioni* manuscripts, see Helena Szépe, *Privilege and Duty in the Serene Republic: Illuminated Manuscripts of Renaissance Venice* (New Haven, CT: Yale University Press, forthcoming); and David S. Chambers, "Merit and Money: The Procurators of St Mark and Their *Commissioni*, 1443–1605," *Journal of the Warburg and Courtauld Institutes* 60 (1997): 23–88.

16. O'Connell, *Men of Empire*, 58.

17. "quamvis piratae Teucri quotidie abigebant pecora et insulanos terra marique capiebant et abducebant, quia triremium Venetarum ductores aut Corcyrae aut Zacynthi aut Craetae pecunias ludunt et eas scortis crapulando consumunt." Bembo, "Autobiographie des Venezianers Giovanni Bembo (1536)," 598–99.

18. For example, *Ire debeas in rettorem Caneae*, 42.

19. BEst, Alfa E. 5. 15.

20. Ibid., 2v, 3r.

21. Massimo Donattini, "Bartolomeo da li Sonetti, il suo Isolario e un viaggio di Giovanni Bembo," *Geografia Antiqua* 3–4 (1994–95): 227.

22. A small island off the northern coast of Cerigo.

23. "e dita Insula principal et sedia del S. Duca de Archipelago loqual nome S. Zuane Crispo loqual vene in Venetia cum una gallia armata cum homini de sue insule videlicet dela suda homini 80 de Milo 50 de S. Herini 40 el resto fino ala summa di 280 homini de Nixia die 5. Zugno 1523. Se parti el qual signoria anni 6 essendo su la sua insula ala caza di Zervi trovandose sua signoria sola cum duo gentilhomini videlicet in a cavalo fu preso da corsaro turcho Et li sui gentilhomini et subditi lo rescatono quella horo instesa da quello corsaro per ducati per la qual cosa el signor Turco hebe per mal che ldicto corsar non have presentato dicto signor a si et cercho di farlo prehender per apicharlo." This passage was partially edited by Donattini, "Bartolomeo da li Sonetti," 228.

24. Arbel, "Colonie d'oltremare," 968.

25. O'Connell, *Men of Empire*, 42.

26. Both Frank Lestringant and Tom Conley have commented on the way in which the genre of the *isolario* lends itself to use as a "taxonomic system" for recording and preserving information. Frank Lestringant, *Le livre des îles: atlas et récits insulaires de la genèse a Jules Verne* (Geneva: Droz, 2002), 57; and Tom Conley, *The Self-Made Map: Cartographic Writing in Early Modern France* (Minneapolis: University of Minnesota Press, 1996), 168–69.

27. His annotation reads: "Skopelos and the island of Alonissos with which Philip and the Athenians are concerned are different, there is another Alonissos in the Ionian archipelago." ("Scopelos et Alonisos Insula de qua inter Philippum et Athenienses differentia erat, est et Altera Alonises Ionia.") BEst, Alfa E. 5. 15, 51v.

28. Livy, *The History of Rome*, 31.28.

29. Stephanus of Byzantium, *De Urbibus*. Aldus Manutius printed an edition of this text in 1502, while Bembo was involved with the Aldine circle.

30. "De hac Sciatho Titus Livius de bello Macedonio lib. secundo ait: Nec Phillipus segnius (iam enim in Macedonico percenerat) adparabat bellum. Perseam puerum admodum datis ex amicorum numero qui aetatem eius regerent cum parte copiarum ad obsidendas angustias, quae ad Pelagoniam sunt, mitit; Sciathum et Peparethum haud ignobilis urbes ne classi hostium praesae aut praemio essent diruit. Sciathus seruat nomen. Stephanus de urbibus ait: Peparethus est una ex Cycladibus. Haec Peparethus insula nunc a nautis dicitur Diadromi, a Sciathiis dicitur Prepathora. Longitudo est XXX M. P., ambitus LX M.P., latitudo VII M. P., Sciathi ambitus est XX M. P. latitudo VII M. P. Stephanus ait: Sciathos insula est Euboeae. Distat autem Sciathos ab Euboea insula XX M passuum. Scopelos autem insula longe est a Sciatho quinque M. P., cuius longitudo est XXX MP, latitudo vero XII millia passuum." Bembo, "Autobiographie des Venezianers Giovanni Bembo (1536)," 597.

31. Arbel, "Venice's Maritime Empire in the Early Modern World," 158.

32. Gaetano Cozzi, "Considerazioni sull'amministrazione della giustizia nella Repubblica di Venezia (sec. XVI-XVI)," in *Florence and Venice: Comparisons and Relations*, ed. Sergio Bertelli and Nicolai Rubinstein (Florence: La Nuova Italia, 1980), 2: 101–33; and Cozzi, "La politica del diritto," in *Stato società e giustizia nella Repubblica Veneta (sec. XV-XVIII)* (Rome: Jouvence, 1981), 17–152.

33. "And about the judgement on which you desired my distinguished father's opinion: on this, in his opinion the judgement merits praise." ("Et del iuditio di quello desiderar la opinion de mio patre dinoto ad quella per sua opinion multo tal iuditio meritar laude.") BSM, CLM 10801, 183r.

34. Lucien Faggion, "Violence, Rites and Social Regulation in the Venetian *Terra Firma* in the Sixteenth Century," in *Aspects of Violence in Renaissance Europe*, ed. Jonathan Davies (Farnham: Ashgate, 2013), 191.

35. For a parallel in modern colonial history, see Patricia van der Spuy, "Infanticide, Slavery and the Politics of Reproduction at Cape Colony, South Africa, in the 1820s," in *Infanticide: Historical Perspectives on Child Murder and Concealment, 1550–2000*, ed. Mark Jackson (Aldershot: Ashgate, 2002), 128–48.

36. Ruff, *Violence in Early Modern Europe*, 153.

37. "Nam quid aliud est dedecorare hoc iudicium meum et male de eo loqui, quam fateri, licere Tauro, regis Minois scribae, comprimere Pasiphaem reginam ipsius Minoir coniugem?" Bembo, "Autobiographie des Venezianers Giovanni Bembo (1536)," 603.

38. Rebecca Armstrong, "Pasiphae in the *Eclogues* and *Ars Amatoria*," in *Cretan Women: Pasiphae, Ariadne, and Phaedra in Latin Poetry* (Oxford: Oxford University Press, 2006), 169–86.

39. Bembo, "Autobiographie des Venezianers Giovanni Bembo (1536)," 599–601. For Latin text, see appendix II.

40. Thelma S. Fenster and Daniel Lord Smail, eds., *Fama: The Politics of Talk and Reputation in Medieval Europe* (Ithaca, NY: Cornell University Press, 2003), 2.

41. Virgil, *The Aeneid*, trans. Robert Fagles (New York: Penguin, 2006), 133–34.

42. On Venetian history in Tana, see Bernard Doumerc, "La Tana au XVe siècle: comptoir ou colonie?" in *État et Colonisation au Moyen Âge et à la Renaissance*, ed. Michel Balard (Lyon: La Manufacture, 1989), 251–66.

43. ASV, Segretario alle voci, Reggimenti (1491–1523), 99r.

44. ASV, Segretario alle voci, Elezioni in Maggior Consiglio (1524–40), reg. 1, 156v–157r.

45. ASV, Capi del Consiglio di Dieci, Lettere, reg. 26 (1526) and reg. 27 (1527). These collections of letters contain no reference to the scandal.

46. "The death of Madonna Cyurω, your wife, whose death has been most troubling to us." BSM, CLM 10801, 182v–183r.

47. "mio patre me havea ordinato per io ve devesse far la debita risposta latine" Ibid., 183r.

48. John M. McManamon, *Funeral Oratory and the Cultural Ideals of Italian Humanism* (Chapel Hill: University of North Carolina Press, 1989).

49. Margaret King, *The Death of the Child Valerio Marcello* (Chicago: University of Chicago Press, 1994).

50. Strocchia, *Death and Ritual in Renaissance Florence*, 116.

51. The passage: Bembo, "Autobiographie des Venezianers Giovanni Bembo (1536)," 604–5.

52. Ibid., 605.

53. As George McClure argues in *Sorrow and Consolation in Italian Humanism* (Princeton, NJ: Princeton University Press, 1991).

54. "Et de primo quidem varie erunt hominum voces . . . ita enim ferme quisque loquitur, ut impellit non veritas, sed voluptas; nec laudis nec infamie modus est." Petrarch, "Critical Edition of Epistola Posteritati," ed. Karl A. E. Enenkel, in *Modelling the Individual: Biography and Portrait in the Renaissance* (Amsterdam: Rodopi, 1998), 256–57.

55. "putantes me in crimen bonis ponere atque infamiam." Bembo, "Autobiographie des Venezianers Giovanni Bembo (1536)," 599.

56. *Librorum Francisci Petrarche impressorum annotatio* (Venice: Simone Bevilacqua, 1503). BL, 11421. k. 13.

57. Bembo, "Autobiographie des Venezianers Giovanni Bembo (1536)," 609.

6. On the Borders of Italy

1. BCA, Ms. A. 117. See Almagià, "The Atlas of Pietro Coppo, 1520."

2. BnF, Fond. Lat. 9663.

3. Slovenia, Piran, Sergej Mašera Maritime Museum; BNM, Ms. Lat. X 146 (=3331).

4. Coppo, *Pietro Coppo. Le "Tabulae."*

5. Pietro Kandler published several early modern chorographies that were modeled on Coppo's in "Corografie dell'Istria." See Erin Maglaque, "Writing the Local Landscape: Renaissance Chorographies of Istria," in *Creating a Third Nature: Gardens and Constructions of Landscape in the Italian Renaissance*, ed. Anatole Tchikine (Philadelphia: University of Pennsylvania Press, forthcoming). The Vavassore map exists in one copy: London, National Maritime Museum, G235.

6. Coppo's own term for Istria. *Del Sito de Listria*, reprinted in Coppo, "Di Pietro Coppo e delle sue opere," 413.

7. On Ptolemy's definition of chorography, see Denis Cosgrove, "Mapping New Worlds: Culture and Cartography in Sixteenth-Century Venice," *Imago Mundi* 44 (1992): 66.

8. Petrus Apianus, *Cosmographicus liber* (Landshut: D. Ioannis Weyssenburger, 1524), 6v–6r.

9. Marcantonio Sabellico, *De vetustate Aquileiae patriae* (Padua: Antonius de Avinione, between 1481 and 1483). In what follows, I refer to the reprint of the text in Sabellico's collected texts in the *Opera*, 118v–136v. Selections from Crijević's *De Epidauro* have been published in *Hrvatiski latinisti: Croatici auctores quae scripserunt*, ed. Veljko Gortan and Vladimir Vratović (Zagreb: Zora, 1999), 1: 449–53. The entire text has been published online in the *Croatiae auctores Latini* database. Sanudo's text has been edited with a critical commentary: *Itinerario per la terraferma veneziana*, ed. Varanini.

10. Barkan, *Unearthing the Past*, 35.

11. "Pomponii Vita M. Antonius Sabellicus. M. Antonio Mauroceno Equiti Salutem," in *Romanae historiae compendium* (Venice, 1499), sig. pi (recto)–pic (verso).

12. Ruth Chavasse, "The First Known Author's Copyright, September 1486, in the Context of a Humanist Career," *Bulletin of the John Rylands University Library of Manchester* 69, no. 1 (1986): 11–37.

13. "De vetustate Aquileiae," in Sabellico, *Opera*, 127. "Antenor potuit, mediis elapsus Achivis, / Illyricos penetrare sinus, atque intima tutus / regna Liburnorum . . . / Hic tamen ille urbem Patavi sedesque locavit." Virgil, *Aeneid*, 1: 242–47. Translation by Fagles, *The Aeneid*, 55.

14. "Uno ferme eodemque tempore Roma gentium domino amisso imperii fulgore ignominiose capta: ac direpta solitudinis: & ruinae plena suo Augusto solo: velut Priamus ille ad aram hercei Iovis miserabiliter condidit." "De vetustate Aquileiae," in Sabellico, *Opera*, 127.

15. "Aquileiam ipsam Roma longe antiquiorem: aequalemque Patavio Altino: & Concordia: quippe quas uno ferme tempore a Troianis: qui cum Antenore venerant conditas affirmare audeant." Ibid., 127.

16. "Cuius cladis phama tantum terroris universae patriae attulit: ut qui in oppidis erant vix se tutos futuros putarent. Frequens fuga nocte illa: qui diem pugnae secuta est: ex villis & agris facta dicitur. Postridie autem cum iam multum diei processisset repente circa Hunnium compluribus locis fumei globi attolli coeperunt: quibus cognitum est hostem adesse: atque momento tempis: quasi inter Barbaros ita convenisset. Quicquid villarum inter sontium & Tiliaventum fuit hostili manu deflagravit. Eram ero per id tempus Tarcenti: quo ob pestilentem annum ex Hunnio concesseram: auditaque clade ad sontium acepta in arcem: qui vico imminet: cum multis mortalibus me receperam: ex eo loco perspectus in universam patriam late patet inde atrocissimum patriae incendium non sine lachrymis spectavi: foedum liquidem fuit interdiu videre tamen culti & amoeni soli fumo & caligne opertum: sed longe foedius atrociusque sub primas tenebras: as per reliquum noctis cernere aciem unam flammarum a sontio amne ad Tiliaventum extensarum: ut nihil medium esse videret: quod non ignis occupasset. . . . Ausim ego affirmare nullo unque tempore tam atroxincendium a mortalibus visum: nidi forte fabulis poetarum credendum putaminibus: qui portentosa illa de phaetonte mendacia confinxere: sed nos haec omnia copiosius in nostris poematibus." "De vetustate Aquileiae," in Sabellico, *Opera*, 136.

17. John McManamon also lists fifteen funeral orations authored by Crijević that circulated in manuscript. "An Incipitarium of Funeral Orations and a Smattering of Other Panegyrical Literature from the Italian Renaissance (ca. 1350–1550)," ac-

cessed February 21, 2014, http://www.luc.edu/media/lucedu/history/pdfs/Incipit _Catalogue.pdf.

18. Ivica Martinović, "Unpublished Manuscript Heritage of the Croatian Latinists in the Libraries and Archives of Dubrovnik: Preliminary Report," 1, 13, 16–17 (paper presented at the Euroclassica Congress, Dubrovnik, March 2005), accessed November 21, 2013, http://www.eduhi.at/gegenstand/ . . . /data/Euroclassica_zbornik _Dubrovnik.doc.

19. "Est Socolitanum castelli nomine saxum / Deserto sub monte loco, quod surgit in auras / Vertice praeruptum summo, ab radicibus altis / Saxum horrendum, ingens et formidabile visu. / Desuper useque adeo specula prospectat ab alta / Undique cinxerunt asperrima saxa fragosis / Rupibus et cautes avulsae a montibus altis. / A tergo hi sese circum flexere theatri / In speciem, quos nec saxosos esse putares; / Sed saxa horrorem sic per declivia vastum / Usque ad radices lapidoso vertice servant / Cunctaque saxorum magnis adoperta ruinis / Vestiri et late videas vastescere circum." Crijević, "De Epidauro," 449.

20. "Tu nunc una duplex Epidaurus et altera fies / Caelestis summoque micantior orbe nitesces, / Syderibus stellata novis, cursabere terra / Altera, nam cives per summa cacumina montis / Elapsi et reduces fato meliore novabunt / Teque restaurandam propiori in littore condent." Ibid., 453.

21. Marin Sanudo, *Città Excelentissima: Selections from the Renaissance Diaries of Marin Sanudo*, ed. Patricia H. Labalme and Laura Sanguineti, trans. Linda L. Carroll (Baltimore: Johns Hopkins University Press, 2008), xxvi.

22. Sanudo, *Itinerario per la terraferma veneziana*, 458.

23. Ibid., 441–44.

24. Sabellico, *Opera*, 10–10v, 32–32v, 48.

25. Michael B. Petrovich, "Croatian Humanists and the Writing of History in the Fifteenth and Sixteenth Centuries," *Slavic Review* 37, no. 4 (1978): 633.

26. Sabellico, *Opera*, 57–59. In 1481 and 1492, another of Coriolanus Cippico's sons, Pietro, erected on the family's house in Trogir classical inscriptions commemorating the major events of his father's life. The first inscription described Coriolanus's naval expedition under Pietro Mocenigo, and the second inscription described the fire that destroyed the original structure, providing an opportunity for Pietro to commemorate its reconstruction. The Venetian Senate contributed to its reconstruction, as recorded in the inscription. When the castle in Trogir was again damaged in 1515—this time, by the Ottomans—the Venetian Senate again paid for the repairs. See Marcantonio Sabellico, "Un carme consolatio di Marcantonio Sabellico a Coriolano Cippico da Traù (1492)," ed. A. Bacotich, *Archivio Storico per la Dalmazia* 12, no. 69 (1931): 433, n. 1.

27. Sabellico, *Opera*, 48.

28. Alvise Cippico, "Un poemetto di Alvise Cippico sulla guerra di Ferrara del 1482," *Archivio storico per la Dalmazia* 10 (1930): 314–39.

29. Ivović, "Humanism in schools," 5–6. On the mobility of scholars between eastern and central Europe, see Marianna D. Birnbaum, *Humanists in a Shattered World: Croatian and Hungarian Latinity in the Sixteenth Century* (Columbus: Slavica Publishers, 1985), esp. 48–76.

30. Julia Haig Gaisser, *Catullus and His Renaissance Readers* (Oxford: Clarendon Press, 1993), 105.

31. "Haec sunt, si quaeris, veneranda volumina, lector, / Quae Coppus miro condidit ingenio. / Aethera et hic narrat, terras depingit et ipsa / aequora; et ex toto praeterit orbe nihil. / Plura doctus oculos pariter delectat et aures. / Quis, rogo, tam pulchrum non legat istud opus?" Giuseppe Mazzatinti, ed., *Inventari dei manoscritti delle biblioteche d'Italia* (Florence: L. S. Olschki, 1924), Vol. 30: Bologna, 59, no. A. 117.

32. Palladio Fosco, *Palladii Fusci Patavini De situ orae Illyrici* (Rome: Antonius Bladus Asulanus, 1540); Palladio Fosco, "Palladio Fosco e il suo *De situ orae Illyrici,*" ed. Salvatore Sabbadini, *Archeografo triestino*, 3rd ser., 13 (1926): 180.

33. Ivović, "Humanism in schools," 5–6.

34. Coriolanus Cippico, *Coriolano Cippico: The Deeds of Commander Pietro Mocenigo in Three Books*, trans. Kiril Petkov (New York: Italica Press, 2014), 1.

35. Cochrane, *Historians and Historiography*, 82.

36. Kristeller, *Iter Italicum*, 2, n. 647. Sabbadini wrote that this text was lost. Fosco, "Palladio Fosco," 180.

37. Degrassi, "Un umanista Isolano."

38. "gia da Iovenil etate contratta nel litteratissimo contubernio del nostro gia humanissimo Sabelico." Coppo, "Di Pietro Coppo e delle sue opere," 377.

39. "desideroso (come scrivete) grandemente di tal cognitione in volgar lengua a sua plena intelligentia (seti voi litteratissimo) et de cadauna altar non molto litterata persona." Ibid., 377.

40. "altre volte scritto et designato le province et lochi de tutta la terra a cerco in latino." Ibid., 377.

41. "avanti che li preditti Argonauti venissero li come dicemo. laqual alhora era habitata in qua in la da Indigeni Aborigeni gente Pastoral. come anchor il resto de Italia al tempo de Iano over Fauno et de Saturno che venero di Grecia: et trovorono gente rude vivente secundo la natura de animali et frutti produceva da si la terra non culta. doppo da quelli redutti a viuer piu humano et domestico al culto dela terra. et haver habitatione soto il culto divino et lege." Ibid., 378.

42. "In piu lochi de Listria si attrovano molte degne antiquita et vestigii de terre antique. qual demostrano gia esser sta habitate da potenti et degni huomeni." Ibid., 379.

43. "Et doppo destruta Roma da Breno bellicosissimo capitano de Franzosi. qual passo de Franza in Italia con Tresento millia ferocissimi combatenti ad acquistarsi nove sede et habitatione . . . per labondante cresciuta multitudine in Franza. Laqual Roma cosi abrugiata et del tutto destruta lassata Breno ando in la dalmatia Ongaria et con prospero successo in Grecia: metendo a terra ogni cosa con asperrima crudelita a focho et ferro senza alcuna pieta. Spogliata prima Listria de tutte sue sustantie et beni. Doppo alquanti anni Totila Re de Goti con numeroso exercito ancor lui venne in Italia. destrusse molte Citta et Fiorenza in tal modo che un gran tempo deserta per il Gottico furor resto senza nome. diche destruta cosi Roma dominatrice del mondo dal Levante al Ponente: Fiorenza et altre famose citta. Molti deli potenti et opulenti de quelle massimamente Romani ala prima con sue richeze et faculta mobile se redussero ala dita Acquilegiense citta et di grande devenuta la fecero grandissima. et a queste terre e Listria. maxime a Pola: et con le loro richeze feceno quelli notabel ediffici. come haveano gia fatto il suo antecessori maxime Romani deliqual ne sono rimasti ancor alquanti mirabel vestigii." Ibid., 379.

44. Barkan, *Unearthing the Past*, 205–7.

45. Sanudo, *Itinerario per la Terraferma veneziana*, 460.

46. Biondo Flavio, *Italy Illuminated*, ed. and trans. Jeffrey A. White (Cambridge, MA: Harvard University Press, 2005), 1: 3–5.

47. "Histriam nunc, non quidem novam (quae ante Caesaris Augusti tempora Italiae censebatur) sed inter ceteras oras ultimo additam, inchoemus." Ibid., 2: 166–67.

48. Balázs Trencsényi and Márton Zászkaliczky, *For the Love of Which Country?: Composite States, National Histories, and Patriotic Discourses in Early Modern East Central Europe* (Leiden: Brill, 2010), 193.

49. Ibid., 195.

50. Flavio, *Italy Illuminated*, 2: 175.

51. Ibid., 2: 175–77.

52. "[i Longobardi populi] del tutto destruger et anichilar la lengua Latina fecero abrugiar tutti i libri Latini si poteno trovar. acio il suo Barbaro parlar et loro regnaselro. et alhora nascete fa vocaboli corotti tra Barbari et Latini el volgar parlar." Coppo, "Di Pietro Coppo e delle sue opere," 382.

53. Trieste and much of the territory of modern-day Slovenian Istria was ruled by the Habsburgs during the fifteenth and sixteenth centuries; thus, Istria was a Venetian peninsula truly "between" these larger Habsburg territories. See Sergij Vilfan, "Towns and States at the Juncture of the Alps, the Adriatic, and Pannonia," in *Cities and the Rise of States in Europe, AD 1000–1800*, ed. Charles Tilly and Wim P. Blockmans (Boulder, CO: Westview Press, 1994), 44–59.

54. Flavio, *Italy Illuminated*, 2: 177.

55. Sanudo, *Itinerario per la Terraferma veneziana*, 456.

56. *Inferno* 9: 112–14: "As at Arles, where the Rhone stagnates, or Pola, near the Gulf of Quarnaro, that confines Italy, and bathes its coast, the sepulchers make the ground uneven." Text and translation from "Divine Comedy," Digital Dante, accessed May 17, 2017, https://digitaldante.columbia.edu.

57. "Sono doi gran Montagne adherente ale Alpe: che seperano la Italia dala Barbara natione. una tra Maistro et Tramontana chiamata Monte Caldiera sopra el Colfo Tergestino. laltra tra Grego Levante sopra el Carner chiamata Monte Mazor. et cose se ha il Sito de Istria." Coppo, "Di Pietro Coppo e delle sue opere," 387.

58. BCA, Ms. A. 117, 152v–153r.

59. Ibid., 153v–154r.

60. Ibid., 154v–155r.

61. Coppo, *Pietro Coppo. Le "Tabulae,"* Tavola V.

62. Appuhn, *A Forest on the Sea*, 169–78.

63. Lauren Benton has similarly written that chorography was used in early modern geography to depict empire as a series of discrete, local spaces. *A Search for Sovereignty: Law and Geography in European Empires, 1400–1900* (Cambridge: Cambridge University Press, 2010), 18.

64. Chambers, *The Imperial Age of Venice*, 24.

65. Dandelet, *The Renaissance of Empire*.

66. An interesting parallel study is Alison Brown's on Florence and its *contado*. Brown examines the ways in which the city adopted classical Roman language into its legislative and administrative vocabulary concerning its empire on the Italian mainland.

"The Language of Empire," in *Florentine Tuscany: Structures and Practices of Power*, ed. William J. Connell and Andrea Zorzi (Cambridge: Cambridge University Press, 2000), 32–47.

Conclusion

1. Maxson, *The Humanist World of Renaissance Florence*; Ross, *Everyday Renaissances*.

2. Lowry, *The World of Aldus Manutius*, 51; and Flavio et al., "Corografie dell'Istria."

3. Grubb, "Memory and Identity."

4. Grubb, "When Myths Lose Power," 52.

5. Chojnacki, *Women and Men in Renaissance Venice*.

6. O'Connell, *Men of Empire*, 57–74.

7. For the Venetian Mediterranean, see Dursteler, *Renegade Women*.

8. Lynn M. Thomas, "Historicising Agency," *Gender & History* 28, no. 2 (2016): 324–39.

9. Ibid., 335.

10. Crouzet-Pavan, *Venice Triumphant*, 185.

11. Francesco Barbaro, *The Wealth of Wives: A Fifteenth-Century Marriage Manual*, trans. and ed. Margaret King (Toronto: Iter Academic Press, 2015), 80.

12. Ibid., 69.

13. Grubb, "When Myths Lose Power," 51. See Queller, *The Venetian Patriciate*; as well as Guido Ruggiero, *Violence in Early Renaissance Venice* (New Brunswick, NJ: Rutgers University Press, 1980).

14. Ibid., 51.

15. This kind of work began with Edward Muir's pathbreaking study, *Civic Ritual in Renaissance Venice* (Princeton, NJ: Princeton University Press, 1981).

16. On the "empirical" school of critique, see the works of Queller and Ruggiero, cited above, as well as Finlay, *Politics in Renaissance Venice*; and on critical reexamination of the myth, see Filippo de Vivo, "Historical Justifications of Venetian Power in the Adriatic," *Journal of the History of Ideas* 64, no. 2 (2003): 159–76.

17. This book offers an answer to Jutta Sperling's call for study of the ways in which Venetian political mythology impacted the lives of women (and indeed families) as well as patrician men. *Convents and the Body Politic*, 72–114.

18. Scott, *The Fantasy of Feminist History*, 19.

Appendix I

1. Bembo, "Autobiographie des Venezianers Giovanni Bembo (1536)," 604–5.

Appendix II

1. Bembo, "Autobiographie des Venezianers Giovanni Bembo (1536)," 599–601.

BIBLIOGRAPHY

Archival Sources

Archivio di Stato, Trieste, Italy (AST)
    Antico archivio di Capodistria, nos. 69, 70, and 71 (microfilm)
Archivio di Stato, Venice (ASV)
    Avogaria di comun
        Balla d'Oro, reg. 165 (1414–1523)
        Libro d'Oro delle nascite, reg. 1
        Matrimoni con notizie dei figli
            Matrimoni di nobili veneti, reg. 106
            Cronaca Matrimoni, reg. 107
    Capi del Consiglio di Dieci
        Lettere, reg. 26 (1526), reg. 27 (1527)
    Dieci savi alle decime in Rialto
        Condizioni di decima della città, 1514
    Miscellanea codici
        Serie I, 17: M.A. Barbaro (with additions by M. Tasca), *Arbori de' patritii veneti*
        Serie I, 24: G. Priuli, *Genealogie di famiglie nobili*
    Notai, Testamenti
        Atti Canal, b. 190
    Segretario alle voci
        Elezioni in Maggior Consiglio (1524–1540), reg. 1
        Reggimenti (1491–1523), reg. 8
    Senato
        Mar, reg. 20 (1522–1525), 21 (1526–1529)
Bayerische Staatsbibliothek, Munich (BSM)
    CLM 10801
Biblioteca Apostolica Vaticana, Vatican City (BAV)
    Vat. Pal. Lat. 1476
Biblioteca Civica, Padua (BCP)
    CM 289
Biblioteca Comunale dell'Archiginnasio, Bologna (BCA)
    Ms. A. 117
Biblioteca Nazionale Marciana, Venice (BNM)
    Ms. Lat. X 124 (=3177)
    Ms. Lat. X 146 (=3331)

Ms. It. VII 27 (=7761)
Ms. It. VII 90 (=8029)
Ms. It. VII 198 (=8383)
Ms. It. VII 538 (=7734)
Bibliothèque nationale de France (BnF)
    Fond. Lat. 9663
Bodleian Library, Oxford (BodL)
    Ms. Canon Misc. 280
Pomorski Muzej Sergej Mašera Library, Piran
    De summa totius orbis, Pietro Coppo (consulted in facsimile)

Early Printed Copies with Manuscript Annotations pre-1800

Biblioteca Estense, Modena (BEst)
    Alfa E. 5. 15: Bartolomeo dalli Sonetti, [pseud.]. *Isolario*. Venice: Guilelmus
        Anima Mia, Tridinensis?, not after 1485.
Biblioteca Nazionale Marciana, Venice (BNM)
    Incun. D 393 D 150: *Institutiones Graecae grammatices*. Venice: Aldus Manutius,
        1497.
Biblioteca Trivulziana, Milan (BTriv)
    Inc. c. 54: Lucretius, *De rerum natura*. Venice: Theodorus de Ragazonibus, 1495.
British Library, London (BL)
    11421. k. 13: Petrarch, *Librorum Francisci Petrarche impressorum annotatio*. Venice:
        Simone Bevilacqua, 1503.

Printed Sources pre-1800

Apianus, Petrus. *Cosmographicus liber*. Landshut: D. Ioannis Weyssenburger, 1524.
Bembo, Giovanni, ed. *In hoc volumine haec continentur: Marci Antonii Sabellici
    annotationes veteres et recentes: ex Plinio: Livio: & pluribus authoribus*. Venice:
    Iacobum Pentium de Leuco, 1502.
Bordone, Benedetto. *Libro di Benedetto Bordone nel quale si ragiona de tutte l'isole del
    mondo*. Venice: Nicolò Zoppino, 1528.
von Breydenbach, Bernhard. *Peregrinatio in terram sanctam*. Mainz: Erhard Reuwich,
    1486.
Coppo, Pietro. *Portolano*. Venice: Augustino di Bindoni, 1528.
———. *Del Sito de Listria*. Venice: Francesco Bindoni and Maffeo Pasini, 1540.
Corner, Flaminio. *Creta Sacra*. Vol. 1. Venice: Jo. Baptistae Pasquali, 1755.
dalli Sonetti, Bartolomeo [pseud.]. *Isolario*. Venice: Guilelmus Anima Mia, Tridinen-
    sis?, not after 1485.
Flavio, Biondo. *Italia illustrata*. Rome: Johannes Philippus de Lignamine, not before
    1474.
———. *Roma instaurata*. Rome: Printer of Statius, before 1471.
Fosco, Palladio. *Catullus una cum commentariis eruditi viri Palladii Fusci Padavini*.
    Venice: Johannes Tacuinus de Tridino, 1496.
———. *Palladii Fusci Patavini De situ orae Illyrici*. Rome: Antonius Bladus Asulanus, 1540.

Institutiones Graecae grammatices. Venice: Aldus Manutius, 1497.

Leto, Pomponio. *Pomponius Laetus de Romanae urbis vetustate noviter impressus.* Rome: Giacomo Mazzocchi, 1515.

——. *Romanae historiae compendium.* Venice: Bernardinus Venetus, de Vitalibus, 1499.

Lo libro chiamado Portolano composto per uno zentilomo veneciano lo qual a veduto tute queste parte anti scrite. Venice: Bernardo Rizo de Novaria, 1490.

Lucretius Carus, Titus. *De rerum natura.* Venice: Theodorus de Ragazonibus, 1495.

Manzuoli, Nicolò. *Nova descrittione della Provincia dell' Istria di Nicolò Manzuoli. Con la vita dei santi di detta provincia.* Venice: Giorgio Bizzardo, 1611.

Mela, Pomponius. *Cosmographia, sive De situ orbis.* Venice: Erhard Ratdolt, 1482.

Petrarch, Francesco. *Librorum Francisci Petrarche impressorum annotatio.* Venice: Simone Bevilacqua, 1503.

Ptolemy, Claudius. *Geographia.* Venice: Iacobum Pentium de Leuco, 1511.

Quirini, Nicolò. *Ioannis Quirini Nicolai Oratio in eximii viri Benedicti Brugnoli laudem.* Venice, n.p., after 1502.

Sabellico, Marcantonio. *De vetustate Aquileiae patriae.* Padua: Antonius de Avinione, between 1481 and 1483.

——. *Opera.* Venice: Albertinus Vercellensis, 1502.

Stephanus of Byzantium. *De urbibus.* Venice: Aldus Manutius, 1502.

Tatio, Giovanni. *La imagine del rettore della bene ordinata città.* Venice: Giolito, 1573.

Vavassore, Giovanni Andrea. *La vera descrittione del Mare Adriatico.* Venice, n.p., 1541.

Zamberto, Bartolomeo. *Euclidis megarensis philosophi platonici mathematicarum disciplinarum janitoris.* Venice: Johannes Tacuinus de Tridino, 1505.

Zeno, Apostolo. *Degl'istorici delle cose veneziane.* Vol. 1. Venice: Il Loviso, 1718.

Modern Editions of Early Manuscript and Printed Sources

Barbaro, Francesco. *The Wealth of Wives: A Fifteenth-Century Marriage Manual.* Translated and edited by Margaret King. Toronto: Iter Academic Press, 2015.

Bembo, Giovanni. "Autobiographie des Venezianers Giovanni Bembo (1536)." Edited by Theodor Mommsen. *Sitzungsberichten der Kaiserlichen Akademie der Wissenschaften* (1861): 581–609.

Buondelmonti, Cristoforo. *Descriptio Insule Crete et Liber Insularum.* Translated and edited by Marie-Anne Van Spitael. Heraklion: Syllogos Politistikos Anaptyxeos, 1981.

——. *Description des îles de l'Archipel.* Translated and edited by Émile Louis J. Legrand. Paris: Leroux, 1897.

——. *Liber insularum archipelagi: Universitäts- und Landesbibliothek Düsseldorf Ms. G 13 Faksimile.* Edited by Irmgard Siebert, Max Plassmann, Arne Effenberger, and Fabian Rijkers. Wiesbaden: Reichert, 2005.

Carbone, Ludovico. "Oratio habita in funere . . . Guarini Veronensis." In *Prosatori latini del Quattrocento.* Edited by Eugenio Garin. Milan: Ricciardi, 1952, 382–417.

Casola, Pietro. *Canon Pietro Casola's Pilgrimage to Jerusalem in the Year 1494.* Translated and edited by M. Margaret Newett. Manchester: University of Manchester Press, 1907.

Cippico, Alvise. "Un poemetto di Alvise Cippico sulla guerra di Ferrara ne 1482."
    Edited by Giuseppe Praga. *Archivio storico per la Dalmazia* 10 (1930): 314–39.
Cippico, Coriolanus. *Coriolano Cippico: The Deeds of Commander Pietro Mocenigo in
    Three Books.* Edited and translated by Kiril Petkov. New York: Italica Press, 2014.
Coppo, Pietro. "Di Pietro Coppo e delle sue opere: documenti inediti e l'opusculo
    Del Sito De Listria ristampato dall' edizione del 1540." Edited by Attilio
    Degrassi. *L'Archeografo triestino: raccolta di opuscoli notizie per Trieste e per
    L'Istria,* 3rd ser., 11 (1924): 319–87.
——. *Pietro Coppo. Le "Tabulae" (1524–1526),* 2 vols. Edited by Luciano Lago and
    Claudio Rossit. Trieste, Italy: Lint, 1986.
Crijević, Iliya. *De Epidauro.* Edited by Veljko Gortan and Vladimir Vratović. *Hrvatiski
    latinisti: Croatici auctores quae scripserunt,* vol. 1. Zagreb: Zora, 1999.
Cyriac of Ancona. *Cyriac of Ancona: Later Travels.* Translated and edited by Ed-
    ward W. Bodnar. Cambridge: Harvard University Press, 2003.
——. *Cyriacus of Ancona and Athens.* Translated and edited by Edward W. Bodnar.
    Brussels: Latomus, 1960.
——. *Cyriacus of Ancona's Journey in the Propontis and the Northern Aegean, 1444–1445.*
    Translated and edited by Edward W. Bodnar and Charles Mitchell. Philadel-
    phia: American Philosophical Society, 1976.
——. "Vita Viri Clarissimi et Famosissimi Kyriaci Anconitani." Translated and edited
    by Edward W. Bodnar and Charles Mitchell. *Transactions of the American
    Philosophical Society,* N.S., 86, no. 4 (1996): 1–246.
dalli Sonetti, Bartolomeo [pseud.]. *Isolario.* Edited by Frederick R. Goff. Amsterdam:
    Theatrum Orbis Terrarum Series of Atlases in Facscimile, 1972.
Flavio, Biondo. *Italy Illuminated.* 2 vols. Translated and edited by Jeffrey A. White.
    Cambridge, MA: Harvard University Press, 2005–16.
——. *Roma instaurata, Rome restaurée.* 2 vols. Translated and edited by Anne
    Raffarin-Dupuis. Paris: Les Belles Lettres, 2005.
Flavio, Biondo, Pietro Coppo, Giovanni Baptisa Goineo, Leando Alberti, and
    Ludovico Vergerio. "Corografie dell'Istria." Edited by Pietro Kandler.
    Archeografo triestino, 1st ser., 2 (1830): 13–100.
Fosco, Palladio. "Palladio Fosco e il suo *De situ orae Illyrici.*" Edited by Salvatore
    Sabbadini. *Archeografo triestino,* 3rd ser., 13 (1926): 176–208.
Ire debeas in rettorem Caneae: la commissio del doge di Venezia al rettore di Canea, 1589.
    Edited by Chryssa A. Maltezou. Venice: Elleniko institouto byzantinon, 2002.
Kohl, Benjamin G., Andrea Mozzato, and Monique O'Connell, eds. "The Rulers of
    Venice, 1332–1524." Renaissance Society of America and ACLS, 2005–2008.
    http://rulersofvenice.org.
McManamon, John, ed. "An Incipitarium of Funeral Orations and a Smattering of
    Other Panegyrical Literature from the Italian Renaissance (ca. 1350–1550)."
    http://www.luc.edu/media/lucedu/history/pdfs/Incipit_Catalogue.pdf.
Noiret, Hippolyte. *Documents inédits pour servir à l'histoire de la domination vénitienne
    en Crète de 1380 à 1485.* Paris: Thorin & Fils, 1892.
Petrarch, Francesco. "Critical Edition of Epistola Posteritati." Translated and edited
    by Karl A. E. Enenkel. *Modelling the Individual: Biography and Portrait in the
    Renaissance* (Amsterdam: Rodopi, 1998).

———. *Letters on Familiar Matters.* Vol. 1. Translated and edited by Aldo S. Bernardo. New York: Italica Press, 2005.

Ptolemy, Claudius. *Geographia: Venice, 1511.* Edited by Raleigh Ashlin Skelton. Amsterdam: Theatrum Orbis Terrarum Series of Atlases in Facsimile, 1969.

The Reports of the Venetian Baili and Provveditori of Corfu (16th Century). Edited by Gerassimos D. Pagratis. Athens: National Hellenic Research Foundation, 2008.

Sabellico, Marcantonio. *Marcantonio Sabellico: De Latinae Linguae Reparatione.* Edited by G. Bottari (Messina: Centro interdipartimentale di studi umanistici, 1999).

———. "Un carme consolatio di Marcantonio Sabellico a Coriolano Cippico da Traù (1492)." Edited by A. Bacotich. *Archivio Storico per la Dalmazia* 12, no. 69 (1931): 418–49.

Sanudo, Marin. *Città Excelentissima: Selections from the Renaissance Diaries of Marin Sanudo.* Edited by Patricia H. Labalme and Laura Sanguineti. Translated by Linda L. Carroll. Baltimore: Johns Hopkins University Press, 2008.

———. *Itinerario per la Terraferma veneziana.* Edited by Gian Maria Varanini. Rome: Viella, 2014.

Statut Piranskega komuna od 13. do 17. stoletja. Edited by Morislac Pahor and Janez Šumrada. Ljubljana, Slovenia: Izdala Slovenska Akademija Znanosti in Umentnosti, 1987. Italian preface.

Testamenti di Isola d'Istria (dal 1391 al 1579). Edited by Giovanni Russignan. Trieste, Italy: Società istriana di archeologia e storia patria, 1986.

Virgil. *The Aeneid.* Translated by Robert Fagles. New York: Penguin, 2006.

Secondary Sources

Akerman, James R. "The Structuring of Political Territory in Early Printed Atlases." *Imago Mundi* 47 (1995): 138–54.

Algazi, Gadi. "Food for Thought: Hieronymus Wolf Grapples with the Scholarly Habitus." In *Egodocuments and History: Autobiographical Writing in Its Social Context since the Middle Ages,* edited by Rudolf Dekker, 21–44. Hilversum, the Netherlands: Verloren, 2002.

———. "Scholars in Households: Refiguring the Learned Habitus, 1480–1550." *Science in Context* 16, nos. 1–2 (2003): 9–42.

Almagià, Roberto. "The Atlas of Pietro Coppo, 1520." *Imago Mundi* 7 (1950): 48–50.

Andrade, Tonio. "A Chinese Farmer, Two African Boys, and a Warlord: Toward a Global Microhistory." *Journal of World History* 21, no. 4 (2010): 573–91.

Antoni, Francesco. "Materiali per una ricerca sui vicedomini di Trieste." *Archeografo Triestino,* 4th ser., 51 (1991): 151–77.

Appuhn, Karl. *A Forest on the Sea: Environmental Expertise in Renaissance Venice.* Baltimore: Johns Hopkins University Press, 2009.

Arbel, Benjamin. "Colonie d'oltremare." In *Storia di Venezia dalle origini alla caduta della Serenissima.* Vol. 5, *Il Rinascimento,* edited by Alberto Tenenti and Ugo Tucci, 947–85. Rome: Istituto della Enciclopedia Italiana, 1996.

———. *Cyprus, The Franks, and Venice: 13th–16th Centuries.* Aldershot: Ashgate Variorum, 2000.

——. *Trading Nations: Jews and Venetians in the Early Modern Mediterranean.* Leiden: Brill, 1995.

——. "Venice's Maritime Empire in the Early Modern World." In *A Companion to Venetian History, 1400–1797,* edited by Eric R. Dursteler, 125–253. Leiden: Brill, 2013.

Arbel, Benjamin, Evelien Chayes, and Harald Hendrix, eds. *Cyprus and the Renaissance (1450–1650).* Turnhout: Brepols, 2013.

Armstrong, Rebecca. *Cretan Women: Pasiphae, Ariadne, and Phaedra in Latin Poetry.* Oxford: Oxford University Press, 2006.

Aslanian, Sebouh David. *From the Indian Ocean to the Mediterranean: The Global Trade Networks of Armenian Merchants from New Julfa.* Berkeley: University of California Press, 2011.

Babinger, Franz. "Notes on Cyriac of Ancona and Some of His Friends." *Journal of the Warburg and Courtauld Institutes* 25, no. 3 (1962): 321–23.

Bacchion, Eugenio. *Il Dominio Veneto du Corfù (1386–1797).* Venice: Edizioni Altino, 1956.

Baernstein, P. Renée, and John Christopoulos, "Interpreting the Body in Early Modern Italy: Pregnancy, Abortion, and Adulthood." *Past and Present* 223, no. 1 (2014): 41–75.

Bahr, Arthur. *Fragments and Assemblages: Forming Compilations of Medieval London.* Chicago: University of Chicago Press, 2013.

Baker, Patrick. *Italian Renaissance Humanism in the Mirror.* Cambridge: Cambridge University Press, 2015.

Balard, Michel, ed. *État et colonisation au Moyen Âge et à la Renaissance.* Lyon: La Manufacture, 1989.

Balard, Michel, and Alain Ducellier. *Le partage du monde: échanges et colonisation dans la Méditerranée médiévale.* Paris: Publications de la Sorbonne, 1998.

Ballinger, Pamela. *History in Exile: Memory and Identity at the Borders of the Balkans.* Princeton, NJ: Princeton University Press, 2002.

——. "Lines in the Water, Peoples on the Map: Maritime Museums and the Representations of Cultural Boundaries in the Upper Adriatic." *Narodna umjetnost: Hrvatski časopis za etnologiju folkloristiku* 43, no. 1 (2006): 15–39.

Barbour, Ruth. "A Thucydides Belonging to Cyriac d'Ancona." *Bodleian Library Record* 5, no. 1 (1954): 9–13.

Barkan, Leonard. *Unearthing the Past: Archaeology and Aesthetics in the Making of Renaissance Culture.* New Haven, CT: Yale University Press, 1999.

Barker, Nicholas. *Aldus Manutius and the Development of Greek Script and Type in the Fifteenth Century.* 2nd ed. New York: Fordham University Press, 1992.

Baron, Hans. *The Crisis of the Early Italian Renaissance: Civic Humanism and Republican Liberty in an Age of Classicism and Tyranny.* Princeton, NJ: Princeton University Press, 1955.

Barsanti, Claudia. "Costantinopoli e l'Egeo nei primi decenni del XC secolo: la testimonianza di Cristoforo Buondelmonti." *Rivista dell'Istituto Nazionale d'Archeologia e Storia dell'Arte* 56 (2001): 83–254.

Beard, Mary. "Officers and Gentlemen? Roman Britain and the British Empire." In *From Plunder to Preservation: Britain and the Heritage of Empire, c. 1800–1940,* edited by Astrid Swenson and Peter Mandler, 49–62. Oxford: Oxford University Press, 2013.

Bec, Christian. *Les marchands écrivains: affaires et humanisme à Florence 1375–1434.* Paris: Mouton, 1967.

Beck, Hans-Georg, Manoussos Manoussacas, and Agostino Pertusi, eds. *Venezia: centro di mediazione tra Oriente e Occidente (secoli XV–XVI): aspetti e problemi.* 2 vols. Florence: L. S. Olschki, 1977.

Bedford, Ronald, Lloyd Davis, and Philippa Kelly, eds. *Early Modern Autobiography: Theories, Genres, Practices.* Ann Arbor: University of Michigan Press, 2006.

Bellavitis, Anna. *Identité, mariage, mobilité sociale. Citoyennes et citoyens à Venise au xvie siécle.* Rome: Ecole française de Rome, 2001.

Benton, Lauren. *A Search for Sovereignty: Law and Geography in European Empires, 1400–1900.* Cambridge: Cambridge University Press, 2010.

Ben-Yehoyada, Naor. "The Moral Perils of Mediterraneanism: Second Generation Immigrants Practicing Personhood between Sicily and Tunisia." *Journal of Modern Italian Studies* 16, no. 2 (2011): 386–403.

Bessi, Benedetta. "Cristoforo Buondelmonti: Greek Antiquities in Florentine Humanism." *Historical Review/La Revue Historique* 9 (2012): 63–76.

Biadene, Susanna, ed. *Carte da navigar: portolani e carte nautiche del Museo Correr, 1318–1732.* Venice: Marsilio, 1990.

Birnbaum, Marianna D. *Humanists in a Shattered World: Croatian and Hungarian Latinity in the Sixteenth Century.* Columbus, OH: Slavica Publishers, 1985.

Bisaha, Nancy. *Creating East and West: Renaissance Humanists and the Ottoman Turks.* Philadelphia: University of Pennsylvania Press, 2004.

Black, Robert. *Humanism and Education in Medieval and Renaissance Italy: Tradition and Innovation in Latin Schools from the Twelfth to the Fifteenth Century.* Cambridge: Cambridge University Press, 2001.

——. "Italian Renaissance Education: Changing Perspectives and Continuing Controversies," *Journal of the History of Ideas* 52, no. 2 (1991): 315–34.

Blair, Ann. *Too Much to Know: Managing Scholarly Information before the Modern Age.* New Haven, CT: Yale University Press, 2010.

Bloise, Delia. "I Vicedomini e i loro registri." In *Le magistrature cittadine di Trieste nel secolo XIV,* 45–50. Rome: Edizioni dell'Ateneo, 1982.

Boese, Helmut, ed. *Die Lateinischen Handschriften der Sammlung Hamilton zu Berlin.* Wiesbaden: Harrassowitz, 1966.

Borsari, Silvano. "I Veneziani delle colonie." In *Storia di Venezia.* Vol. 3, *La formazione dello stato patrizio,* edited by Giorgio Cracco, Girolamo Arnaldi, and Alberto Tenenti, 127–58. Rome: Enciclopedia Italiana, 1996.

——. *L'Eubea veneziana.* Venice: Deputazione di storia patria per le Venezie, 2002.

Botley, Paul. "Learning Greek in Western Europe, 1476–1516." In *Literacy, Education and Manuscript Transmission in Byzantium and Beyond,* edited by Catherine Holmes and Judith Waring, 199–224. Leiden: Brill, 2002.

Bouwsma, William James. *Venice and the Defense of Republican Liberty: Renaissance Values in the Age of the Counter Reformation.* Berkeley: University of California Press, 1968.

Branca, Vittore, ed. *La sapienza civile: studi sull'umanesimo a Venezia.* Florence: L.S. Olschki, 1998.

——. *Lauro Quirini Umanista.* Florence: L. S. Olschki, 1977.

——. "L'umanesimo." In *Storia di Venezia*. Vol. 4, Il Rinascimento, edited by Alberto Tenenti and Ugo Tucci, 723–56. Rome: Enciclopedia Italiana, 1996.

——. *Mercanti scrittori: ricordi nella Firenze tra Medioevo e Rinascimento*. Milan: Rusconi, 1986.

——. *Umanesimo europeo e umanesimo veneziano*. Florence: Sansoni, 1963.

Branca, Vittore, and Sante Graciotti, eds. *L'Umanesimo in Istria*. Florence: L. S. Olschki, 1983.

Braudel, Fernand. *The Mediterranean and the Mediterranean World in the Age of Phillip II*. 2nd ed. Translated by Siân Reynolds. London: William Collins, 1972.

——. *Une leçon d'histoire de Fernand Braudel*. Paris: Arthaud, 1986.

Brewer, John. "Microhistory and the Histories of Everyday Life." *Cultural and Social History* 7, no. 1 (2010): 87–109.

Bromberger, Christian. "Towards an Anthropology of the Mediterranean." *History and Anthropology* 17, no. 1 (2006): 91–107.

Brown, Alison. "The Language of Empire." In *Florentine Tuscany: Structures and Practices of Power*, edited by William J. Connell and Andrea Zorzi, 32–47. Cambridge: Cambridge University Press, 2000.

Bühler, Curt Ferdinand. "Variants in the First Atlas of the Mediterranean." *Gutenberg Jahrbuch* 32 (1957): 94–97.

Burckhardt, Jacob. *The Civilization of the Renaissance in Italy*. Translated by S. G. C. Middlemore. 1990; repr., London: Penguin Books, 2004.

Burke, Ersie. "Our Daughters and Our Future: Elite Greco-Venetian Marriages, 1520–1610." In *Marriage in Premodern Europe: Italy and Beyond*, edited by Jacqueline Murray, 169–98. Toronto: Centre for Reformation and Renaissance Studies, 2012.

Busetto, Giorgio. "Coppo, Pietro." In *Dizionario biografico degli Italiani*, 28. Rome: Istituto dell'Enciclopedia italiana, 1983.

Byars, Jana. "From Illegitimate Son to Legal Citizen: Noble Bastards in Early Modern Venice." *Sixteenth Century Journal* 42, no. 3 (2011): 643–63.

Campana, Augusto. "The Origin of the Word 'Humanist.'" *Journal of the Warburg and Courtauld Institutes* 9 (1946): 60–73.

Campbell, Julie D., and Anne R. Larsen, eds. *Early Modern Women and Transnational Communities of Letters*. Farnham: Ashgate, 2009.

Campbell, Tony. *The Earliest Printed Maps, 1472–1500*. Berkeley: University of California Press, 1987.

Carlton, Genevieve. "Making an Impression: The Display of Maps in Sixteenth-Century Venetian Homes." *Imago Mundi* 64, no. 1 (2012): 28–40.

Castellani, Giorgio. "Giorgio da Trebisonda, maestro di eloquenza a Vicenza e a Venezia." *Nuovo Archivio Veneto* 11, no 1. (1896): 123–42.

Celenza, Christopher S. *The Lost Italian Renaissance: Humanists, Historians, and Latin's Legacy*. Baltimore: Johns Hopkins University Press, 2004.

Chambers, David S. *The Imperial Age of Venice, 1380–1580*. London: Thames & Hudson, 1970.

——. "Merit and Money: The Procurators of St Mark and Their *Commissioni*, 1443–1605." *Journal of the Warburg and Courtauld Institutes* 60 (1997): 23–88.

Chavasse, Ruth. "The First Known Author's Copyright, September 1486, in the Context of a Humanist Career." *Bulletin of the John Rylands University Library of Manchester* 69, no. 1 (1986): 11–37.

———. "Humanism Commemorated: The Venetian Memorials to Benedetto Brugnolo and Marcantonio Sabellico." In *Florence and Italy: Renaissance Studies in Honour of Nicolai Rubinstein*, edited by Peter Denley and Caroline Elam, 455–61. London: Westfield Publications in Medieval Studies, 1988.

———. "The *studia humanitatis* and the Making of a Humanist Career: Marcantonio Sabellico's Exploitation of Humanist Literary Genres." *Renaissance Studies* 17, no. 1 (2003): 27–38.

Chojnacka, Monica. *Working Women of Early Modern Venice*. Baltimore: Johns Hopkins University Press, 2001.

Chojnacki, Stanley. *Women and Men in Renaissance Venice: Twelve Essays on Patrician Society*. Baltimore: Johns Hopkins University Press, 2000.

Ciccolella, Federica. *Donati Graeci: Learning Greek in the Renaissance*. Leiden: Brill, 2008.

Cleall, Esme, Laura Ishiguro, and Emily J. Manktelow. "Imperial Relations: Histories of Family in the British Empire." *Journal of Colonialism and Colonial History* 14, no 1. (2013): n.p.

Clough, Cecil H. "The Cult of Antiquity: Letters and Letter Collections." In *Cultural Aspects of the Italian Renaissance: Essays in Honor of Paul Oskar Kristeller*, edited by Cecil H. Clough, 33–67. Manchester: Manchester University Press, 1976.

Cochrane, Eric W. *Historians and Historiography in the Italian Renaissance*. Chicago: University of Chicago Press, 1981.

Cochrane, Eric W., and Julius Kirschner. "Deconstructing Lane's Venice." *Journal of Modern History* 47, no. 2 (1975): 321–34.

Colin, Jean. *Cyriaque d'Ancône: le voyageur, le marchand, l'humaniste*. Paris: Maloine, 1967.

Colley, Linda. *The Ordeal of Elizabeth Marsh: A Woman in World History*. London: Harper Press, 2007.

Conley, Tom. *The Self-Made Map: Cartographic Writing in Early Modern France*. Minneapolis: University of Minnesota Press, 1996.

———. "Virtual Reality and the *Isolario*," *Annali d'Italianistica* 14: "Hodoeporics: On Travel Literature" (1996): 121–30.

Connell, William J. "The Humanist Citizen as Provincial Governor." In *Florentine Tuscany: Structures and Practices of Power*, edited by W. J. Connell and Andrea Zorzi, 144–64. Cambridge: Cambridge University Press, 2000.

Cosgrove, Denis. "Mapping New Worlds: Culture and Cartography in Sixteenth-Century Venice." *Imago Mundi* 44 (1992): 65–89.

Cowan, Alexander. *Marriage, Manners and Mobility in Early Modern Venice*. Aldershot: Ashgate, 2007.

Cozzi, Gaetano. "Considerazioni sull'amministrazione della giustizia nella Repubblica di Venezia (sec. XVI-XVI)." In *Florence and Venice: Comparisons and Relations*. Vol. 2. Edited by Sergio Bertelli and Nicolai Rubinstein, 101–33. Florence: La Nuova Italia, 1980.

———. "La politica del diritto." In *Stato società e giustizia nella Repubblica Veneta (sec. XV–XVIII)*, 17–152. Rome: Jouvence, 1981.

Crescenzi, Victor. *Esse de Maiori Consilio. Legittimità civile e legittimazione politica nella Repubblica di Venezia (sec. XIII-XVI)*. Rome: Istituto Palazzo Borromini, 1996.

Crljenko, Marija Mogorović. "The Position of Women in 'Istrian Marriage Pattern' (15th–16th centuries)." In "Donne a Venezia: spazi di libertà e forme di potere (sec. XVI–XVIII)," *Storia di Venezia* (2008), http://www.storiadivenezia.net /sito/donne/Mogorovic_Position.pdf

——. "Women, Marriage, and Family in Istrian Communities in the Fifteenth and Sixteenth Centuries." In *Across the Religious Divide: Women, Property, and the Law in the Wider Mediterranean (ca. 1300–1800)*, edited by Jutta Sperling and Shona Kelly Wray, 137–57. New York: Routledge, 2010.

Crouzet-Pavan, Elisabeth. *Venice Triumphant: The Horizons of a Myth*. Translated by Lydia G. Cochrane. Baltimore: Johns Hopkins University Press, 2002.

Damen, Giada. "The Trade in Antiquities between Italy and the Eastern Mediterranean (ca. 1400–1600)." PhD diss., Princeton University, 2012.

Dandelet, Thomas J. *The Renaissance of Empire in Early Modern Europe*. Cambridge: Cambridge University Press, 2014.

Darovec, Darko. *Auscultauerint cum notario: Istrian Notaries and Vicedomini at the Time of the Republic of Venice*. Venice: Cafoscarina, 2015.

——. "Ruolo dei vicedomini Istriani nella redazione degli atti notarili in rapporto ad uffici affini dell' area Adriatica." *Acta Histriae* 18, no. 4 (2010): 789–822.

Davidson, Nicholas. "'As Much for Its Culture as for Its Arms': The Cultural Relations of Venice and Its Dependent Cities, 1400–1700." In *Mediterranean Urban Culture, 1400–1700*, edited by Alexander Cowan, 197–214. Exeter: University of Exeter Press, 2000.

Davis, James C. *A Venetian Family and Its Fortune, 1500–1900: The Donà and the Conservation of Their Wealth*. Philadelphia: American Philosophical Society, 1975.

De Luca, Lia. "Le immigrazioni in Istria nel Cinquecento e Seicento: un quadro d'insieme." *Ateneo Veneto* CXCIC, ser. 3 11/I-II (2012): 49–82.

De Vivo, Filippo. "Historical Justifications of Venetian Power in the Adriatic." *Journal of the History of Ideas* 64, no. 2 (2003): 159–76.

——. *Information and Communication in Venice: Rethinking Early Modern Politics*. Oxford: Oxford University Press, 2007.

Degrassi, Attilio. "Podestà e Vicedomini d'Isola." *Atti e Memorie della Società Istriana di Archeologia e Storia Patria*, n.s., 17 (Venice, 1969): 9–12.

——. "Un umanista Isolano del Cinquecento: Francesco Egidio." *Atti e memorie della Società istriana di archeologia e storia patria* 37 (1925): 235–45.

Diller, Aubrey. "The Library of Francesco and Ermolao Barbaro." *Italia Medioevale e Umanistica* 6 (1963): 253–62.

Dionisotti, Carlo. *Gli umanisti e il volgare fra Quattro e Cinquecento*. Florence: Felice Le Mournier, 1968.

Djikic, Maya, and Keith Oatley. "The Art in Fiction: From Indirect Communication to Changes of the Self." *Psychology of Aesthetics, Creativity, and the Arts* 8, no. 4 (2014): 498–505.

Djikic, Maya, Keith Oatley, Sara Zoeterman, and Jordan B. Peterson. "On Being Moved by Art: How Reading Fiction Transforms the Self." *Creativity Research Journal* 21, no. 1 (2009): 24–29.

Donati, Claudio. *L'idea di nobiltà in Italia: secoli XIV-XVIII.* Rome: Laterza, 1988.

Donattini, Massimo. "Bartolommeo da li Sonetti, il suo Isolario e un viaggio di Giovanni Bembo." *Geografia Antiqua* 3–4 (1994–95): 211–36.

——. *Spazio e modernità: libri, carte, isolari nell'età delle scoperte.* Bologna: CLUEB, 2000.

Doumerc, Bernard. "Il dominio del mare." In *Storia di Venezia: Il Rinascimento. Politica e cultura.* Vol. 4, *Il Rinascimento*, edited by Alberto Tenenti and Ugo Tucci, 113–80. Rome: Enciclopedia Italiana, 1996.

——. "La Tana au XVe siècle: comptoir ou colonie?" In *État et Colonisation au Moyen Âge et à la Renaissance*, edited by Michel Balard, 251–66. Lyon: La Manufacture, 1989.

Dursteler, Eric R. *Renegade Women: Gender, Identity, and Boundaries in the Early Modern Mediterranean.* Baltimore: Johns Hopkins University Press, 2011.

——. *Venetians in Constantinople: Nation, Identity, and Coexistence in the Early Modern Mediterranean.* Baltimore: Johns Hopkins University Press, 2006.

Edwards, Catharine. *Writing Rome: Textual Approaches to the City.* Cambridge: Cambridge University Press, 1996.

Elliott, John H. "A Europe of Composite Monarchies." *Past and Present* 137 (1992): 48–71.

Embiricos, Alexandre. *La renaissance crétoise.* Vol. 1, *La littérature.* Paris: Société d'édition "Les belles lettres," 1960.

Faggion, Lucien. "Violence, Rites and Social Regulation in the Venetian *Terra Firma* in the Sixteenth Century" In *Aspects of Violence in Renaissance Europe*, edited by Jonathan Davies, 184–204. Farnham: Ashgate, 2013.

Fenster, Thelma, and Daniel Lord Smail, eds. *Fama: The Politics of Talk and Reputation in Medieval Europe.* Ithaca, NY: Cornell University Press, 2003.

Ferraro, Joanne M. *Marriage Wars in Late Renaissance Venice.* Oxford: Oxford University Press, 2001.

——. *Nefarious Crimes, Contested Justice: Illicit Sex and Infanticide in the Republic of Venice, 1557–1789.* Baltimore: Johns Hopkins University Press, 2008.

Finlay, Robert. *Politics in Renaissance Venice.* New Brunswick, NJ: Rutgers University Press, 1980.

Fleet, Kate. "Italian Perceptions of the Turks in the Fourteenth and Fifteenth Centuries." *Journal of Mediterranean Studies* 5 (1995): 159–72.

Fortini Brown, Patricia. "Becoming a Man of Empire: The Construction of Patrician Identity in a Republic of Equals." In *Architecture, Art, and Identity in Venice and Its Territories, 1450–1750*, edited by Nebahat Avcioğlu and Emma Jones, 231–49. Farnham: Ashgate, 2013.

——. "Between Observation and Appropriation: Venetian Encounters with a Fragmentary Classical Past." In *Pietre di Venezia: spolia in se spolia in re*, edited by Monica Centanni and Luigi Sperti, 221–40. Rome: L'Erma di Bretschneider, 2016.

——. *Private Lives in Renaissance Venice: Art, Architecture, and the Family.* New Haven, CT: Yale University Press, 2004.

——. "Ritual Geographies in Venice's Colonial Empire." In *Rituals of Politics and Culture in Early Modern Europe: Essays in Honour of Edward Muir*, edited by Mark Jurdjevic and Rolf Strøm-Olsen, 43–89. Toronto: Centre for Reformation and Renaissance Studies, 2016.

———. "The Venetian Loggia: Representation, Exchange, and Identity in Venice's Colonial Empire." In *Viewing Greece: Cultural and Political Agency in the Medieval and Early Modern Mediterranean*, edited by Sharon E. J. Gerstel, 207–35. Turnhout: Brepols 2016.

———. *Venice and Antiquity: The Venetian Sense of the Past*. New Haven, CT: Yale University Press, 1996.

Frick, Carole Collier. *Dressing Renaissance Florence: Families, Fortunes, and Fine Clothing*. Baltimore: Johns Hopkins University Press, 2002.

Gaeta, Franco. "Storiografia, coscienza nazionale e politica culturale nella Venezia del Rinascimento." In *Storia della cultura veneta*. Vol. 3, *Dal primo Quattrocento al concilio di* Trento, no. 1, edited by Girolamo Arnaldi and Manlio Pastore Stocchi, 1–91. Vicenza: Neri Pozza, 1980–81.

Gaisser, Julia Haig. *Catullus and His Renaissance Readers*. Oxford: Clarendon Press, 1993.

Galantino, Francesco. *Storia di Soncino, con documenti*. Vol. 1. Milan: Bernardoni, 1869.

Garin, Eugenio. *Italian Humanism: Philosophy and Civic Life in the Renaissance*. Oxford: Blackwell, 1965.

Geanakoplos, Deno John. *Greek Scholars in Venice: Studies in the Dissemination of Greek Learning from Byzantium to Western Europe*. Cambridge, MA: Harvard University Press, 1962.

Georgopoulou, Maria. *Venice's Mediterranean Colonies: Architecture and Urbanism*. Cambridge: Cambridge University Press, 2001.

Gerstel, Sharon E. J. *Rural Lives and Landscapes in Late Byzantium: Art, Archaeology, and Ethnography*. Cambridge: Cambridge University Press, 2015.

Ghezzo, Michele Pietro, ed. "Città e sistema Adriatico alla fine del medioevo." *Atti e memorie della Società dalmata di storia patria* 26 (Venice, 1997).

Ghobrial, John Paul. "The Secret Life of Elias of Babylon and the Uses of Global Microhistory." *Past and Present* 222 (2014): 51–93.

Gilbert, Felix. "Biondo, Sabellico, and the Beginnings of Venetian Historiography." In *Florilegium historiale: Essays Presented to Wallace K. Ferguson*, edited by John Gordon Rowe and W. H. Stockdale, 276–93. Toronto: University of Toronto Press, 1971.

———. "Humanism in Venice." In *Florence and Venice: Comparisons and Relations*. Vol. 1, *Quattrocento*, edited by Sergio Bertelli, Nicolai Rubinstein, and Craig Hugh Smith, 13–26. Florence: La Nuova Italia, 1979.

Gluzman, Renard. "Resurrection of a Sunken Ship: The Remarkable Salvage of the Venetian *marciliana* That Saved Cattaro from Barbarossa." *Archivio Veneto*, 6th ser., no. 8 (2014): 29–78.

Goffman, Daniel, and Christopher Stroop. "Empire as Composite: The Ottoman Polity and the Typology of Dominion." In *Imperialisms: Historical and Literary Investigations, 1500–1800*, edited by Elizabeth Sauer and Balachandra Rajan, 129–46. New York: Palgrave Macmillan, 2004.

Goldthwaite, Richard A. *Private Wealth in Renaissance Florence*. Princeton, NJ: Princeton University Press, 1968.

Gothein, Percy. *Francesco Barbaro: Früh-Humanismus und Staatskunst in Venedig*. Berlin: Verlag Die Runde, 1932.

Grafton, Anthony. *Defenders of the Text: The Traditions of Scholarship in an Age of Science, 1450–1800*. Cambridge, MA: Harvard University Press, 1991.

Grafton, Anthony, and Lisa Jardine. *From Humanism to the Humanities: Education and the Liberal Arts in Fifteenth- and Sixteenth-Century Europe*. Cambridge, MA: Harvard University Press, 1986.

Greene, Molly. *Catholic Pirates and Greek Merchants: A Maritime History of the Mediterranean*. Princeton, NJ: Princeton University Press, 2010.

——. *A Shared World: Christians and Muslims in the Early Modern Mediterranean*. Princeton, NJ: Princeton University Press, 2000.

Gregory, Brad S. "Is Small Beautiful? Microhistory and the History of Everyday Life." *History and Theory* 38, no. 1 (1999): 100–110.

Grendler, Paul F. *Schooling in Renaissance Italy: Literacy and Learning, 1300–1600*. Baltimore: Johns Hopkins University Press, 1989.

Grivaud, Gilles. *Entrelacs chiprois. Essai sur les lettres et la vie intellectuelle dans le royaume de Chypre (1191–1570)*. Nicosia: Moufflon Publications, 2009.

Grossberg, Lawrence. "Identity and Cultural Studies: Is That All There Is?" In *Questions of Cultural Identity*, edited by Stuart Hall and Paul du Gay, 87–107. London: Sage, 1996.

Grubb, James S. *Family Memoirs from Venice (15th to 17th Centuries)*. Rome: Viella, 2009.

——. *Firstborn of Venice: Vicenza in the Early Renaissance State*. Baltimore: Johns Hopkins University Press, 1988.

——. "Memory and Identity: Why Venetians Didn't Keep Ricordanze." *Renaissance Studies* 8, no. 4 (1994): 375–87.

——. *Provincial Families of the Renaissance: Private and Public Life in the Veneto*. Baltimore: Johns Hopkins University Press, 1996.

——. "When Myths Lose Power: Four Decades of Venetian Historiography." *Journal of Modern History* 58, no. 1 (1986): 43–94.

Guglielminetti, Marziano. "Per un sottogenere della letteratura di viaggio: gl'isolari fra quatro e cinquecento." In *La letteratura di viaggio dal Medioevo al Rinascimento: generi e problemi*, edited by Silvia Benso, 107–17. Alexandria: Edizione dell'Orso, 1989.

Guillén, Claudio. "Notes toward the Study of the Renaissance Letter." In *Renaissance Genres: Essays on Theory, History, and Interpretation*, edited by Barbara Kiefer Lewalski, 70–101. Cambridge, MA: Harvard University Press, 1986.

Hale, John, ed. *Renaissance Venice*. London: Faber and Faber, 1973.

Hall, Catherine. "Making Colonial Subjects: Education in the Age of Empire." *History of Education* 37, no. 6 (2008): 773–87.

Hankins, James. "The 'Baron Thesis' after Forty Years and Some Recent Studies of Leonardo Bruni." *Journal of the History of Ideas* 56, no. 2 (1995): 309–38.

——, ed. *Renaissance Civic Humanism: Reappraisals and Reflections*. Cambridge: Cambridge University Press, 2000.

Harley, J. B., and David Woodward, eds. *The History of Cartography*. Vol. 3, *Cartography in the European Renaissance*. Chicago: University of Chicago Press, 2007.

Harris, Jonathan, Catherine Holmes, and Eugenia Russell, eds. *Byzantines, Latins, and Turks in the Eastern Mediterranean World after 1150*. Oxford: Oxford University Press, 2012.

Harris, William V., ed. *Rethinking the Mediterranean*. Oxford: Oxford University Press, 2005.

Hasluck, F. W. "Depopulation in the Aegean Islands and the Turkish Conquest," *Annual of the British School at Athens* 17 (1910/1911): 151–81.

Holton, David. "Classical Antiquity and Cretan Renaissance Poetry." *Journal of the Hellenistic Diaspora* 27, nos. 1–2 (2001): 87–101.

Holton, David, ed. *Literature and Society in Renaissance Crete*. Cambridge: Cambridge University Press, 1991.

Horden, Peregrine, and Nicholas Purcell. *The Corrupting Sea: A Study of Mediterranean History*. Oxford: Oxford University Press, 2000.

Horodowich, Elizabeth. *Language and Statecraft in Early Modern Venice*. Cambridge: Cambridge University Press, 2008.

——. "The Gossiping Tongue: Oral Networks, Public Life and Political Culture in Early Modern Venice." *Renaissance Studies* 19, no. 1 (2005): 23–45.

——. "The New Venice: Historians and Historiography in the 21st Century Lagoon." *History Compass* 2 (2004): 1–27.

Howard, Deborah. *Venice and the East: The Impact of the Islamic World on Venetian Architecture 1100–1500*. New Haven, CT: Yale University Press, 2000.

Hurlburt, Holly. *Daughter of Venice: Caterina Corner, Queen of Cyprus and Woman of the Renaissance*. New Haven, CT: Yale University Press, 2015.

Ivetić, Egidio. *L'Istria moderna 1500–1797: una regione confine*. Verona: Cierre Edizioni, 2010.

——. *Un confine nel Mediterraneo. L'Adriatico orientale tra Italia e Slavia (1300–1900)*. Rome: Viella, 2014.

Ivović, Sandra. "Humanism in Schools: Italian Humanists as Teachers in the 15th-Century Ragusa and Dalmatian Communes." *Croatiae auctores Latini*. http://www.ffzg.unizg.hr/klafil/dokuwiki/doku.php/z:humanism-eastern-adriatic. Accessed 26 October 2017.

Jacoby, David. "The Demographic Evolution of Euboea under Latin Rule, 1205–1470." In *The Greek Islands and the Sea*, edited by Julian Chrystostomides, Charalambos Dendrinos, and Jonathan Harris, 132–79. Camberley: Porphyrogenitus, 2004.

Jasanoff, Maya. *Edge of Empire: Conquest and Collecting in the East, 1750–1850*. London: Fourth Estate, 2005.

Jovanović, Neven. "Dubrovnik in the Corpus of Eastern Adriatic Humanist *Laudationes urbium*." *Dubrovnik Annals* 16 (2012): 23–36.

Judde de Larivière, Claire. *Naviguer, commercer, gouverner: Économie maritime et pouvoirs à Venise (XVᵉ–XVI siècles)*. Leiden: Brill, 2008.

Jurdjevic, Mark. "Hedgehogs and Foxes: The Present and Future of Italian Renaissance Intellectual History." *Past and Present* 195 (May 2007): 241–68.

Kandler, Pietro. "L'Archivio di Capodistria." *L'Istria* 38–39 (1852): 177–180, and 182–84.

Karmon, David. *The Ruin of the Eternal City: Antiquity and Preservation in Renaissance Rome*. Oxford: Oxford University Press, 2011.

Kent, F. W. *Household and Lineage in Renaissance Florence: The Family Life of the Capponi, Ginori, and Rucellai*. Princeton, NJ: Princeton University Press, 1977.

Kiel, Machiel. "The Smaller Aegean Islands in the 16th–18th Centuries According to Ottoman Documents." *Hesperia Supplements*. Vol. 40, *Between Venice and Istanbul: Colonial Landscapes in Early Modern Greece* (2007): 35–54.

King, Margaret. *The Death of the Child Valerio Marcello*. Chicago: University of Chicago Press, 1994.

———. "The Social Role of Intellectuals: Antonio Gramsci and the Italian Renaissance." *Soundings* 61, no. 1 (1978): 23–46.

———. *Venetian Humanism in an Age of Patrician Dominance*. Princeton, NJ: Princeton University Press, 1986.

———. "The Venetian Intellectual World." In *A Companion to Venetian History, 1400–1797*, edited by Eric R. Dursteler, 571–614. Leiden: Brill, 2013.

———, ed. and trans. "Introduction." In *The Wealth of Wives: A Fifteenth-Century Marriage Manual*. Toronto: Iter Academic Press, 2015: 1–63.

Kitromilides, Paschalis M. "Law and Humanism in Cretan Culture: The Evidence of an Early Seventeenth-Century Library Catalogue." In *Pepragmena tou V diethnous kretologiou synedriou*. Vol. 2, 182–96. Iraklion, 1985.

Klapisch-Zuber, Christiane. *Women, Family, and Ritual in Renaissance Italy*. Chicago: University of Chicago Press, 1985.

Klapisch-Zuber, Christiane, and David Herlihy. *Tuscans and Their Families: A Study of the Florentine Catasto of 1427*. New Haven, CT: Yale University Press, 1985.

Krekić, Bariša. *The Urban Society of Eastern Europe in Premodern Times*. Berkeley: University of California Press, 1987.

Kristeller, Paul Oskar, ed. *Iter Italicum: A Finding List of Uncatalogued or Incompletely Catalogued Humanistic Manuscripts of the Renaissance*. 6 vols. London: Warburg Institute, 1963–96.

———. "Petrarch's 'Averroists': A Note on the History of Aristotelianism in Venice, Padua, and Bologna." *Bibliothèque d'Humanisme et Renaissance* 14, no. 1 (1952): 59–65.

———. "The Humanist Movement." In *Renaissance Thought: The Classic, Scholastic, and Humanistic Strains*, 3–23. New York: Harper & Row, 1961

———. *Renaissance Thought and Its Sources*. Edited by Michael Mooney. New York: Columbia University Press, 1979.

Kuehn, Thomas. *Illegitimacy in Renaissance Florence*. Ann Arbor: University of Michigan Press, 2002.

Labalme, Patricia H. *Bernardo Giustiniani: A Venetian of the Quattrocento*. Rome: Edizioni di storia e letteratura, 1969.

———. "The Last Will of a Venetian Patrician (1489)." In *Philosophy and Humanism: Renaissance Essays in Honor of Paul Oskar Kristeller*, edited by Edward P. Mahoney, 483–501. New York: Columbia University Press, 1976.

Lane, Frederic C. "Family Partnerships and Joint Ventures in the Venetian Republic." *Journal of Economic History* 4, no. 2 (1944): 178–96.

———. *Venice: A Maritime Republic*. Baltimore: Johns Hopkins University Press, 1973.

Lazzarini, Lino. *Paulo de Bernardo e i primordi dell'umanesimo in Venezia*. Geneva: L. S. Olschki, 1930.

Lestringant, Frank. *Le livre des îles: atlas et récits insulaires de la genèse a Jules Verne*. Geneva: Droz, 2002.

Liang, Yuen-Gen. *Family and Empire: The Fernández de Córdoba and the Spanish Realm.* Philadelphia: University of Pennsylvania Press, 2011.

Loenertz, Raymond-Joseph. *Les Ghisi: Dynastes vénitiens dans l'Archipel 1207–1390.* Florence: L. S. Olschki, 1975.

Lowry, Martin. *The World of Aldus Manutius: Business and Scholarship in Renaissance Venice.* Oxford: Blackwell, 1979.

Lupher, David A. *Romans in a New World: Classical Models in Sixteenth-Century Spanish America.* Ann Arbor: University of Michigan, 2003.

Luttrell, Anthony T. "The Latins and Life on the Smaller Aegean Islands, 1204–1453." *Mediterranean Historical Review* 4, no. 1 (1989): 146–57.

Maffei, Elena. "Attività notarile in aree bilingui: i vicedomini a Trieste e in Istria nel 1300." *Nuova Rivista Storica* 83 (1999): 489–542.

Maglaque, Erin. "The Literary Culture of the Venetian Mediterranean." *Italian Studies* 73, no. 1 (forthcoming).

——. "Writing the Local Landscape: Renaissance Chorographies of Istria." In *Creating a Third Nature: Gardens and Constructions of Landscape in the Italian Renaissance,* edited by Anatole Tchikine. Philadelphia: University of Pennsylvania Press, forthcoming.

Majer, Francesco. *Inventario dell'Antico Archivio Municipale di Capodistria.* Koper: Cobol & Priora, 1904.

Malcolm, Noel. *Agents of Empire: Knights, Corsairs, Jesuits and Spies in the Sixteenth-Century Mediterranean World.* London: Allen Lane, 2015.

Mallett, Michael E., and John R. Hale. *The Military Organization of a Renaissance State: Venice, c.1400–1617.* Cambridge: Cambridge University Press, 1984.

Markesinis, Basile. "Janos Lascaris, la bibliothèque d'Avramis à Corfou et Le Paris, Gr. 854." *Scriptorium* 54 (2000): 302–6.

Martin, John, and Dennis Romano, eds. *Venice Reconsidered: The History and Civilization of an Italian City-State, 1297–1797.* Baltimore: Johns Hopkins University Press, 2000.

Martinović, Ivica. "Unpublished Manuscript Heritage of the Croatian Latinists in the Libraries and Archives of Dubrovnik: Preliminary Report." Paper presented at the Euroclassica Congress, Dubrovnik, March 2005. http://www.eduhi.at /gegenstand/ . . . /data/Euroclassica_zbornik_Dubrovnik.doc.

Maxson, Brian. *The Humanist World of Renaissance Florence, 1400–1480.* Cambridge: Cambridge University Press, 2014.

Mazzatinti, Giuseppe, ed. *Inventari dei manoscritti delle biblioteche d'Italia.* Vol. 30. Florence: L. S. Olschki, 1924.

McClure, George W. *Sorrow and Consolation in Italian Humanism.* Princeton, NJ: Princeton University Press, 1991.

McKee, Sally. *Uncommon Dominion: Venetian Crete and the Myth of Ethnic Purity.* Philadelphia: University of Pennsylvania Press, 2000.

McManamon, John M. *Funeral Oratory and the Cultural Ideals of Italian Humanism.* Chapel Hill: University of North Carolina Press, 1989.

Meserve, Margaret. *Empires of Islam in Renaissance Historical Thought.* Cambridge, MA: Harvard University Press, 2008.

——. "News from Negroponte: Politics, Popular Opinion, and Information in the First Decade of the Italian Press." *Renaissance Quarterly* 59, no. 2 (2006): 440–480.

Mitchell, Charles. "Ex libris Kiriaci Anconitani." *Italia Medioevale e Umanistica* 5 (1962): 283–99.

Morteani, Luigi. "Isola ed i suoi statuti." *Atti e Memorie della Società Istriana di Archeologia e Storia Patria* 4, nos. 1–4 (1887–88).

Moss, Ann. *Printed Commonplace-Books and the Structuring of Renaissance Thought.* Oxford: Oxford University Press, 1996.

Mueller, Reinhold C. "Aspects of Venetian Sovereignty in Medieval and Renaissance Dalmatia." In *Quattrocento Adriatico: Fifteenth-Century Art of the Adriatic Rim*, edited by Charles Dempsey, 29–56. Bologna: Nuova Alfa Editoriale, 1996.

Muir, Edward. *Civic Ritual in Renaissance Venice.* Princeton, NJ: Princeton University Press, 1981.

Nagel, Alexander, and Christopher Wood. *Anachronic Renaissance.* New York: Zone Books, 2010.

Nardi, Bruno. *Saggi sulla cultura veneta del Quattro e Cinquecento.* Edited by Paolo Mazzatini. Padua: Antenore, 1971.

Nauert, Charles. "Renaissance Humanism: An Emergent Consensus and Its Critics." *Indiana Social Studies Quarterly* 33 (1980): 5–20.

Nederman, Cary J. "Humanism and Empire: Aeneas Sylvius Piccolomini, Cicero and the Imperial Ideal." *Historical Journal* 36, no. 3 (1993): 499–515.

O'Connell, Monique. *Men of Empire: Power and Negotiation in Venice's Maritime State.* Baltimore: Johns Hopkins University Press, 2009.

——. "The Sexual Politics of Empire: Civic Honor and Official Crime outside Renaissance Venice." *Journal of Early Modern History* 15 (2011): 331–48.

Olin, John C. *Erasmus, Utopia, and the Jesuits: Essays on the Outreach of Humanism.* New York: Fordham University Press, 1994.

Paci, Gianfranco, and Sergio Sconocchia, eds. *Ciriaco d'Ancona e la cultura antiquaria dell'umanesimo. Atti del convegno internazionale di studio.* Parma: Diabasis, 1998.

Palmer, Ada. *Reading Lucretius in the Renaissance.* Cambridge, MA: Harvard University Press, 2014.

Panagiotakes, Nikolaus M. "The Italian Background of Early Cretan Literature." *Dumbarton Oaks Papers* 49 (1995): 281–323.

Parroni, Piergiorgio. "Maestri di grammatica a Pesaro nel Quattrocento." *Res Publica Litterarum* 5, no. 1 (1982): 205–20.

Pastore Stocchi, Manlio. "Scuola e cultura umanistica fra due secoli." In *Storia della cultura veneta.* Vol. 3, *Dal primo Quattrocento al concilio di Trento*, no. 1, 93–121. Edited by Girolamo Arnaldi and Manlio Pastore Stocchi. Vicenza: Neri Pozza, 1980–81.

Pertusi, Agostino. "L'umanesimo greco della fine del secolo XIV agli inizi del secolo XVI." In *Storia della cultura veneta.* Vol. 3, *Dal primo Quattrocento al concilio di Trento*, no. 1, 177–264. Edited by Girolamo Arnaldi and Manlio Pastore Stocchi. Vicenza: Neri Pozza, 1980–81.

Pesaro, Marco Francesco. *Catalogo della libreria d'un illustre patrizio veneto.* Padua: Stamperia del Seminario, 1805.

Petrovich, Michael B. "Croatian Humanists and the Writing of History in the Fifteenth and Sixteenth Centuries." *Slavic Review* 37, no. 4 (1978): 624–39.

Povolo, Claudio. "Note per uno studio dell'infanticidio nella Repubblica di Venezia nei secoli XV–XVIII." *Atti dell'Istituto Veneto di Scienze, Lettere ed Arti* 137 (1978–79): 115–31.

Purcell, Nicholas. "Colonization and Mediterranean History." In *Ancient Colonizations: Analogy, Similarity, and Difference*, edited by Henry Hurst and Sara Owen, 115–39. London: Duckworth, 2005.

Queller, Donald E. *Two Studies on Venetian Government.* Geneva: Droz, 1977.

——. *The Venetian Patriciate: Reality versus Myth.* Urbana: University of Illinois Press, 1986.

Queller, Donald, and Thomas F. Madden. "Father of the Bride: Fathers, Daughters, and Dowries in Late Medieval and Early Renaissance Venice." *Renaissance Quarterly* 46 (1993): 685–710.

Rabil, Albert, Jr. *Erasmus and the New Testament: The Mind of a Christian Humanist.* San Antonio, TX: Trinity University Press, 1972.

Raby, Julian. "Cyriacus of Ancona and the Ottoman Sultan Mehmed II." *Journal of the Warburg and Courtauld Institutes* 43 (1980): 242–46.

Ragone, Giuseppe. "Il Liber Insularum Archipelagi di Cristoforo dei Buondelmonti: filologia del testo, filologia dell'immagine." In *Humanisme et culture geographique à l'epoque du Concile de Constance*, edited by Didier Marcotte, 177–218. Turnhout: Brepols, 2002.

Raines, Dorit. *L'Invention du mythe aristocratique: L'image de soi du patriciat vénitien au temps de la Sérénissime.* 2 vols. Venice: Istituto Veneto di Scienze, Lettere ed Arti, 2006.

Revest, Clémence. "Les discours de Gasparino Barzizza et la diffusion du style cicéronien dans la première moitié du XVe siècle. Premiers aperçus." *Mélanges de l'École française de Rome* 128, no. 1 (2016): 47–72.

Roberts, Sean. *Printing a Mediterranean World: Florence, Constantinople, and the Renaissance of Geography.* Cambridge, MA: Harvard University Press, 2013.

Romano, Dennis. *Housecraft and Statecraft: Domestic Service in Renaissance Venice, 1400–1600.* Baltimore: Johns Hopkins University Press, 1996.

——. *Patricians and Popolani: The Social Foundations of the Venetian Renaissance State.* Baltimore: Johns Hopkins University Press, 1987.

Romney, Susanah Shaw. *New Netherland Connections: Intimate Networks and Atlantic Ties in Seventeenth-Century America.* Chapel Hill: University of North Carolina Press, 2014.

Roper, Lyndal. *Oedipus and the Devil: Witchcraft, Religion and Sexuality in Early Modern Germany.* London: Routledge, 1994.

Ross, J. B. "Venetian Schools and Teachers Fourteenth to Early Sixteenth Century: A Survey and a Study of Giovanni Battista Egnazio." *Renaissance Quarterly* 29, no. 4 (1976): 521–66.

Ross, Sarah G. *Everyday Renaissances: The Quest for Cultural Legitimacy in Venice.* Cambridge, MA: Harvard University Press, 2016.

Rothman, Natalie E. *Brokering Empire: Trans-Imperial Subjects between Venice and Istanbul.* Ithaca, NY: Cornell University Press, 2011.

Rothschild, Emily. *The Inner Life of Empires: An Eighteenth Century History.* Princeton, NJ: Princeton University Press, 2011.

Rublack, Ulinka. *The Crimes of Women in Early Modern Germany.* Oxford: Oxford University Press, 2001.

Ruff, Julius R. *Violence in Early Modern Europe.* Cambridge: Cambridge University Press, 2001.

Ruggiero, Guido. *The Boundaries of Eros: Sex Crime and Sexuality in Renaissance Venice.* Oxford: Oxford University Press, 1985.

———. *Violence in Early Renaissance Venice.* New Brunswick, NJ: Rutgers University Press, 1980.

Rundle, David, ed. *Humanism in Fifteenth-Century Europe.* Oxford: Society for the Study of Medieval Languages and Literature, 2012.

Sabbadini, Remigio. *Le scoperte dei codici latini e greci nè secoli XIV e XV.* Florence: G. C. Sansoni, 1905.

Saint-Guillain, Guillaume. "Les conquérants de l'Archipel: l'empire Latin de Constantinople, Venise et les premiers seigneurs des Cyclades." In *Quarta Crociata: Venezia, Bizanzio, Impero Latino*, edited by Gherardo Ortalli, Giorgio Ravegnani, and Peter Schreiner, 125–233. Venice: Istituto Veneto di Scienze, Lettere ed Arti, 2006.

Salzberg, Rosa. "Masculine Republics: Establishing Authority in the Early Modern Venetian Printshop." In *Governing Masculinities in the Early Modern Period: Regulating Selves and Others*, edited by Susan Broomhall and Jacqueline Van Gent, 47–65. Farnham: Ashgate, 2011.

Scholz, Bernhard F. "Self-Fashioning by Mail: The Letters of a Renaissance Misfit." In "Correspondences: A Special Issue in Letters," special issue, *Prose Studies: History, Theory, Criticism* 19, no. 2 (1996): 136–48.

Scott, Joan Wallach. *The Fantasy of Feminist History.* Durham, NC: Duke University Press, 2011.

Shaw, James. *The Justice of Venice: Authorities and Liberties in the Urban Economy, 1550–1700.* Oxford: Oxford University Press, 2006.

Slot, Ben J. *Archipelagus turbatus: les Cyclades entre colonisation latine et occupation ottomane c. 1500–1718.* Istanbul: Nederlands Historisch-Archaeologisch Instituut, 1982.

Smyth, Adam. *Autobiography in Early Modern England.* Cambridge: Cambridge University Press, 2010.

Sperling, Jutta. *Convents and the Body Politic in Late Renaissance Venice.* Chicago: University of Chicago Press, 1999.

———. *Roman Charity: Queer Lactations in Early Modern Visual Culture.* New York: Columbia University Press, 2017.

Špoljarić, Luka. "Power and Subversion in the Ducal Palace: Dalmatian Patrician Humanists and Congratulatory Orations to Newly Elected Doges." In *Neo-Latin Contexts in Croatia and Tyrol: Challenges, Prospects, Case Studies*, edited by Luka Špoljarić, Neven Jovanović, Johanna Luggin, and Lav Šubarić. Vienna, forthcoming.

Stanković, Petar. *Biografia degli uomini distinti dell'Istria.* Vol. 2. Trieste, Italy: Marenigh, 1829.

Stöckly, Doris. *Le système de l'incanto des galées du marché a Venise (fin XIIᵉ-milieu XVᵉ siècle)*. Leiden: Brill, 1995.

Stoler, Ann Laura. "Tense and Tender Ties: The Politics of Comparison in North American History and (Post)Colonial Studies." *Journal of American History* 88, no. 3 (2001): 829–65.

——, ed. *Haunted by Empire: Geographies of Intimacy in North American History*. Durham, NC: Duke University Press, 2006.

Stouraiti, Anastasia. "Collecting the Past: Greek Antiquaries and Archaeological Knowledge in the Venetian Empire." In *Re-imagining the Past: Antiquity and Modern Greek Culture*, edited by Dimitris Tziovas, 29–46. Oxford: Oxford University Press, 2014.

Strocchia, Sharon. *Death and Ritual in Renaissance Florence*. Baltimore: Johns Hopkins University Press, 1992.

Szépe, Helena. *Privilege and Duty in the Serene Republic: Illuminated Manuscripts of Renaissance Venice*. New Haven, CT: Yale University Press, forthcoming.

Tateo, Francesco. "Coccio, Marcantonio, detto Marcantonio Sabellico." In *Dizionario biografico degli Italiani*, 26. Rome: Istituto dell'Enciclopedia italiana, 1982.

——. "Marcantonio Sabellico e la svolta del classicismo quattrocentesco." In *Florilegum historiale: Essays Presented to Wallace K. Ferguson*, edited by John Gordon Rowe and W. H. Stockdale, 41–64. Toronto: University of Toronto Press, 1971.

Taylor, Barbara. "Historical Subjectivity." In *History and Psyche: Culture, Psychoanalysis, and the Past*, edited by Sally Alexander and Barbara Taylor, 195–210. Basingstoke: Palgrave Macmillan, 2012.

——. "Separations of Soul: Solitude, Biography, History." *American Historical Review* 114, no. 3 (2009): 640–51.

Tenenti, Alberto. *Piracy and the Decline of Venice, 1580–1615*. London: Longmans, 1967.

Thiriet, Freddy. *La Romanie Vénitienne au Moyen Âge: le développement et l'exploitation du domaine colonial vénitien*. Paris: E. de Boccard, 1959.

Thomas, Lynn M. "Historicising Agency." *Gender & History* 28, no. 2 (2016): 324–39.

Tolias, George. "The Politics of the *Isolario*: Maritime Cosmography and Overseas Expansion during the Renaissance." *Historical Review/La Revue Historique* 9 (2012): 27–52.

Tracy, James. "From Humanism to the Humanities: A Critique of Grafton and Jardine." *Modern Language Quarterly* 51 (1990): 122–43.

Trencsényi, Balázs, and Márton Zászkaliczky. *For the Love of Which Country?: Composite States, National Histories, and Patriotic Discourses in Early Modern East Central Europe*. Leiden: Brill, 2010.

Trexler, Richard C. "Infanticide in Florence: New Sources and First Results." *History of Childhood Quarterly* 1, no. 1 (1973): 98–116.

Trivellato, Francesca. "Is There a Future for Italian Microhistory in the Age of Global History?" *California Italian Studies* 2, no. 1 (2011): 1–23.

Tsironis, Niki, ed. *The Book in Byzantium: Byzantine and Post-Byzantine Bookbinding*. Athens: Greek Society of Bookbinding, National Hellenic Research Foundation, 2008.

Tsougarakis, Dimitrios. "Some Remarks on the 'Cretica' of Cristoforo Buondelmonti." *Ariadnē* 3 (1985): 88–108.

Turner, Hilary L. "Christopher Buondelmonti and the *Isolario.*" *Terrae Incognitae* 19 (1987): 11–28.

Twinam, Ann. *Public Lives, Private Secrets: Gender, Honor, Sexuality and Illegitimacy in Colonial Spanish America.* Stanford, CA: Stanford University Press, 1999.

Urbanc, Mimi. "Contested Slovene Istria: A Distinctive Region of Its Own or Merely Part of a Larger Supranational Region?" *Die Erde* 138, no. 1 (2007): 77–96.

van der Spuy, Patricia. "Infanticide, Slavery and the Politics of Reproduction at Cape Colony, South Africa, in the 1820s." In *Infanticide: Historical Perspectives on Child Murder and Concealment, 1550–2000,* edited by Mark Jackson, 128–48. Aldershot: Ashgate 2002.

Veracini, Lorenzo. *Settler Colonialism: A Theoretical Overview.* Basingstoke: Palgrave Macmillan, 2010.

Viggiano, Alfredo. "Note sull'amministrazione veneziana in Istria nel secolo XV." *Acta Histriae* 3 (1994): 5–20.

Vilfan, Sergij. "Towns and States at the Juncture of the Alps, the Adriatic, and Pannonia." In *Cities and the Rise of States in Europe, AD 1000–1800,* edited by Charles Tilly and Wim P. Blockmans, 44–59. Boulder, CO: Westview Press, 1994.

Weiss, Roberto. *The Renaissance Discovery of Classical Antiquity.* Oxford: Blackwell, 1969.

Wilson, Bronwen. *The World in Venice: Print, the City, and Early Modern Identity.* Toronto: University of Toronto Press, 2005.

Wilson, Nigel G. *From Byzantium to Italy: Greek Studies in the Italian Renaissance.* London: Duckworth, 1992.

Wolff, Larry. *Venice and the Slavs: The Discovery of Dalmatia in the Age of Enlightenment.* Stanford, CA: Stanford University Press, 2002.

Woodward, David. *Five Centuries of Map Printing.* Chicago: University of Chicago Press, 1975.

——. *Maps as Prints in the Italian Renaissance: Makers, Distributors, and Consumers.* London: The British Library, 1996.

Wren Christian, Kathleen. *Empire without End: Antiquities Collections in Renaissance Rome, c. 1350–1527.* New Haven, CT: Yale University Press, 2010.

Zabughin, Vladimir. *Giulio Pomponio Leto: saggio critico.* Rome: La Vita Letteraria, 1909–12.

Zakythinos, Dionysios A. "Corsaires et pirates dans les mers grecques au temps de la domination Turque," *L'Hellenisme Contemporain* 10–11 (April-May 1939): 695–738.

Zeldes, Nadia. "Jewish Settlement in Corfu in the Aftermath of the Expulsions from Spain and Southern Italy, 1492–1541." *Mediterranean Historical Review* 27, no. 2 (2012): 175–88.

INDEX

CPSIA information can be obtained
at www.ICGtesting.com
Printed in the USA
LVOW12*1930030518

575867LV00006B/156/P